EUROPEAN STUDIES

24

EUROPEAN STUDIES

An Interdisciplinary Series in European Culture, History
and Politics

Executive Editor

Menno Spiering, University of Amsterdam
m.e.spiering@uva.nl

Series Editors

EUROPEAN STUDIES

An Interdisciplinary Series in European Culture, History
and Politics

24

MEDIA AND CULTURAL
POLICY
IN THE EUROPEAN UNION

Edited by

Katharine Sarikakis

Amsterdam - New York, NY 2007

Le papier sur lequel le présent ouvrage est imprimé remplit les prescriptions
de "ISO 9706:1994, Information et documentation - Papier pour documents -
Prescriptions pour la permanence".

The paper on which this book is printed meets the requirements of
'ISO 9706: 1994, Information and documentation - Paper for documents -
Requirements for permanence'.

ISBN-13: 978-90-420-2175-4
©Editions Rodopi B.V., Amsterdam - New York, NY 2007
Printed in The Netherlands

NOTE FOR CONTRIBUTORS

European Studies is published several times a year. Each issue is dedicated to a specific theme falling within the broad scope of European Studies. Contributors approach the theme from a wide range of disciplinary and, particularly, interdisciplinary perspectives. Past issues have focused on such topics as Britain and Europe, France and Europe, National Identity, Middle and Eastern Europe, Nation Building and Literary History, Europeanisation and Euroscepticism.

The Editorial board welcomes suggestions for other future projects to be produced by guest editors. In particular, *European Studies* may provide a vehicle for the publication of thematically focused conference and colloquium proceedings. Editorial enquiries may be directed to the series executive editor.

Subscription details and a list of back issues are available from the publisher's web site: www.rodopi.nl.

CONTENTS

AUTHORS IN THIS VOLUME

GILLIAN DOYLE is based at Centre for Cultural Policy Research (CCPR) in the Department for Theatre, Film & Television Studies at the University of Glasgow. Her teaching and research interests are related to media economics and media policy. She is on the editorial board of the *Journal of Media Economics* and of *Media and Cultural Politics*. She is Treasurer and Membership Secretary of the Media, Communications and Cultural Studies Association (MeCCSA) and is also President-Elect of the Association for Cultural Economics International (ACEI). She is the author of *Media Ownership* and of *Understanding Media Economics*, both published by Sage. She has served as a consultant for the Council of Europe's Committee of Experts on Media Concentrations and Pluralism (MM-CM).

ELISABETH DUMONT is a Research Officer at the University of Liège, (Ulg-Lema), coordinating international projects on cultural tourism, development as well as heritage conservation. She specifically focuses on cultural changes and quality of life. One of the projects she coordinates, PICTURE, funded by the EU sixth framework programme, focuses on the Proactive management of the Impact of Cultural Tourism upon Urban Resources and Economies. She is the editor of the *Strategic Urban Governance Framework for the Development of Cultural Tourism* due at the end of the project. She also knows the other side of the coin as she worked in the private sector related to culture. Among others, she took part in the launch of a start-up selling cultural products over the Internet and worked as a marketing and business development manager for a major publishing company. She has volunteered across the world and still does in a local cultural centre.

PETER HUMPHREYS is Professor at the University of Manchester, UK, where he has taught comparative European politics since 1986. He has published extensively on comparative media and telecommunications policy. He is author of *Media and Media Policy in Germany* (Berg, 1994), *Mass Media and Media Policy in Western Europe* (MUP, 1996) and (with Seamus Simpson) *Globalisation, Convergence and European Telecommunications Regulation* (Edward Elgar, 2005). Since 1996 he has been involved in a series of ESRC-funded research projects examining aspects of European media or telecoms regulation. His current three-year project, which commenced in February 2005, is entitled *Globalisation, Regulatory*

Competition and Audiovisual Regulation in Five Countries (the US, Canada, Britain, France and Germany).

DAVID HUTCHISON teaches at Glasgow Caledonian University. He was for many years the Course Leader of the university's BA in Communication and Mass Media, and has been associated, since its inception, with the Scottish Centre of Journalism Studies, a joint venture between Caledonian and Strathclyde Universities. He has been a member of the BBC's General Advisory Council and of the Scottish Film Council (now Scottish Screen). He is the author of *Media Policy* (1999). His recent published papers have been concerned with a number of topics including foreign coverage in the Canadian news magazine, *Maclean's*, and the representation of Glasgow on television. He is currently working on a comparative study of OFCOM and the Canadian Radio-television and Telecommunications Commission and co-editing a collection of essays, *The Media in Scotland.*

SONJA KRETZSCHMAR is Lecturer in Communication Sciences at the Institute of Communication Sciences, Westfälische Wilhelms-Universität Münster. Her research interests are in the field of International and Inter-cultural Communication, Journalism, European Television and Mobile Communication. She is author of the book *Fremde Kulturen im Euro-päischen Fernsehen* (Foreign Cultures on European Television). She has taught at the Universities of Erfurt, Munich, Münster and as a visiting professor at the University of Leipzig. She is a trained journalist and has worked in several print, radio, TV and online-media, among others three years at *Tagesthemen*, for the German public service broadcaster ARD. She is currently working on a research project on Mobile Communication and Journalism.

CAROLINE PAUWELS is Professor in national and European communication policy at the Vrije Universiteit Brussel and was formerly a full time researcher at the National Fund for Scientific research. She is also Head of the Department of Communication Studies of the VUB. Since 2000, she directs the Centre for Media, Information and Telecommunication (SMIT), employing 20 fulltime researchers working on ICT usage, national and transnational media policy within the emergence of an information and knowledge society. In 1998 she has been appointed as an expert for the Flemish Mediaraad and in 2002 she has been appointed as an expert in the Strategic Digital Platform of the flemish ministry. Her current domains of interest are in the field of

European audiovisual policymaking, the entertainment economy, convergence issues, and media concentration and antitrust policy. She has published several articles on media policy-related issues.

BEN VAN ROMPUY is a Researcher at the Institute for European Studies (IES) in Brussels. He holds a Master's degree in Communication Studies and in International and European Law from the Vrije Universiteit Brussel. After graduating in 2006, he started working on a PhD on the dialectics between the EU and the WTO as regards competition policy in the telecommunications and audiovisual sector.

KATHARINE SARIKAKIS is Senior Lecturer in Communications Policy and Postgraduate Research Director at the Institute of Communications Studies, University of Leeds. Her research interests are in the field of European and international communications and the role of institutions in supra-and international communications policy processes. She is the author of *Powers in Media Policy* (Peter Lang 2004) *British Media in a Global Era* (Arnold 2004) the co-editor of *Ideologies of the Internet* (Hampton Press 2006) the co-author of *Media Policy and Globalization* (Edinburgh University Press 2006) and the managing editor of the *International Journal of Media and Cultural Politics*. She is an Honorary Research Scholar at Hainan University, China. She has served as Vice-President elect of the International Association of Mass Communications Researchers (2000-2004) and a Secretary General for the European Consortium for Communication Research (2000-2002).

HEDWIG DE SMAELE is Professor in Communication Sciences at the Catholic University of Brussels/Katholieke Universiteit Brussel (K.U.Brussel). Before that, she was a research fellow, a postdoctoral researcher of the Research Foundation – Flanders and a lecturer in politics and mass media at Ghent University. Her Ph.D (2001) looks at the transition of mass media in Russia. Recent research projects include the study of Russian mass media and information climate, audiovisual policy in the enlarged European Union, impact of EU media policy on the programming of European broadcasters and the inflow of American television fiction, media and democratisation processes and political communication in new democracies. She has published in journals such as *European Journal of Communication, Trends in Communication* and *Javnost/The Public*.

JACQUES TELLER holds a PhD degree in Civil Engineering. He is Lecturer at the University of Liège (Belgium) and Technical University of Compiègne (France). He is presently working as Senior Researcher in LEMA – Centre for Architectural and Urban Design Studies. He was the coordinator of the SUIT project (2000-2003) – Sustainable development of Urban historical areas through an active Integration within Towns, supported by the Fifth EU Framework Programme of Research. He is presently a scientific coordinator of the PICTURE research project (2004-2007) – Proactive management of the Impact of Cultural Tourism upon Urban Resources and Economies - financed by the European Commission, Sixth Framework Programme of Research, Topic 3.6 the protection of cultural heritage and associated conservation strategies.

LIZA TSALIKI is Lecturer at the Department of Communications and Mass Media at the National Kapodistrian University of Athens; prior to that she was the director of international collaborations at the Hellenic Culture Organization (www.cultural-olympiad.gr) for the past three years. Her current interests involve ICTs, and the Internet in particular, and democratic participation; the public sphere; oral histories; cultural policy-making; city narratives. She is the author of articles published in the *European Journal of Communication* and *First Monday* among others and serves on the editorial board of the *International Journal of Media and Cultural Politics*.

SOPHIE DE VINCK joined the research centre SMIT-IBBT of the Vrije Universiteit Brussel in October 2005 as a Research Assistant (Aspirant) of the Research Foundation - Flanders (FWO-Vlaanderen). She is currently preparing her Ph.D. Her research focuses on the policies of the European Union towards the creation of economically competitive and culturally diverse content industries in the digital age.

MARK WHEELER is a Senior Lecturer in the Department of Law, Governance and International Relations, London Metropolitan University (City Campus). He is the author of *Politics and the Mass Media* (Blackwells, 1997), *Hollywood: Politics and Society* (British Film Institute, 2006) and co-author (with Petros Iosifidis and Jeanette Steemers) of *European Television Industries* (British Film Institute, 2005). He has contributed refereed articles to the *European Journal of Communications, Democratisation, Convergence,* the *Canadian Journal of Communications* and the *Harvard International Journal of Press/Politics*. He is a research officer for the British Screen Advisory Council (BSAC).

EUROPEAN STUDIES 24 (2007): 13-21

INTRODUCTION

THE PLACE OF MEDIA AND CULTURAL POLICY IN THE EU

Katharine Sarikakis

The role of the European Union in the sphere of media and culture has known an increasing importance in the last two decades, not only for national markets and societies that are directly associated with the EU polity but also for non EU states influenced by international agreements. As media and cultural policy has attracted the attention of the academy and policymakers, so have the institutions of the EU dedicated resources to the development of policies that target European or EU dimensions of such policies. Most notable difficulties in this process have been questions of jurisdiction – whether the EU *does* have jurisdiction upon the media and generally cultural sector – as well as philosophical questions about the *raison d' être* – whether the EU *should* have jurisdiction in these areas.

The varying perspectives and sociocultural contexts of European states, as well as the complexities deriving from the tensions between traditions of public service, which are regarded inherently 'European', and the intensified privatisatisation of such culture, including the field of media are some of the problems that are closely related to the directions to which the polity may be developing. They belong to fundamental questions about the nature of governance of the European political and cultural space, affecting one way or another the ways in which European citizens experience their cultures, and that of others, and actively create them. Even more so, policy affects the ways in which citizens, including those of a 'precarious' status, nation states and EU institutions relate to one another, to actively construct their living space.

The significance of cultural and media policy cannot be overestimated, as it transcends the fields of technology, politics, economics and
social life in a number of ways. Not only have media and culture industries become increasingly central in the economies of European countries, they have also become the terrain of contestation and consensus
regarding self-governance and cultural identity. The polity had to deal
with these questions in its transformation from an economic coalition to
a political and cultural entity. Media and cultural policies are themselves
expressions of conflict of economic interests and political ideological
positions. They have an impact upon rights, the legitimation of the polity, and the conditions for the materialisation of citizenship. They occupy
a peculiar position in the European Union agenda. Not only have they
entered the arena of EU jurisdiction under complex and contradictory
conditions, but they have also become the terrain where the essence and
future of the polity is taking shape. Or at the very least, this is the domain where worldviews about the identity of the EU conflate and con-
test its present. The historical development of European integration has
been characterised by a continuous, albeit neither homogenous nor
seamless, integration of national and regional markets, accompanied by
the establishment of institutions whose roles and relation to each other –
and the member states – has grown more complex as their competencies
increased.

These changes have been driven by an economic imperative of market integration, underwritten by a web of international relations en-
trenched in a Cold War atmosphere based on the politics of fear. On the
one hand, the –ideology of – fear of and threat from a Communist Europe was exemplified in the race to 'annex' the coal and steel markets of
(Western) Germany to the Western European markets. On the other
hand, the fear of another intereuropean war that would break down the
social fabric of Europe provided the ideological foundation for the pursuit of peace for Europe through the path of – economic first – interde-
pendence. Within this changing climate of international relations, the
first attempts of European market integration saw the rise of institutions
that by their very definition would proclaim the importance of cultural
integration – or perhaps cultural hegemony – for social cohesion in the
continent. The European Parliament and the European Court of Human
Rights have bestowed the European polity a political and social contract

with Europe's citizens that exceeds, albeit not unproblematically, the mere economistic priorities maintained in EU policy for several decades.

The way to the recognition of media and culture as important fields for EU action has similarly reflected and embodied the conflicting perceptions about the raison d' être of the polity, specifically, and the politics of integration, in general. In this process of the EU's searching for an identity, or more cynically, in its attempt to legitimise itself, the politics of citizenship and citizens' representation has been underwritten by the consistent 'quiet power' of Parliamentary intervention into the discourses and debates that the polity has generated alongside its increasing realms of jurisdiction. The role of media institutions and cultural industries in the formation of European identity and of – predominantly – political integration has been identified by the EP from the early days of the institution in landmark reports that called for early action in the field at an EU level.

As media and culture entered the arena of supranational debate in the early 1980s, the privatisation of public owned services and infrastructure was setting foot on the European continent. The EP was mostly concerned about the effects of a de facto expansion of private media corporations and the lack of active involvement of the polity in steering media development towards European centred aims, but had, apart from a *symbolic* role, enjoyed no legislative powers. Respectively, the polity had no legitimate means to initiate policy in the media and culture fields, as the foundational treaties and agreements only later (with the entry into force of Treaty of Maastricht 1993 Article 128[1] on culture; and Treaty of

---

[1] According to ARTICLE 128

1. The Community shall contribute to the flowering of the cultures of the Member States, while respecting their national and regional diversity and at the same time bringing the common cultural heritage to the fore.

2. Action by the Community shall be aimed at encouraging cooperation between Member States and, if necessary, supporting and supplementing their action in the following areas:
   – improvement of the knowledge and dissemination of the culture and history of the European peoples;
   – conservation and safeguarding of cultural heritage of European significance;
   – non-commercial cultural exchanges;
   – artistic and literary creation, including in the audiovisual sector.

3. The Community and the Member States shall foster cooperation with third countries and the competent international organizations in the sphere of culture, in particular the Council of Europe.

4. The Community shall take cultural aspects into account in its action under other

Amsterdam 1999 with the Protocol on the system of Public Broadcasting)[2] introduced the clauses related to culture and media as a policy field.

The development of a European approach to media and cultural policy has parallelled the institutional maturation of European integration and more distinctively that of the European Parliament, which has evolved into a major legislative organ. This 'shared' route has come to epitomise the gradual development of the European polity based on the principles of deliberation and cosmopolitanism. The extent to which both principles are followed through and the ways in which they are defined is a matter of contestation. Nevertheless, the de facto cosmopolitan nature of the EU is reflected on the institutional cultures and internationality of governance, but also in the ways in which it seeks, internal conflicts and drifts notwithstanding, to assign a political and cultural significance upon a space that is having difficulties to define itself.

The communicative space of the EU, as one of political deliberation at an 'elite' and rather distant level, but also as one of human expression, existence and connectivity, at the everyday level, presents us (and policymakers) with a set of interesting questions. If the 'Unity in Diversity' scope of European orientation is believed to be instrumental in the process of legitimisation of the polity and vital for its continuation, then it is worth examining the ways in which 'diversity' may be understood, addressed, utilised and promoted within this communicative space. Entangled with the idea of European citizenship, the development of cultural

provisions of this Treaty.
5. In order to contribute to the achievement of the objectives referred to in this Article, the Council:
- acting in accordance with the procedure referred to in Article 189b and after consulting the Committee of the Regions, shall adopt incentive measures, excluding any harmonization of the laws and regulations of the Member States. The Council shall act unanimously throughout the procedures referred to in Article 189b;
- acting unanimously on a proposal from the Commission, shall adopt recommendations.
    [2] 'The provisions of the Treaty establishing the European Community shall be without prejudice to the competence of Member States to provide for the funding of public service broadcasting insofar as such funding is granted to broadcasting organisations for the fulfilment of the public service remit as conferred, defined and organised by each Member State, and insofar as such funding does not affect trading conditions and competition in the Community to an extent which would be contrary to the common interest, while the realisation of the remit of that public service shall be taken into account.'

policy in the EU demonstrates clarity but also confusion in its constitutional and political foundations. The Commission is for example clear about the role of European citizenship, largely expressed as cultural citizenship but with political rights. 'This idea of European citizenship reflects the fundamental values that people throughout Europe share and on which European integration is based. Its strength lies in Europe's immense cultural heritage'. (European Commission 2002, 3). At the same time, the definition of 'fundamental values' remains vague and intentionally broad. These may be more concretely expressed in the Charter of Fundamental Rights of the European Union. In particular Articles 10 and 11[3] express the EU (supranational) values of freedom of expression, as well as freedom to rights of cultural significance (right to freedom of thought conscience and religion), as well as Articles 13 (freedom of the arts and sciences) and 22 that state the EU's commitment to cultural linguistic and religious diversity.

However apart from these legally expressed values, as the rights accompanying EU citizenship, there are few instances of EU 'common consciousness' that can point to a 'European' imagined community. These are most visible in relatively small scale programmes, such *Socrates* where the exchange of students among universities in Europe has created generations of young Europeans with some experience of their neighbours' cultures or in projects such as the European Union Youth Orchestra or the European Union Chamber Orchestra, projects leaning rather towards the High Arts spectrum of cultural policy. On the other end, we have a few examples of cultural production addressed at larger audiences, such as Eurosport, and a history of failed attempts to create

---

[3] *Article 10*
Freedom of thought, conscience and religion
1. Everyone has the right to freedom of thought, conscience and religion. This right includes freedom to change religion or belief and freedom, either alone or in community with others and in public or in private, to manifest religion or belief, in worship, teaching, practice and observance.
2. The right to conscientious objection is recognised, in accordance with the national laws governing the exercise of this right.
 Article 11
Freedom of expression and information
1. Everyone has the right to freedom of expression. This right shall include freedom to hold opinions and to receive and impart information and ideas without interference by public authority and regardless of frontiers.
2. The freedom and pluralism of the media shall be respected.

and sustain pan-European television channels. Audiovisual production remains domestic in its origin and consumption, despite the support mechanisms employed in the last fifteen years, while the press remains firmly located within the national and regional spaces. It seems that the potential of media and cultural expression in constructing and reflecting an imagined community, bound perhaps at the very least by its common ground of difference, sense of transcendence and transition, is affected by the politics of particularism of culture(s), as well as of the structural economic conditions of production. Within this context, Europe's communicative space is one of tension and contradiction about not only the 'big' questions concerning the EU and its future, but also those confronted at the level of the everyday life, such as experiencing and living cultural and political citizenship.

In particular, the questions permeating the debate around Europe's role of media and cultural policy concern the priorities expressed in Europe's communicative space, as represented through policy and deliberation. To what extent does this assumed or aspired cosmo-or Europolitanism of living (in) the EU find a reflective political basis? How does policy mediate and shape diversity in culture and society in Europe? This collection of articles comes to address the historical transformation of policies at an EU level and opens the field to possible future reflection, taking into account the recent EU enlargement, the role of the EU within the Member States and, of course, the ways in which the EU may seek to see and define itself through citizenship policy and the regulation of cultural expression and information.

There are three factors raising the question of a re-examination of media and cultural policy in the EU. First, the globalisation of communication systems, including those of the production of culture pose a set of questions that the nation-state would need to address within a platform of supranational governance. This renders the governing capabilities of, and scepticism against, the EU a significant factor in the well-being of local populations in the continent. Second, the transantional flows of people and integration of markets challenge the traditional formulations of citizenship connectedness and social cohesion. These concepts have been clearly associated with media and cultural industries and their role in shaping and expressing ideas about the human condition. Against the backdrop of the shift from local to global and back to local, the EU's role in mediating certain forms of association among citizens, nations

and its members to the world (through for example the recent enlargement and the processes of accession) is increasingly judged against, until
recently considered, 'secondary' priorities, those of cultural diversity and
creativity and expression, that is, against the soft power of cultural preservation and leadership. The political will is the third factor that becomes
immensely important in the governance of cultural and social relations,
the maintenance of economic and the pursuit of social cohesion. As the
European Union space becomes more diverse, by the inclusion of Eastern European countries, but also due to complex flows of internal and
incoming migration and human displacement, the need for public policy
that takes account of the increased heterogeneity of Europe's social
making, its cultural exposition, as well as its place within the global net
of economic and political relations becomes more acute.

The study of EU media and cultural policy has generated increasing
interest among scholars over the last decade. Among a good number of
publications around specific policy objects, such as television, or objectives, such as ownership, the question of diversity in communications
policy has largely been addressed in terms of cultural diversity, as related
to cultural initiatives or as a synonym for 'pluralism' of content in the
study of media ownership concentration. Moreover, the study of EU
media and cultural policy tends to be fragmented, largely addressing
specific policy 'moments'. As such, detailed policy analysis of a micro-or
mesoscopic nature cannot provide an analysis of the bigger picture and
map the trajectory of policy development. At the same time, 'culture' and
'media' are often treated as distinct questions of categorization that reflect epistemological approaches to the study of policy. Without dismiss-
ing the rationale and purposefulness of such distinction, this volume
seeks to show the usefulness of addressing media and cultural policy as
parts of the same whole. Media are understood as manifestations of
cultural praxis that integrates questions of identity as well as of equity. At
the same time, 'culture' policy is to be found in the most unexpected
places, such as the so-called structural funds for Europe's peripheries or
the policies surrounding EU citizenship.

Although many of the most significant works are discussed at appropriate junctures throughout this volume, it is worth mentioning that
book-length monographs in the field of media policy are rather rare.
Among the major books addressing EU media policy are Sophia
Kaitatzi-Whitlock's *Europe's Political Communication Deficit* (2006: Arima),

David Ward's *The European Union Democratic Deficit and the Public Sphere* (2004: IOS Press), Alison Harcourt's *The European Union and the Regulation of Media Markets* (2004: Manchester University Press); Katharine Sarikakis's *Powers in Media Policy* (2004: Peter Lang) and Richard Collins's *Audiovisual and Broadcasting Policy in the European Union* (1994: John Libbey), as well as Peter Humphreys' *Media Policy in Western Europe* which, although including a great deal of material on EU policy, is largely focused on policies in western Europe generally (1996: Manchester University Press). Finally, the publications by the Euromedia Research Group explore media policies in European countries but not at an EU level (for instance *The Media in Europe* (2004: Sage) and *Media Policy* (1999: Sage). Most books are focused on the audiovisual policy development, as this area has produced most regulation or attracted most attention. This volume aims to make a case for a renewed look at the trajectory of media policies in the EU by bringing together analyses of specific media policies, as well as policy questions that transcend specific 'media' or cultural mediations. As such:

— it offers a historical and socio-political analysis of major media policies in the European Union addressing the most recent developments and contextualising them;
— it turns its attention to areas largely neglected by scholarly publishing, such as the press, journalism and the newsroom, media in the enlarged Europe from the perspective of diversity in media and culture and
— it addresses media and cultural policies as an interrelated part of EU construction, through questions of identity and political representation.

As an overarching aim, however, the articles in this issue provide an analysis of media and cultural policy in the Union through a sense of urgency and the prism of diversity. The concept is left intentionally undefined, as each case studied reveals a different perspective of how diversity may be understood and defined. All the same, the basic question these articles are addressing is about the ways in which the EU seeks to understand, protect and promote, or undermine, diversity through media and cultural policies. The articles address the context of EU policy by taking into account broader, contextual questions about social cohesion and the place of the EU in the world (Sarikakis) and citizenship (Tsaliki), as well as questions around specific media and policy objects, national sovereignty and state support for culture (Pauwels et al, Dumondt and Teller), market liberalisation and ownership (Doyle) the role and future of public service broadcasting and the audiovisual sector in the enlarged Europe (Humphreys, de Smaele, Wheeler), and the role of diversity in the newsroom and the lack of EU policy in the press (Hutchison, Kretzschmar). The articles are looking at media and cultural policies not in order to provide a prescription of diversity and the role of policy, but in order to revisit policy from the perspective of an open-ended question, and to argue that commitment and political will are urgently needed to address the complex issues of cohesion, citizenship, and European integration, all of which depend on the quality of the conditions determining access to and creation of culture, expression and meaningful participation in Europe's communicative space.

References

European Commission 2002 *A Community of Cultures* Directorate-General for Press and Communication. Brussels.

Charter of Fundamental Rights of the European Union Official Journal of the European Communities C 364/8.

EUROPEAN STUDIES 24 (2007): 23-43

CAN STATE AID IN THE FILM SECTOR STAND
THE PROOF OF EU AND WTO LIBERALISATION EFFORTS?

Caroline Pauwels, Sophie De Vinck and Ben Van Rompuy

Abstract

State aid granted to the European national film sectors has traditionally been legitimised on the basis of notions of national identity, the
public interest and cultural diversity. While the economic value of
these industries has contributed to their importance in the eyes of
national policy-makers, this has also put state aid regimes under pressure on a European and global level, where a liberalisation agenda
has come increasingly to the fore from the 1980s on. The research
question raised in this article is therefore whether state aid in the film
sector will be able to stand the proof of EU and WTO liberalisation
efforts. Considering the evolution of primary and secondary EU
legislation, as well as the on going debates within the WTO, it seems
that the biggest threat to the sector's aid regimes comes not from the
regulation itself, but from the ambivalence and vagueness of its application. Not all points to a liberalising evolution however. The EU
itself has set up a number of programmes intended to support the
film sector, while the recent adoption of the Unesco Convention on
the Protection and Promotion of the Diversity of Cultural Expressions can be seen as a counterweight as well. The actual strength and
impact of these counterbalances in practice, however, is doubtful
and/or unclear. The question remains therefore whether the WTO
and the EU will be able to wander from their path dependent future,
as a liberalist approach lies at the base of both. In consequence, political willingness will prove to be crucial in the following years, beginning with the review of present EU state aid regulation in 2007.

Introduction

The concept of state support for the audiovisual industries, the film sector in particular, has been around in the EU Member States for quite some time. It has resulted in a complex interplay of both direct and indirect aid mechanisms. The legitimations for this public aid centre on notions of national identity, the public interest and cultural diversity. This last notion has often been coupled with issues of cultural 'imperialism' (or, as Chalaby prefers, 'primacy'), most often associated with a dominance of US culture over the rest of the world (Chalaby 2006). Thus, it is generally argued by its proponents that governmental cinema policies are necessary to 'counter an excess of imported images which would erode the social texture and the sovereignty and cultural identity of a country' (Unesco 2001). Although it does not lie within the scope of this article to give an overview of the different definitions of cultural diversity, we wish to refer to the recently adopted Unesco Convention on the Protection and Promotion of the Diversity of Cultural Expressions. In this document, cultural diversity is defined as referring to '*the manifold ways in which the cultures of groups and societies find expression*' (Unesco 2005). Smaller countries in particular tend to explicitly privilege the fostering (or protecting) of national cultural values and/or cultural diversity in the context of state aid for film. Two main conditions for the preservation of cultural diversity are hereby put forward: the ability of governments to protect and stimulate domestic production and the subsequent circulation and exchange of these local productions (Aas 2001, Unesco 2001, Marcus 2005).

It is, however, important not to forget that the issue of cultural diversity transcends the question of stimulating domestic production and distribution. While state funding for the film and audiovisual industries is all too often targeted at an increase in the number of national productions, a crucial question has to do with what constitutes this domestic production from a qualitative point of view (Unesco 2001). Moreover, not only the supply side needs stimulation in order to realise a culturally diverse society, the demand side is equally important but particularly difficult to grasp (Unesco 2001).

Aside from the cultural dimension, the fact that the film and other cultural industries have an increasing economic weight as well (Throsby 2001), contributes to the importance and support granted by these governments. The growing trade deficit between the EU and the US in the audiovisual sector – more than 8 billion US dollar in 2000 – is significant in this regard (European Commission 2003c).

Precisely this economic value, however, has put national cultural policy-making under increasing pressure on a European and global level, as state support may effectively lead to market distortions. As such it is deemed incompatible with the liberal(ising) philosophy that has gained ground from the 1980s onwards, specifically on a European and world level.

At the same time, the goal of preserving cultural diversity has recently resurfaced on the global policy agenda as well, with the adoption of the Unesco Convention at the end of 2005 as a provisional peak.

All of this goes to show that state aid in the audiovisual sector is increasingly situated in the centre of two tension fields. On the one hand, balancing cultural (diversity) and economic (competitiveness) objectives is a crucial, yet difficult exercise. On the other hand, in a globalising and multi-level context, the national states' aim of protecting national sovereignty in audiovisual policy-making is often butted against increasing liberalising interference from regulatory and policy organs on a supranational level, the EU and WTO in particular.

In the subsequent paragraphs, we will address the characteristics of those EU and WTO provisions that are of particular concern for the film industries in order to assess to which extent existing state aid schemes are indeed threatened by an EU and WTO-led liberalisation of the sector. In concrete terms, we will consider the evolution of primary and secondary EU legislation, before moving to an overview of the WTO debates on these matters and their (provisional) outcome. Furthermore, it is important to have a closer look at the industrial support programmes the EU itself has set up in order to encourage the development of European audiovisual industries, such as the MEDIA programmes, their interaction with state aid legislation and the structural impact they may have had on the audiovisual sector.

The constitutional framework

The EU's approach towards state support measures in the audiovisual sector is one of the contentious issues of its competition policy. While the provisions contained in Articles 81 (concerted practices) and 82 (abuse of dominant position) of the EC Treaty also affect the conduct of undertakings in the audiovisual sector, the state aid regime is specifically addressed in Articles 87 to 89 EC Treaty.

According to Article 87(1), state aid is incompatible with the common market insofar as it affects trade between Member States and, by favouring certain companies or the production of certain goods, distorts or threatens to distort competition. The concept of state aid is defined very large, including both direct and indirect advantages given by a state. This general prohibitive rule is, however, not absolute. Rather, the Treaty stipulates that certain categories of aid can benefit from an automatic or discretionary exemption because of their beneficial impact (Articles 87(2) and 87(3) EC Treaty). Since the Maastricht Treaty included a cultural derogation in Article 87(3)(d) EC Treaty, in addition to the incorporation of culture amongst the Community's policies (Article 151 EC Treaty), aid in view of culture promotion and heritage conservation too has become eligible for such an exemption. While cultural diversity is in this way inserted in the evaluation of state aid mechanisms, the hierarchy between cultural objectives and the Commission's responsibility to preserve undistorted competition is not spelled out clearly in the Treaty (Herold 2004, 14). Matters are further complicated by the fact that derogations to fundamental principles of Community law are generally construed strictly, and that there are no indications that this is any different for sub-close d) (Mayer-Robitaille 2004, 503 ; Smith 2004, 63). Indeed, it is clear from the Article itself that the cultural derogation can only be invoked as long as the aid 'does not affect trading conditions and competition (…) to an extent that is contrary to the common interest'. Since it is the European Commission's task to make this assessment, Member States can only implement support mechanisms for the film sector after they have been notified and authorised by the Commission. Furthermore, the Commission can also abolish state aid regimes a posteriori. This leaves the European Commission with a wide discretion as to decide whether or not to permit a particular aid scheme (European Commission 2001b ; Nitsche 2001, 145 ; Pauwels 1995, 451-455 ; Quigley and Collins 2003, 81-82).

As a result, the tensions between national sovereignty and European supranationality on the one hand, cultural concerns and economic prerogatives on the other, remain highly controversial as far as primary EU legislation concerns. The Commission has consequently tried to clarify its approach with regard to state aid for film through secondary legislation. However, despite these serious attempts to clarify EU policy guidelines, the final outcome remains just as ambivalent.

Application of the legal framework in practice

Despite recent controversy over the EU actions in this field, worries about the sustainability of national aid mechanisms for the film sector are certainly not new. Since the late 1980s, conflicts between the Member States and the European Commission have arisen as a consequence of actions taken against state aid in the film sector. First of all, an early attempt to establish a set of detailed rules on aid to the film and television industry was turned down due to the strong opposition of several Member States (Rawlinson 1993, 55). Furthermore, provisions included in German, Danish, Italian and Greek support mechanisms, amongst others, have had to give way under pressure from the Commission (Pons 1996). It must, however, be stressed that only a few cases were treated during this period, for the simple reason that aid schemes for the audiovisual sector were only very rarely notified by the Member States (European Commission 2001a, 6). Moreover, the Commission's attention was limited to possible breaches of the fundamental freedoms of the Treaty. As long as a notified aid measure did not discriminate against nationals of other Member States, it was considered compatible with the common market (Dony 1996, 116-117; Loman 1992, 136-138).

This all changed in 1998, when the Commission received a complaint about exclusionary effects created by the French system of support for film production. The Commission assessed and confirmed the complaint, upon which the French authorities modified several provisions of the aid scheme. France, in turn, however insisted on an equal treatment of the support measures of other Member States, thereby initiating a specific and one hoped more generic policy towards state aid to film production. The Commission thus announced that it would review the schemes in other Member States under the specific criteria adopted in the French decision: 1) guarantees must be given by the Member State in order to ensure that the content of the aided production is cultural, 2) the producer must be free to spend at least 20% of the film budget in other Member States without any loss of aid, 3) the aid intensity must be limited to 50% of the total budget of the film, except in case of low budget films and 4) aid supplements for certain activities[1] are not allowed (European Commission 1998).

By mid-2000 the Commission had given its consent to the national support mechanisms of five EU Member States.[2] Even though the Commission's activities in this regard in practice did not result in an endangerment of the state support mechanisms, the fact that it was interfering more overtly and explicitly nevertheless gave rise to heated discussions between the Member States, in particular within the Council of Ministers. Several Member States felt that the EU was intruding in a national policy domain, attacking their own prerogatives and as such undermining the principle of subsidiarity (Council of the European Union 2000a, 2000b). The rising controversy entailed the Commission to publish a Communication on the matter in 2001 (European Commission 2001a).

This first 'Cinema Communication' signified a change in the Commission's strategy in a number of ways. First of all, it can be seen as the prelude to a more transparent policy-making, with clearer criteria and policy guidelines set out until June 2004 (and subsequently until 2007, as the regime has been extended in March 2004). As such it aims at providing more legal certainty (Council of the European Union 2001 ; European Commission 2004a ; European Parliament 2002). Moreover, despite the fact that the Commission stuck to its four compatibility criteria, some changes were made in view of the Member States' concerns. To give an example, the limitation of aid intensity to 50% of the film budget, one of the most contested provisions, was modified to allow for more flexibility. Exceptions for 'difficult' and 'low budget' films could from now on be defined by the Member States themselves, an indication of the recognized need for a more situation-specific approach (European Commission 2001a, 8-10).

Nevertheless, not all aspects of the Commission's approach, as consolidated in the Communication of 2001 (and the follow-up communication of 2004), can be evaluated in a positive way. One of the most deplorable changes in this context is that the Commission distanced itself from its earlier opinions on the close relation between the cultural and

[1] In its decision, the Commission only mentioned two activities for which aid supplements would not be allowed, namely pornographic works and publicity. Which other activities would fall under the scope of this criterion, remained unclear.

[2] France (European Commission 1998), the Netherlands (case N486/97), Germany (case N4/98), Ireland (cases NN49/97 and N32/97) and Sweden (case N748/1999).

industrial dimension of film production. In particular the Communication states that the cultural derogation (Article 87(3)(d) EC Treaty) can only be applicable to state aid that is strictly targeted at culture-enhancing goals. Not only does this interpretation go beyond what was said in the French Decision (European Commission 1998 ; Van Rompuy 2005, 62-65). It also entails an inconsistency in the Communication itself: on the one hand, the Commission acknowledges the double nature of the audiovisual sector and underlines that the rationale behind support measures for this sector is based on both cultural and industrial considerations; but on the other hand, it attempts to strictly distinguish between aid to the creation of a cultural product (film) and aid to the film industry. It therefore comes as no surprise that the European Parliament, in its Report on the Commission Communication, questioned 'whether the Treaty, which puts forward a purely cultural solution, provides the flexibility which is necessary when dealing with the unavoidably dual nature (cultural and industrial) of the audiovisual sector' (European Parliament 2002, 11-12).

Practical consequences of the seemingly narrowed juridical ground to authorise film aid schemes, came to the fore when the European Commission released a discussion document in December 2003. In this document, the Commission expressed its worries about so-called territorialisation requirements, which oblige the receiver of aid, as a condition of eligibility for the full aid amount, to spend a certain amount of the film budget within the country. According to the Commission, such conditions result in adverse industrial effects and thus are not defendable on a purely cultural basis, especially when they are defined in excess of the effective aid amount.[3] Consequently, three options were proposed to alter the existing compatibility criterion related to the admissible level of territorialisation (80% of the film budget, cfr. supra). According to the first option, territorialisation requirements which exceed the effective aid amount provided under the scheme would be no longer accepted (for instance, an aid intensity of 50% of the film budget would correspond at most with a 50% level of territorialisation). The second option was to limit territorialisation requirements to those posts identified in the film budget as cultural or artistic. And the third option was to prohibit the use of territorialisation requirements, but in this case the criteria which

---

[3] This is the case when a Member State, for instance, imposes a territorialisation requirement of 75% of the film budget in order to qualify for aid, even though the aid intensity is lower (for instance 50% of the film budget).

limit in principle the aid intensity to 50%, would be adjusted upwards (European Commission 2003a). The consultation exercise that was subsequently organised, however, led to a virulent and polemic discussion during which Member States and representatives from the audiovisual sector unanimously opposed the Commission's proposal. Given such a strong support for the existing rules, the Commission decided to extend the validity of the compatibility criteria, as set out in the Communication of 2001, until June 2007 (European Commission 2004a), thus not enforcing its initial plan of 'severing' the application of territorialisation provisions.

Even though a (provisional) status quo has been preserved on the Commission guidelines, the EU interference in public support for the film sector is not clear-cut yet. Unresolved tensions between cultural and economic aims as well as between the different policy-making levels, continue to exist (Herold 2004 ; Van Rompuy 2005).

It is, for instance, telling that all Member States rejected a further tightening of the rules on national film policies, even though only a small minority of them imposes territoriality requirements which exceed the effective aid amount. Moreover, the often-heard argument that the Commission had not provided evidence that the territorialisation criterion was unable to prevent undue distortion of competition (EFCA 2004 ; FIAPF 2004), demonstrates how fundamentally the legitimacy of the Commission's action was questioned. In response, the Commission announced to carry out an extensive study on the cultural and economic impact of territoriality requirements, notably on co-productions (European Commission 2004a, 2). The importance of the outcome of this study can therefore not be underestimated, especially in the light of the next review of the communication in 2007.

Additionally, the Commission's attempt to isolate cultural from industrial aspects of film production, gives rise to many questions with regard to its actual view on the hybrid nature of cinematographic works. In particular, it remains to be seen to what extent industrial-political elements of national support mechanisms will still be considered as legitimate. The fact that several Member States have had to modify territoriality provisions in order to win the Commission's approval of a notified aid scheme (Van Rompuy 2005) may be seen as indicative in this context. At the least, it reveals the ambiguity of the statement that 'the Commission has never prohibited any national audiovisual aid scheme', frequently used to counter the Member States' concerns (for instance Reding 2001, 2003).

Rather, even if severe liberal attacks on film subsidies have been turned down by Member States, it is just as valid to emphasise that the Commission's strict interpretation of the legal framework continues to threaten legitimations for film subsides in the middle and long term.

Further pressures arising on a global level: the WTO and state aid for film

The future of state aid in the audiovisual sector is not only dependent on the EU's balancing act between cultural and economic considerations. More and more, it is also to be situated in the context of international trade law. In particular, the external pressure of the WTO on the maintenance of national support measures for film should certainly not be overlooked.

Although a thorough technical analysis of the WTO regulation would lead us too far, it is nevertheless relevant to take a closer look at the compatibility of national state aid schemes for film with the WTO framework.

Because of the fundamental differences that exist between the legal treatment of (subsidies to) goods and services within the WTO framework, the issue of classification is first of all decisive. However, the respective scope of the goods (GATT) and services (GATS) provisions is not always clear and thus remains, at least to a certain extent, a matter of interpretation. Traditionally, the legal nature of the medium of film is seen as being twofold: although cinematographic works are explicitly mentioned in Article IV GATT, rental activities as well as the distribution and exhibition of a film are considered as services (Herold 2003, 3-4; Weber 2004, 370). Furthermore, in the view of technological convergence, the traditional boundaries between the different WTO agreements further become blurred, leading to more complexities and vagueness (Pauwels and Loisen 2006).

a) GATT

Although drafted to liberalise the world trade through generally applicable rules, the GATT includes some exceptions that seem to recognise a certain specificity for culture (Herold 2003 ; Weber 2004). For instance, Article IV GATT on screen quotas can be seen as an acknowledgement of the validity to pursue cultural policy aims in the film sector. Its practical implications are however limited since screen quotas are, at least in Europe, rarely used anymore as an instrument to support the national film industry (Cottier 1994, 750 ; Herold 2003).

Likewise, paragraph f) of Article XX GATT justifies the restriction of free trade in the case of measures that are taken to protect national treasures of artistic, historic or archaeological value. Although it is interesting to note that this provision recognises the relationship between culture and national identity (Bernier 1998, 114), the practical use of this exemption for the purpose of audiovisual support measures has been rather low. Indeed, stretching the scope of the term 'treasures' to a more general cultural exemption, would clearly depart from its intended meaning (Herold 2003, 3 ; Weber 2004, 372). Consequently, there are few reasons to assume that national film support measures would not be subject to the general rules of the GATT. As a result, potential conflicts with the GATT framework occur in at least two respects.

First of all, there seems to be an inherent contradiction between film support mechanisms and the principle of national treatment (Article III GATT), which prohibits discriminatory measures against 'like products' from other contracting parties that are intended to protect domestic production. The outcome of the Canadian Periodical case is instructive in this context. According to the Appellate Body, the Canadian measures to protect its magazine industry (e.g. 'funded' postal rates) were not granted directly in the form of payments to domestic producers and therefore could not be justified by Article III:8(b) GATT, which provides for an exception from the national treatment imperative for direct subsidies. As a result, the postal subsidy was deemed incompatible with Article III GATT (Bernier 1998, 116-117). This decision has potentially far-reaching consequences for film support, since it implies that indirect forms of subsidies granted to cinematographic producers (for instance, tax remittances and fiscal measures) are challengeable (Herold 2003, 4).

Secondly, questions may arise as to whether national film support mechanisms are compatible with the WTO *Agreement on Subsidies and Countervailing Measures* (SCM). This agreement, which gives effect to Articles VI and XVI GATT, disciplines the use of subsidies on goods and regulates the actions that can be taken against their possible harmful effects. A distinction is made between prohibited and actionable subsidies. Traditional film support instruments, focusing on film production, fall under the latter and are thus 'actionable', i.e. they can be challenged (either through countervailing action or through the dispute settlement procedure) when they adversely affect the interests of other GATT members (Herold 2003, 5). This, however, requires the complaining member to demonstrate that such adverse trade effects do exist. As a result, even though the definition of 'adverse effects' is relatively broad (Herold 2003), the US would find it difficult to challenge European film subsidies, given the dominance of its film productions on the European market (Cottier 1994, 754). Nevertheless, this still leaves the door open for film producers from other countries who might have a strong argument when they feel affected by these subsidies. The possibility of an action under the SCM Agreement should therefore not be dismissed (Bernier 1998, 119 ; Herold 2003, 5).

b) GATS

Unlike the GATT, the GATS contains no specific rules on the treatment of subsidies. Article XV GATS, however, indicates that members shall enter into negotiations on the matter to avoid the distortive effects that subsidies may have on trade in services. The current Doha Round of negotiations will possibly determine the regulation of subsidies to services and is therefore also of particular relevance to our discussion.

In the meantime, state support for film services remains compatible with the WTO framework. This is to a large extent the result of the compromise solution that was accepted after the Uruguay Round (1986-1994), during which the US took on the rest of the world in a debate over cultural trade (Gournay 2002, 57 ; Smiers 2003, 175-176). At the end of these negotiations, the EU and its Member States were able to stay clear of any commitments on audiovisual services, excluding these from the scope of the principles of national treatment and market access, as well as − through a detailed list of exceptions - from the most-favoured-nation principle (Pauwels and Loisen 2003, 294-296). Nevertheless, as for the regulation on subsidies, the possible threat posed by GATS lies in the commitments that might be exacted in the future (Cottier 1994, 756 ; Weber 2004, 377).

The observations made for the EU thus seem to be applicable to the global (WTO) level as well. Although state support for the film sector has been put under pressure by the WTO's liberalisation efforts in the past, the current situation is one of standstill. However, as the EU has only been able to postpone the issue to subsequent negotiation rounds, legal uncertainty remains. Moreover, with ambiguity and vagenuess reigning on a number of issues, the question of whether national state aid can stand the WTO test in the existing framework, is not resolved.

Future developments thus have to be followed with great care. The economic considerations and liberalisation agenda that lie at the base of the WTO, in itself constitute a continuing external pressure on the sustainability of EU and national support measures. The Unesco Convention on the Protection and Promotion of the Diversity of Cultural Expressions (approved in October 2005), can be seen as a potential counterweight to the WTO's liberalising agenda, balancing the economy-culture tension field by emphasising the Member States' right to establish distinct cultural policies. However, the actual impact of this instrument, in particular its relation to WTO regulations, remains to be seen (De Vinck 2005, 72-77). For the moment, the Commission seems, at least in rhetoric, to hold on to its defensive stance in the matter:

> La convention UNESCO donne un poids politique, et dans une certaine mesure juridique, à la position constante de l'Union européenne à l'OMC sur les services audiovisuels. Il n'y a pas eu et il n'y aura pas, tant que je serai Commissaire en charge de l'Audiovisuel, d'offre de l'Europe dans ce domaine. Autrement dit: pas de marchandage «agriculture» contre «audiovisuel»! (Reding 2005, 2)

EU support for the cultural industries

As we have seen, national state aid regimes for the film sector have come under increasing scrutiny from the 1980s and especially 1990s on, on the global as well as the EU level. While the EU has often been identified as a pro-liberalisation actor, threatening the continuation of such state support schemes, it has, perhaps paradoxically, itself taken a number of initiatives in support of the cultural industries. From the end of the 1980s onwards, the EU has indeed set up a number of industrial policies targeted at the production and subsequent cross-border distribution of such European audiovisual content, including films (Biltereyst 1998, 83). The fear for a EU-led abolishment of state aid through the competition legislation and regulation is thus put in perspective. Significantly, however, these EU initiatives are set up as *industrial*, not *cultural* programmes.

The aim is to create European cultural content industries that are both economically competitive – in particular vis-à-vis the US – and offer sufficiently culturally diverse content. As such the EU discourse for legitimation of supportive mechanisms is a replica of the discourse on a national level. In order to achieve these objectives, supranational support instruments at a European level are deemed necessary next to existing regional and national measures, all the while emphasising the notion of subsidiarity and complementarity between national and Community mechanisms and policies (European Commission 2003b, 11 ; European Commission 2004b, 39).

From the start, it is thus clear that EU initiatives are again confronted with the necessary but difficult balancing of both economic versus cultural and subsidiarity versus supranationality concerns. Moreover, questions have arisen concerning the actual economic and cultural structural impact of these measures.

In view of the limited legal base for EU cultural interventions, it should come as no surprise that the first initiatives in view of supporting the European cultural industries were set up by another pan-European actor, the Council of Europe, through the set-up of the Eurimages fund (in 1988) and Audiovisual Eureka (launched in 1989 and abolished in 2003) (Biltereyst 1998, 82-84; European Audiovisual Observatory 2005; Pauwels 1995, 549).

Specifically for the EU, such initiatives as eContentplus , culture 2000 and i2i Audiovisual, as well as the (meanwhile abolished) action plan 16/9 or (more indirectly) via the Structural Funds, cultural projects have been financed.

Yet the foremost support has come from the MEDIA programmes (*Mesures pour Encourager le Développement de l'Industrie Audiovisuelle*), which have made several funds available for the European audiovisual industries (Europa 2004; Europa 2005a; Europa 2005b; European Commission 2004b; Pauwels 1995, 548-549).

The MEDIA programme first existed as a pilot phase for a couple of years during the late-1980s, became official with the launch of MEDIA I (200 million euro for the period 1991-1995), and was sustained through the adoption of MEDIA II (310 million euro for the period 1996-2000) (Biltereyst 1998, 83-84 ; Pauwels 1995,548).

In January 2001, the Media Plus and Media Training programmes received a budget of 400 million euro for continued support to the sector, split into 50 million euro for training and 350 million for creation, promotion[4] and pilot projects. It runs until 2006, after which a MEDIA

---

[4] This was new as it had not been identified as a specific priority for MEDIA II (European Commission 2003b, 3).

2007 programme may replace it. According to the Commission's proposal, more than one billion euro should be put aside for this programme during the period 2007-2013, for projects related to pre-production as well as post-production in the audiovisual sector, thus combining the two existing parts in an attempt to structurally simplify the Community's intervention in the audiovisual sphere. It is explicitly designed to take into account the changes brought about by digitisation and the enlargement of the EU (European Commission 2004b, 3, 5, 8, 13-14; Europa 2005b; Europa 2005c; Wheeler 2004, 352-353).

The Commission itself positively evaluates its industrial audiovisual support programmes, saying that 'The MEDIA Plus and Training programmes have become essential instruments for the European audiovisual industry and have recognised European added value for the sector' (European Commission 2004b, 5).

Applications for financial support from MEDIA have increased substantially over the years, with a rise of 120% between 2001 and 2003. However, as the budget has not been raised accordingly, this means that there is an increase in unmet needs (and related frustrations), with only 279 of the 778 applications receiving a positive reply (a 33.5% increase compared to 2001) (European Commission 2003b, 8).

Although the enormous increase of the budget as it is proposed for MEDIA 2007 might be seen as a positive signal, we must keep in mind that similar proposals have been made in the past, but that the budgets have a tendency to shrink considerably during the process leading to the set-up of the programmes. Thus for the first MEDIA programme, the Commission had initially proposed a budget of 250 million euro, with professionals even calling for 1 billion euro, only to see it cut to 200 million euro (Pauwels 1995, 551-552). Seeing how the negotiations on the EU budget for 2007-2013 diminished the global financial package as it was foreseen by European Parliament and the Commission, it is assumed that MEDIA 2007 will have to do with less financial means altogether (Temmerman and De Preter, 2006).

Significant are moreover the global discrepancies in the budget allocations for so-called 'hardware' and 'software' programmes. Compared to e.g. the 3.625 billion euro budget for 'Information Society Technologies' within the sixth R&D Framework Programme (2002-2006), the funds for MEDIA and other content-stimulating programmes are negligible. Even if we add all content and culture related programmes for the same period, the total budget remains less than 2 billion euro (Preston 2003). In comparison: the 'Centre National de la Cinématographie' (CNC), which is competent for distribution of the French state aid for the film and audiovisual industries, had a budget of 475.7 million euro in 2004 only (CNC 2005).

The level of structural impact the EU industrial policies can have on an economic level is thus questionable. The growing trade deficit with the US is a significant sign in this regard (European Commission 2003c). Emanating from an industrial logic, the EU's approach has moreover been criticised for rewarding lobbying and favouring the bigger companies, which in turn accelerates the concentration process in the audiovisual sector. While this industrial philosophy might spur growth in EU production, it does not necessarily promote 'European' culture and diversity. (Biltereyst 1998, 86; Picard 2001, 17-18). The possible cultural effect of the investments that have been done is thus put in perspective as well. In view of these criticisms, a number of authors have negatively evaluated the effect of the EU support programmes, emphasising their small budgets, fragmentation and the overall lack of coordination (Biltereyst 1998, 84; Pauwels 1995, 581-582 ; Wheeler 2004, 353). Moreover, as for the national state aid measures, one may question whether the principle of organising such financing of the cultural industries on a EU level can pass the WTO test. Even if these programmes arise from a market-centred, industrial philosophy, they might conflict with the WTO liberalisation agenda (cfr. supra).

Conclusions

In assessing to which extent state aid in the audiovisual sector is threatened by WTO and EU-led liberalisation, three main observations have come to the fore. First of all, the biggest problem seems to be the vague concepts included in the legal framework and the uncertain interpretations made on the basis thereof. On the EU level, we can definitely distinguish goodwill within both the Commission and the ECJ regarding the sustainability of national state aid regimes. Faced with Member States' concerns that their competence to set up state aid measures would be endangered by the existing legal uncertainty, the Commission tried to clarify its approach in 2001. The publication of the Cinema Communication can be seen as a legitimation and support for the idea of state aid in the film sector. A clear-cut regime has, however, not been established yet. Indeed, the compatibility of national aid schemes remains uncertain in view of the Commission's strict interpretation of the seemingly straight-forward compatibility criteria. Political goodwill is thus the most crucial factor, making the continuing legitimacy of state aid arbitrarily dependent on the political ideology and approach of the actors concerned.

Secondly, the policy outcome is not the result of one actor, but rather arises from the complex and dynamic interplay between different stakeholders. On the EU level, this can be observed between the different institutions (e.g. the ECJ and the Commission have not always been on the same wavelength in addressing the issues at stake), as well as between the institutions and the Member States. On several occasions, the Member States have successfully exerted pressures on the EU regulatory process, exemplified by the rejection of the Commission's proposal to tighten the territorialisation criterion. Nevertheless, between the different Member States as well, a consensus cannot always be found. In this context, we must keep in sight that the EU is a constructed supranational entity, a patchwork of different backgrounds, political traditions and sometimes conflicting policy goals. The traditional oppositions between cultural protectionists and liberalisation proponents may prove difficult to reconcile in the future, thus potentially putting the future consensus at risk. The systematic erosion of EU support to film through MEDIA e.g. is indeed illustrative of this lack of consensus amongst Member states.

Thirdly, the interinstitutional dialectics are not only important on the European level, but are increasingly at play globally as well. As we have seen, the WTO framework encompasses a number of provisions that are applicable to film subventions, as such possibly affecting the EU and Member States' margin for action. Again, the general view seems to be one of vagueness and unpredictability, with especially the issue of classification (virtual goods vs. virtual services) considered to be a difficult exercise towards the future. While the settlement of the audiovisual dossier has been postponed, thus giving the EU and its Member States a certain breathing space, it is certain that the conflictuous liberalisation agenda will resurface sooner rather than later. The eventual outcome is greatly dependent on the interplay between the different actors in the global arena, but often this negotiational process results in a move towards more liberalisation. Very recently, another international organisation, Unesco, has positioned itself in the middle of the battle ground as well, with the adoption of its Convention on the Protection and Promotion of the Diversity of Cultural Expressions. It remains however to be seen what the input and impact of this actor will be, since no clear hierarchy between the different instruments has been established. In sum, the uncertainty about the future of audiovisual aid persists from a global perspective as well.

The year 2007 will in any case put the case to the test, as this year is set out to be a new turning point in the establishment of EU state aid regulation, including a review of the Cinema Communication. At this time, it is uncertain to which sides of the tension fields (economy vs. culture, subsidiarity vs. supranationality) the balance will tip, but history has made clear that political willingness will be crucial. With both the EU and the WTO traditionally arising from a liberalisation perspective, the question is just how far from their path dependent project they will be able to wander. Yet as past experiences and the following quote from Cameron attest, things are not always as bleak as they seem:

> There will be difficult issues to resolve along the way, notably those related to intellectual property rights and the desire of some countries to protect their unique cultural heritage. Still, if the basic telecom agreement demonstrated anything, it is that the WTO is an extremely creative and flexible body when its Members have the will to achieve something. In audiovisual, as in telecom, if there is a will, there will be a way. (Cameron 2004, 33)

References:

Aas, Nils Klevjer. 2001. Challenges in European Cinema and Film Policy. url (Consulted April 2006): http://www.obs.coe.int/online_ publication/reports/aas.html.

Bernier, Ivan. 1998. Cultural Goods and Services in International Trade Law. In *The Culture/Trade Quandary. Canada's Policy Options*, ed. Dennis Browne, 108-148. Ottawa: Centre for Trade Policy and Law.

Biltereyst, Daniel. 1998. Television Programming Dynamics and Policy Responses. The European Policy to Protect Local Television Content Against US Imports. In *Media Dynamics & Regulatory Concerns in the Digital Age*, eds. Leen d'Haenens and Frieda Saeys, 69-90. Berlin: Quintessenz Verlags.

Cameron, Kelly. 2004. Telecommunications and Audio-visual Services in the Context of the WTO: Today and Tomorrow. In *The WTO and Global Convergence in Telecommunications and Audio-Visual Services*, eds. Damien Geradin and David Luff, 21-33. Cambridge: Cambridge University Press.

Chalaby, Jean K. 2006. American Cultural Primacy in a New Media Order. A European Perspective. *The International Communication Gazette* 68: 33-51.

CNC. 2005. Le bilan 2004 du CNC. url (Consulted December 2005): www.cnc.fr/d_stat/bilan2004/.

Cottier, Thomas. 1994. Die völkerrechtlichen Rahmenbedingungen der Film-förderung in der neuen Welthandelsorganisation WTO-GATT. *Zeitschrift für Urheber- und Medienrecht* 38: 749-759.

Council of the European Union. 2001. Press release on the 2381st Council Meeting (Cultural/Audiovisual affairs) of 5 November 2001, no. 13126/01.

Council of the European Union. 2000a. Note from the Presidency to the Au-diovisual/Cultural Affairs Council: National Subsidies to the Film and Audiovisual Industries, no. 11558/00.

Council of the European Union. 2000b. Press release on the 22261st Council Meeting (Cultural/Audiovisual affairs) of 16 May 2000, no. 8394/00.

Dony, Marianne. 1996. Les aides à l'audiovisuel à la lumière du traité de Maastricht. In *L'actualité du droit de l'audiovisuel européen*, ed. Carine Doutrelepont, 111-124. Bruxelles: Bruylant.

Europa. 2005a. Culture in the Digital Era. url (consulted December 2005): http://europa.eu.int/information_society/soccul/cult/index_en.htm.

Europa. 2005b. Audiovisual: Introduction. August, url (Consulted December 2005): http://europa.eu.int/scadplus/leg/en/lvb/l24109.htm.

Europa. 2005c. Audiovisual: MEDIA 2007: Programme of Support for the European Audiovisual Sector. January, url (Consulted December 2005): http://europa.eu.int/scadplus/leg/en/lvb/l24224a.htm.

Europa. 2004. 'Culture 2000' programme. April, url (Consulted December 2005): http://europa.eu.int/scadplus/leg/en/lvb/l29006.htm.

European Audiovisual Observatory. 2005. Communication. url (Consulted December 2005): www.obs.coe.int/about/oea/org/eureka.html.

European Commission. 2005a. i2010 – a European Information Society for Growth and Employment. Communication from the Commission to the Council, the European Parliament, the European Economic and Social Committee and the Committee of the Regions, SEC(2005) 229 final.

European Commission. 2004a. Communication from the Commission to the Council, the European Parliament, the Economic and Social Committee and the Committee of the Regions on the follow-up to the Commission Communication on certain Legal Aspects Relating to Cinematographic and Other Audiovisual Works of 26.09.2001, COM(2004) 171 final.

European Commission. 2004b. Proposal for a Decision of the European Parlia-ment and the Council Concerning the Implementation of a Programme of Support for the European Audiovisual Sector (MEDIA 2007), COM(2004) 470 final.

European Commission. 2003a. Discussion Document on the Adjustment of Compatibility Criteria for State Aid to Cinema and TV Programme Produc-tion Spelled Out in the Cinema Communication of 26.09.2001.

European Commission. 2003b. Report From the Commission to the Council, the European Parliament, the European Economic and Social Committee and the Committee of the Regions. Report on the Implementation and the Mid-term Results of the Media Plus and Media Training Programmes (2001-2005) and on the Results of the Preparatory Action 'Growth and Audiovisual: 2i Audiovisual', COM (2003) 725 final.

European Commission. 2003c. Communication From the Commission to the Council, the European Parliament, the European Economic and Social Committee and the Committee of the Regions. The Future of European Regulatory Audiovisual Policy, COM(2003) 784 final.

European Commission. 2001a. Communication From the Commission to the Council, the European Parliament, the Economic and Social Committee and the Committee of the Regions on Certain Legal Aspects Relating to Cinematographic and Other Audiovisual Works, COM(2001) 534 final.

European Commission. 2001b. Communication From the Commission on the Application of State Aid Rules to Public Service Broadcasting. Official Journal of the European Communities, 2001/C 320/04: 5-11.

European Commission. 1998. Commission Decision of 24 June 1998 on state aid no. N3/98 (France) Soutien à la production cinématographique.

European Film Companies Alliance (EFCA). 2004. *Transcript of Efca's Oral Intervention: Draft Guidelines on State Aids to the Audiovisual Sector*. Brussels: European Film Companies Alliance.

European Parliament. 2002. Report on the Commission Communication on Certain Legal Aspects Relating to Cinematographic and Other Audiovisual Works, no. A5-0222/2002 final.

FIAPF. 2004. Letter to the European Commission, DG Education and Culture. February, url (Consulted February 2006): www.fiapf.org/pdf/paulgerlocalspendlet.pdf.

Herold, Anna. 2004. EU Film Policy: Between Art and Commerce. European Diversity and Autonomy Papers. www.eurac.edu/documents/edap/2004_edap03.pdf.

Herold, Anna. 2003. European Public Film Support within the WTO Framework. *Iris Plus Legal Observations of the European Audiovisual Observatory* (June): 2-8.

Gournay, Bernard. 2002. *Exception Culturelle et Mondialisation*. Paris: Presses de Sciences Po.

Idate. 2000. Final Evaluation of the 16:9 Action Plan. Final Report. November, url (Consulted December 2005): http://europa.eu.int/comm/information_society/evaluation/pdf/report1691_en.pdf

Loman, J.M.E., K.J.M. Mortelmans, H.H.G. Post, and J.S. Watson. 1992. *Culture and Community Law Before and After Maastricht*. Deventer: Kluwer Law and Taxation.

Marcus, Carmen. 2005. *Future of Creative Industries. Implications for Research Policy*. Brussels : European Commission.

Mayer-Robitaille, Laurence. 2004. Le statut ambivalent au regard de la politique communautaire de concurrence des accords de nature culturelle et des aides d'Etat relatives à la culture. *Revue Trimestrielle de droit européen*, 40, no. 3: 477-503.

Nitsche, Ingrid. 2001. *Broadcasting in the European Union. The Role of Public Interest in Competition Analysis*. The Hague: T.M.C. Asser Press.

Pauwels, Caroline and Jan Loisen. 2006. Cultural Diversity as Commitment or Compromise. The Interinstitutional Bargaining Between WTO and Unesco in the Audiovisual Dossier. In *Beyond Borders: the Globalization of Cultural Regulation*, ed. Nicola Simpson. Forthcoming.

Pauwels, Caroline and Jean-Claude Burgelman. 2003. Policy Challenges Resulting From the Creation of a European Information Society: A Critical Analysis. In *the European Information Society. A Reality Check*, ed. Jan Servaes, 59-85. Bristol/Portland: Intellect.

Pauwels, Caroline and Jan Loisen. 2003. The WTO and the Audiovisual Sector: Economic Free Trade vs Cultural Horse Trading? *European Journal of Communication* 18, no. 3: 291-314.

Pauwels, Caroline. 1995. *Grenzen en mogelijkheden van een kwalitatief cultuur- en communicatiebeleid in een economisch geïntegreerd Europa. Een kritische analyse en prospectieve evaluatie aan de hand van het gevoerde en te voeren Europese omroepbeleid*. Brussels: Unpublished Doctoral Dissertation VUB.

Picard, Robert G. 2001. *Expansion and Limits in EU Television Markets: Audience, Advertising, and Competition Issues*. Aix en Provence: Paper presented to the workshop on Competition in Media and Advertising Markets, University of Aix Marseille-II of October 12-13.

Pons, Jean-François. 1996. La politique de Concurrence Européenne dans le domaine audiovisuel. *Competition Policy Newsletter* 2, no. 3: 6-9.

Preston, Paschal. 2003. European Union ICT Policies: Neglected Social and Cultural Dimensions. In *The European Information Society: a reality check*, ed. Jan Servaes, 33-57. Bristol: Intellect.

Quigley, Conor, and Anthony Collins. 2003. *EC State Aid Law and Policy*. Oxford: Hart Publishing.

Rawlinson, Frank. 1993. The Role of Policy Frameworks, Codes and Guidelines in the Control of State Aid. In *State Aid: Community Law and Policy*, ed. Ian Harden, 52-60. Köln: Bundesanzeiger.

Reding, Vivianne. 2005. *De la télévision sans frontières à l'audiovisuel sans frontières* (Speech). Beaune: Rencontres cinématographiques de Beaune, 22 October 2005.

Reding, Vivianne. 2003. *EU Media Policy: Culture and Competition* (Speech). Madrid: 5Th Conference on Competition Law, 27 March 2003.

Reding, Vivianne. 2001. *A New Approach to the Development of the Audiovisual Sector* (Speech). Mons: Informal meeting of Audiovisual Ministers, 5 oktober 2001.

Smiers, Joost. 2003. *Arts under Pressure. Promoting Cultural Diversity in the Age of Globalization.* London: Zed Books.

Smith, Rachael Craufurd. 2004. Community Intervention in the Cultural Field: Continuity or Change? In *Culture and European Union Law*, ed. Rachael Craufurd Smith, 19-78. Oxford: Oxford University Press.

Temmerman, Jan and Jeroen De Preter. 2006. Ook MEDIA-programma kreunt onder besparingsdruk Britse premier Tony Blair. *De Morgen*, April 13th, p. 8.

Throsby, David. 2001. *Economics and Culture.* Cambridge: Cambridge University Press.

Unesco. 2001. Cinema and audiovisual media. A survey on national cinematography. Conclusions – maintaining cinematographic diversity. url (consulted April 2006): http://www.unesco.org/culture/industries/cinema/html_eng/divers.shtml

Van Rompuy, Ben. 2005. *Nationale steunmaatregelen voor de filmsector in een economisch geïntegreerd Europa. Een inventarisatie en kritische doorlichting van de inhoud en implementatie van het communautair mededingingsbeleid t.a.v. staatssteun voor film.* Brussels: Unpublished Master's Dissertation VUB.

Weber, Olaf. 2004. From Regional to Global Freedom of Trade in Audio-visual Goods and Services ? A Comparison of the Impact on the Audio-visual Sector of the Preferential Trade Zones Established by the European Communities and the World Trade Organization. In *Culture and European Union Law*, ed. Rachael Craufurd Smith, 353-382. Oxford: Oxford University Press.

Wheeler, Mark. 2004. Supranational Regulation. Television and the European Union. *European Journal of Communication* 16: 349-369.

EUROPEAN STUDIES 24 (2007): 45-64

CULTURAL DIVERSITY AND SUBSIDIARITY: THE CASE OF CULTURAL TOURISM IN THE EUROPEAN UNION[1]

Elisabeth Dumont and Jacques Teller

Abstract

This article takes the example of cultural tourism to highlight the specificities of European Cultural Policies. It argues, that, although it is often presented as a way of supporting a diversity of approaches, styles and objectives, the subsidiarity principle can sometimes endanger the cultural diversity it seeks to protect. Tourism for instance, has long been considered as a self-regulating activity and cultural tourism is often seen as 'sustainable by nature'. Experience however shows that local authorities often lack an understanding of all the intricacies and consequences of cultural tourism development. Without proper tools for assessing and preventing negative impacts, local actors may lose control over its development, miss on benefits and endanger the diversity of cultures currently existing and co-existing in the European Union.

[1] Many thanks to members of the staff of the Committee for Culture and Education at the European Parliament for agreeing to answer our questions. Many thanks to all the experts interviewed in the context of PICTURE and those that returned a questionnaire. This article has been prepared in the framework of the PICTURE project 'Pro-active management of the Impact of Cultural Tourism upon Urban Resources and Economies'. The PICTURE project is financed by the European Commission, Sixth Framework Programme of Research, under the theme 'Policy support and anticipating scientific and technological needs', Priority 3 'Underpinning the economic potential and cohesion of a larger and more integrated European Union', Topic 3.6. 'The protection of cultural heritage and associated conservation strategies'. The contract number of the PICTURE project is SSP1-CT-2003-502491.

Introduction

Cultural tourism is the form of tourism that has the highest growth expectations (ATLAS 2005; Ashworth 2001) in an industry that is now number one in the world and the fastest growing economic sector, in terms of foreign exchange earnings and job creation (WTO 2004). Cultural tourism is located at the nexus of the process of globalisation of culture and that of fragmentation of culture and reinforcement of local identities. As a transversal activity, its development involves a variety of stakeholders with different backgrounds and different experiences. This position and array of backgrounds mean on the one hand, that tourism development often proves intricate, with diverging points of views, conflicts of interests and power relations and, on the other hand, that regulation will have to take into account the diversity of the enterprise and the diversity of cultures tourism brings together.

This article takes the example of cultural tourism to highlight the specificities of European Cultural Policies. The European Union considered it was not the role of an international institution to define the notion of culture. The European Union further argues that its originality lies in the diversity of its cultures, a position reflected in the motto recently proposed in the project of European Constitution – 'United in Diversity.' One could question whether Europe proves more culturally diverse than other continents or whether referral to this concept hides the current difficulty to adopt voluntary cultural policies at European level. The article hence starts with an introduction to the difficulty of agreeing on common definitions of politically charged notions such as culture, cultural tourism or cultural diversity. Throughout, it will look at cultural diversity as the peaceful co-existence, respect and equal value given to all types of culture and their expressions in the Union. It will also consider how cultural tourism and EU policies facilitate or hinder the protection of or quest for cultural diversity.

After discussing key concepts, the article will move to end users' expectations from the European Union in cultural policies at large and more specifically in the development of cultural tourism, based on results from surveys carried out at a European level. Although culture was not explicitly part of the Treaty of Rome establishing the European Economic Community in 1957, it can be argued that the mere idea of Europe is both a common heritage and a cultural project. The Treaty of Maastricht in 1992 definitively acknowledged this dimension of the

European construction and established competencies of the European Union in the domain of culture. The Maastricht treaty, as well as the 1996 first report on the consideration of cultural aspects in European community action, the 1996 cohesion policy and culture first framework programme in support of culture (2000-2004) will be more specifically discussed.

The action of the European Union in the domains of culture and cultural tourism still remains limited by the subsidiarity principle, which leaves the initiative to set up cultural policies to local operators (countries, regions, municipalities or private actors). Although it is presented as a way of supporting a diversity of approaches, styles and objectives, these actors often lack the tools to ensure that their policies will in fact not harm cultural diversity, or else, they may have agendas other than the protection of diversity. Experience in cultural tourism indeed shows that without proper tools for assessing and preventing negative impacts of tourism, local actors may lose control over its development and miss on benefits. The paper will then argue, that, if rights come with duties, duties also come with rights and, even if not obligatory, guidance should be provided to help countries and municipalities face their duties and foster sustainability, while allowing respect for local specificities.

Politics of Definition and Difficulties of Implementation

The preservation of cultural heritage falls under the scope of numerous European Union policies. First and foremost Article 151 of the Treaty (ex. Article 128) states that 'The Community shall contribute to the flowering of the cultures of the Member States, while respecting their national and regional diversity and at the same time bringing common cultural heritage to the fore'.

The concept of Culture proves very difficult to define. It varies dramatically in space and time and it is often stamped with subjectivity. As stated in European Commission documents, 'it is not for an institution to define the content of the concept of culture' (CEC, 1996 a). According to UNESCO, 'culture consists of all distinctive, spiritual and material, intellectual and emotional features which characterise a society or a social group' (UNESCO 1982). This definition seems very broad, possibly too much to be operational in any way. It nevertheless reflects the fact that, for these institutions, 'culture is no longer restricted to "highbrow" culture (…). Today the concept also covers popular culture, mass-produced culture, everyday culture' (CEC, 1998).

As a concept, tourism does not meet unanimity either. Consultants in tourism and statistics makers would tend to define it as a travel with at least one night away from home, while local authorities or politicians tend to include day-trippers and locals in tourism. This has an influence on the definition of policies and understanding of statistics. In Venice, for instance, 68,9 % of all tourism comes from excursionists (Manente & Rizzi, qtd. UNESCO 1994). Disregarding them would seriously impede any work on carrying capacity. Without a proper understanding of the concepts and a minimum of agreement on them, all different stake-holders will find it very hard to communicate, reach agreement and face the challenges of tourism development, protection of cultural diversity being one of them.

As cultural tourism is made up of two notions hard to circumscribe such as culture and tourism, it proves very difficult to address at a European-wide level. Definitions of cultural tourism abound among official tourist instances, statistics makers, policy makers, research groups and on the Internet. Some of them focus on the supply-side, some of them on the demand side of this market. Some refuse to categorise or include many restrictions and risk becoming too broad (eg: ICOMOS, International Tourism Charter, 2002) while others prove very specific, intending to allow a market analysis, but risking leaving out many facets of cultural tourism (eg: ATLAS 1995).

In the context of the PICTURE project[2], experts' interviews were used to elaborate a bottom-up (coming from field work rather than from literature) definition of cultural tourism. Interviews were carried out in different countries (mainly European) such as Belgium, France, the Netherlands, Spain but also, for instance Lebanon, with experience in their region of origin or/and others. Their fields of expertise, though all in one way or another related to cultural tourism, varied from town planning, infrastructure and architecture, to local involvement, passing through heritage, archaeology, tourism in itself, economy or culture. Their level of decision-making was local, regional, national or suprana-tional, and they originated from the public (elected or not) and private sector. Yet, in spite of the diversity in these profiles, they all, without

---

[2] Pro-active management of the Impact of Cultural Tourism upon Urban Re-sources Economies. See www.picture-project.com.

exception, showed unease when asked to give their own definition. The fact is they all expressed an agenda in their replies. Discourse is power as Foucault argued. Giving a definition means including certain things, aspects and leaving out some others. This usually takes place on the basis of what turns out more convenient for the speaker, whether this careful selection be conscious or unconscious.[3]

Delineating cultural tourism depends on many factors such as the purpose of the definition (understanding the concept, defining the scope of what should be included in the term, allow the production of statistics, …), the background (origin, education, etc.), the position (tourism professional or heritage conservationist) and the purpose (for instance, making cultural assets profitable versus protecting them) of the people producing the definition. Even though it is important to agree on meaning, it is also important to be aware of the difficulties and political implications of giving a definition (Dumont, Ruelle, Teller, 2005).

The concept of cultural diversity poses the same type of challenges. In its Human Development report, UNDP explains that 'individuals can have multiple identities that are complementary : ethnicity, language, religion and race, as well as citizenship'(2004:2). It further gives examples of gender and politics. In its universal declaration on cultural diversity, UNESCO avoids giving a definite list where choices may be considered political. Rather, it defines cultural diversity as 'the value through which differences are mutually related and reciprocally supportive'(2000:13). If this concept is used and debated in academic, human rights and international cultural circles, its malleability renders it hard to use it for demonstrations or applications. In this paper cultural diversity will be used to refer to the diversity of cultures found in the European Union, between countries and within countries.

The European Commission has been directly involved in the negotiation about UNESCO's Convention on the Protection and the Promotion of the Diversity of Cultural Expressions, and the ratification of the convention by the European Union is now under way. Ratification would undoubtedly reinforce the weight of culture in European Institutions, as

---

[3] For more information on the difficulty to define cultural tourism, see Dumont, Teller, Origet du Clouzeau. 2005. 'Pour une définition européenne du tourisme culturel' in Espaces, 231, novembre: 14-17, or Dumont, Ruelle, Teller. 2004. 'Circumscribing cultural tourism: Towards a criteria-based approach'. Picture Position Paper to be downloaded on www.picture-project.com.

the convention requires parties to consider the objectives of cultural diversity and the terms of the Convention when applying and interpreting their trade obligations. It is hence consistent with existing policies, whose focus is already placed on the protection and promotion of European cultural diversity. Given the ethnic variety of other continents or nations (for instant Vietnam that counts about 50 different population groups) it is questionable whether Europe proves more culturally diverse than other areas of the world. When asked about the relevancy of insisting on the cultural diversity in Europe, a high official of the secretariat of the Committee for Culture and Education at the European Parliament argues that Europe does not exactly prove more diverse than other continents but what makes the difference is the amount of respect and protection of cultural diversity. 'All over the European Continent, diversity is recognised as a good point, as something that deserves respect and protection.' (Interview January 2006).

This care for cultural diversity finds an expression at European level through the principle of cultural exception (even though this mainly concerns economic competition) and through the European institutions internal procedures. The contacts with local population and cultural stakeholders largely rely on the work of European deputies who are expected to bring forward the concerns of their constituencies. With the best of will however, it proves hard for one individual to reflect the diversity of the very large areas that s/he sometimes represents. Other types of contact thus take place, such as the recently started newsletter for cultural and educational stakeholders, as well as hearings during Parliamentary meetings or meetings between members of Parliament and workers of cultural centres. Associations can request a hearing during Parliamentary meetings or a meeting with members of the secretariat of the Committee for Culture and Education in order to draw attention on existing or subsisting problems, to report on the progress made or suggest new projects. These actions demonstrate the Committee's commitment to participation and respect of cultural diversity, but the form it takes can make it hard for cultural stakeholders not regrouped in an association or without access to official circles to make their voices heard.

End-users' Expectations in terms of Cultural Tourism

According to a survey sent to 250 small-and-medium-sized European towns in the context of PICTURE project and 25 direct interviews with professionals directly or indirectly related to tourism, the European Union has an important role to play in tourism development. As one of our experts phrases it: 'reducing the border effect makes it obligatory to reinforce, indeed to adopt regulations and common ways of operating' (Liège, archaeology).[4]

The sample for questionnaires included 250 small-and-medium- sized towns in Europe, covering the different areas of the European Union: East, South, West and North, including candidate countries. It was divided into developing destinations − where local authorities seek to further increase the number of visitors − and mature destinations − where the issue is no longer to increase but to manage the number of visitors (eg.: increase the share of overnight tourists or develop carrying capacity measures). Interviews with experts were realised on the basis of semi-conducted direct interviews on a qualitative, explorative mode. A fair representative sample of each country was not sought after. Experts were rather chosen on the basis of their reputation in their respective domains. Diversity was however looked for, not only in the communities of origin but also in the area of expertise, sector and level of decision-making or influence (local, regional, national or international). In order to avoid receiving a monolithic image it was decided to interview, along with tourism specialists, experts whose core expertise does not lie in tourism but face its development everyday (town planners, archaeologists, representatives of local neighbourhoods, etc.).

Most towns agree on the role the European Union should play in cultural tourism development. They locate it, on the one hand, in the promotion of networks, exchanges, good practices at supranational or supraregional level and, on the other hand, in funding. About 57% of towns where tourism is in development and nearly half (47%) of mature destinations mention funding. An expert, mayor of a town declared world heritage by UNESCO, confirms this feeling and explains that he spent the first three months in his position looking for European Funds,

---

[4] All quotations in this section come from interviews with experts all over Europe. The town, region or other level of expertise of the expert is mentioned, followed by its domain.

and that it is these Funds that have allowed him to foster a sustainable development of his town:

> I devoted every minute of my first months to a search for European funds. We succeeded in getting some for the rehabilitation of the left side of the river – bring the river closer to town – a project of 1000 millions (pesetas), and the plan terminates exactly in the creation of the future convention centre. Alarza bridge, the convention centre, the environment centre San Seguno, the Hipica, the aim is to regain a lot of things. And the 'INTERREG' for improving accessibility to the historical centre is something else we worked on (Avila, tourism).

Promoting twinning, networks, exchanges between towns with similar typologies, disseminating good practices, experience and expertise in general appear nearly as important. It is brought up by 37% of towns where tourism is developing and more than half (52%) of towns where it is mature. As one expert phrases it 'A network can help to establish a network of experience' (Amiens, heritage). Surprisingly, the more mature a town, the stronger the need for guidance. This probably reflects growing awareness of the challenges of tourism but also means guidance will prove increasingly necessary in a world where tourism grows faster.

Tourism promotion, mainly the sustainable form of tourism, as well as technical and procedural advice, also come to light but to a lesser extent. About 20% of developing towns insist on the need of guidelines, support, help and a slightly lesser (18,75%) percentage of mature town agree and mention technical advice. This often relates to EU paperwork that sometimes proves obscure for small municipalities. Yet, mature towns seem to take some distance, put everything into perspective and argue for a European tourism strategy.

Another expert questions this method, since tourism is a world phenomenon and rather argues for diffusion and promotion of knowledge, thus agreeing with the respondents of the questionnaires:

> Efforts have not only been European but international, at world level, through charters and so on, (...).. There, we arrive at a problem of, in a way, level of jurisdiction and regulation (...). And to know whether we need to translate these recommendations into laws, including national laws, that's another problem. I can hardly make a comparison; it is (hesitation) how to make something we produce efficient. Well, if we need to do it that way in order to make it efficient, I don't know and actually, I am not sure about it. I think that the main role, to start with, is the diffusion of that type (sustainable) of thinking (Liège, archaeology).

In the face of the rapid growth of cultural tourism and its correlated challenges, there exists a strong call for a clear definition and regulation that would allow an effective cultural tourism policy at local and global level. We face the paradox of a concept nearly impossible to define and the need to have a clear definition to implement an effective cultural tourism policy, as well as the paradox of one of the biggest economic sector where people are left to their own devices. PICTURE's first answer to this has been to suggest criteria to assess the sustainability of tourism, such as principle of participation (involvement of the local population), principle of precaution (respect of cultural diversity), principle of durability (promote a pro-active approach in order to focus on long-term challenges), principle of integration (respect of the different pillars of sustainable development) (Dumont, Teller, Origet du Clouzeau, 2005). Also, the team is currently developing a framework for the strategic urban governance of cultural tourism and a tool for its impact assessment.

Subsidiarity Principle and EU culture and cultural tourism policies

The recent acceleration of European integration (common monetary unit, enlargement process etc.) combined with the growing speed of globalisation raised real anxieties among citizens of the Union that what they perceive as their culture, in the broader meaning, may be harmed by foreign or centralised regulation (Sørensen and Vaever, 1992, Cram, 2001, Batt, 2001). Therefore, Article 151 of the Treaty adopts a very cautious approach regarding the subsidiarity principle. Point 5 of this Article explicitly requires that the Council activities be limited to incentive measures, excluding any harmonisation of the laws and regulations of the Member Sates. It also states that the Council shall act unanimously in cultural matters. According to this principle, the European Union will have to act 'as something which guarantees the existence and flowering of cultures rather than something which dilutes the European cultural identities' (CEC, 1998).

Unlike culture, tourism does not constitute a Community policy in itself and, by virtue of the principle of subsidiarity, primarily comes within the remit of the Member Sates. Article 2 of the Treaty lists the promotion of sustainable development of economic activities as one of the Community's tasks. Article 3(u) of the Treaty provides for Community action to comprise measures in the field of tourism for the purposes set out in Article 2. Accordingly, the action of the European Union in the domain of tourism has traditionally been conceived as an extension of its wider economic policy, though largely limited to incentives and support programmes.

It was proposed in the Constitutional Treaty to remove the unanimity barrier for decisions relating to culture and to introduce a new title (Article III-281) specifically dedicated to tourism in order to enable the European Union to adopt measures to complement actions within the Member States. Such modifications could prove beneficial for the coherence of the Community's action in the domains of culture and tourism, especially as the European Commission designated cultural tourism as a key area of tourism development in Europe (Richards, 1996). In the meantime the European Union influence on cultural tourism remains largely indirect as it relies on other sectoral policies, such as transport, culture or regional development.

The Culture 2000 Framework and Regional Funds

Unlike for tourism so far, specific policies for culture exist at European level. The EU adopted its first framework programme, Culture 2000, in support of culture in 1998 (CEC, 1998). It seeks to integrate into a unified framework the different incentive measures scattered until then along three main incentive programmes, Kaleidoscope, Ariane and Raphael. This programme introduces the idea of a European cultural area, 'which is open, varied and founded on the principle of subsidiarity, cooperation between all those involved in the cultural sector, the promotion of a legislative framework conducive to cultural activities and ensuring respect for cultural diversity, and the integration of the cultural dimension into Community policies as provided for in the Article 151(4) of the Treaty' The idea of a common European cultural area promotes the view that most cultural trends in Europe progressively gain a transnational character, while the preservation of cultural diversity and mutual knowledge are obviously very important aspects.

The main objective of the framework programme is the promotion of cultural dialogue as well as mutual knowledge of the cultures and histories of the European peoples. The Culture 2000 Framework hence stresses the role of culture in socioeconomic development in view of ensuring direct recognition of culture as an economic factor and as a drive of social integration and citizenship. Three main types of actions were proposed in support of this programme: limited innovative and/or experimental actions (multimedia development, cooperation between cultural and socio-cultural operators for instance); significant integrated actions (mobility of artists, training for instance); and special cultural events (European Capital of Culture for instance).

Six years after the launch of this programme, it is generally accepted that cultural projects are better and more easily supported through European Regional Funds than Culture 2000 fund (FEAP, 2004). This can be explained by the fact that only 0,03% of the European Union's budget has been allocated to the Culture 2000 programme, while Regional Funds account for over one third of the budget (Pire, 2002). Besides, Regional Funds are primarily directed to support regional development and increase social cohesion. Cultural projects supported by these funds have thus to be based on strong socio-economic objectives, which are often directly or indirectly related to cultural tourism. It has been estimated for instance that, in France, some 10% of Regional Funds for the period 2000-2006 will directly benefit the tourism sector (Guicheney & Rouzade, 2004). Arguably the conditions of access to these Regional Funds constitute a very efficient lever to foster a genuine cultural tourism policy respectful of the cultural diversity of European Regions.

Culture and Tourism in other European policies

The importance and transversality of culture is taken seriously in the EU: whenever an area of EU policy has consequences for culture, the cultural aspect needs to be taken into account (Interview high official in the Committee for Culture and Education at the European Parliament, January 2006). Point 4 of article 151 of the Treaty thereby states that 'the Community shall take cultural aspects into account in its action under other provisions of the Treaty, in particular in order to respect and promote the diversity of its cultures' Point 5 of Article 151 (see above) does not affect the bases on which a number of harmonisation measures with a cultural dimension have already been, and continue to be, taken into account in other EU competency areas. We find among these the social and human resources policy, the cohesion and regional development policy or the competition policy.

A First Report on the consideration of cultural aspects in European Community action was issued by the Commission in 1996 (CEC, 1996 a). It was rapidly followed by a report more specifically addressing the impact of cohesion policies on cultural development and derived employment (CEC, 1996 b). The contribution of Structural Funds to the preservation and conservation of cultural heritage is quite important. Funding may be dedicated to projects concerning historic buildings, large industrial remnants or even entire urban historical areas. Yet here again the action of the EU is mostly oriented towards incentive actions and operational projects, not a specifically coordinated policy at European level.

Tourism is also affected by a number of European policies (CEC, 2001), but, unlike cultural matters, tourism is predominantly viewed as an economic activity. It has thus been traditionally addressed by the Enterprise Directorate General of the European Commission. Though, one of the experts interviewed in the PICTURE project explains that even if the industry of tourism is the first provider of jobs in Europe, its fragmented structure (mainly small and local entrepreneurs or retailers) does not allow it to easily reach a strong representation at the European level (Interview Tourism Consultant, mainly at European level)

Two other experts insist on the difficulty to reach an agreement on tourism strategies within Europe, since member states hold most competencies over tourism and do not share common visions about the role of public institutions in its development. Tourism is hence framed by alternative approaches at the moment, allowing some partial influence on policy. However this fragmentation does not allow the development of a true 'Destination Europe' strategy. The organisation of trans-national cultural 'routes' or 'itineraries' represents one solution to the question of sharing expertise and working with different localities on global agendas.

The Subsidiarity Principle and frameworks for action

The strength of the subsidiarity principle currently seems to impede the adoption of common strategic rules and principles guiding cultural tourism at a European level. Voluntary schemes and guidance systems aim to improve the management of cultural tourism. Examples include European eco-labelling, local agenda 21, WTO guidance or integral quality management of urban tourism. However, all of these schemes lack any constraining authority. This appears problematic as impacts upon cultural heritage often prove irreversible, while local authorities tend to underestimate negative impacts of tourism and often focus on its short-term economic benefits.

PICTURE surveys bring to light the overwhelmingly attractive and positive image of tourism within small-and-medium-sized towns. However, they also highlight knowledge gaps, lack of attention for impacts assessment, holistic or long term approaches. Strikingly, the more mature a tourist destination becomes, the more nuanced the positive connotations of tourism become. In our survey, for instance, one fifth of developing destinations nuanced their answers and half of mature towns tuned down their optimism.[5]

Without the proper tools for assessing and preventing negative impacts of tourism, countries lose control over and very often, benefits of tourist developments to the profit of private companies. This can lead to destruction of heritage, prettification, lost authenticity or subcultures rather than expected positive socio-economic impacts. For instance, the PICTURE project highlights that the development of cultural tourism can have very divergent impacts on the urban landscape. On the one hand, the growth of this industry can constitute a strong rationale for conserving a small town's remarkable skyline and natural environment, as it has been the case in the small city of Telč (Czech Republic). A counter-example can be found in the case of Český Krumlov, that was nominated as UNESCO World heritage site the same year as Telč (1992). In this latter case though, the urban landscape was largely altered by new tourist facilities, new buildings and changes in public spaces. There is a risk that the nature of the place passes from a heritage to a mere attraction site whose image is largely driven by consumers' demands (Zukin, 1993, Urry 1990). The city of Amiens (France) is another interesting case as the recently adopted tourism strategy fostered a deep reinvestment in the urban landscape of the city. Still the Perret tower, a modern building of the 1950s, is now threatened for deterring the image of the city, while, though not meeting current criteria of 'sexy architecture' it certainly contributes to the identity of the city. The balance between integration in the landscape and promotion of the local (built) diversity therefore proves very difficult for many tourism destinations but it is also a source of cultural diversity, as it reflects different eras, and different backgrounds and is approached in diverse ways throughout Europe.

---

[5] More information on this can also be found in Deliverable 3 of Picture Project: Multi-dimensional matrix of impacts, by Dumont, Ruelle, Teller to be found on www.picture-project.com/ in the 'deliverables' section.

It has to be further stressed that landscape concerns largely extend beyond aesthetic considerations. In the case of Telč, special efforts had to be made in order to preserve a balance between services for the tourists and for the local population. Obviously the mix of services and uses of public spaces forms part of the identity of a place. Unfortunately such factors are sometimes disregarded in large rehabilitation projects, concentrating heavily on the upgrading of the physical environment with few, if any, resources for supporting the social and cultural fabric of the locality. Aware of this issue, the city of Syracuse (Italy) is now directing part of local and European funds allocated to the development of tourism towards educational and cultural projects.

Indeed, in many places where large, organised cultural enterprises have seen the light, there are complaints about the obliteration of alternative cultural offers as funding is canalised to these enterprises. These are usually partly financed by public monies, which leaves little room for the expression of local artists, sometimes less fancy or marketable, or artists who do not share the same vision of culture as that put forward by the authorities (Massart, 2004, Delgado Ruiz, 2000). Bilbao's Guggenheim, this icon of cultural tourism, has 'been criticised for taking over most of Bilbao's public budget for cultural activities (Zallo 1995)' (Gomez & Gonzalez 2001), while its franchise aspect restricts choice of art exhibited, which is not made at local level or in a participative manner. Culture and heritage become commodities, mere instruments in the consumption game. They increasingly develop into a top-down business model, with elites deciding what needs to be produced and sponsoring it, according to expected profitability. The needs and desires of locals are often disregarded and cultural diversity disappears in the search for the typical or the need to produce one profitable type of artefact (Lask, 2005).

According to a high official from the secretariat of the Committee for Culture and Education at the European Parliament, however, problems arise more from a lack of budget than a lack of will. He insists that currently, only 7 cents per European citizen goes to culture while he argues that more than ten times that amount would be necessary to answer all demands. In such a situation, priorities appear of utmost importance and the crucial questions are who makes decisions on funding and spending: for example on a big eye-catching project or a variety of small local and discrete projects? There is a lot of demand from associations and organisations to provide funds or assistance, the Committee for Culture wants to intervene and display more proactivity but the subsidiarity principle impedes many of these actions, at least in the short term.

The choice of cultural activities and the treatment given to culture depends on the Member States but some effort is being made to influence specific Member States. For instance, a resolution can be adopted in the Parliament to try and stop some practices and without singling out one state, it is possible to use informal negotiations or bilateral agreements to preserve cultural diversity in spite of national policies. Such negotiations and resolutions recommend a set of actions. They do not bear any constraining effect, yet political consequences. The subsidiarity principle is not as strict as it seems but it still exerts power. It prevents immediate progress but 'we should give time to try and find a procedure that suits everybody and answers all expectations' (Interview high official in the Committee for Culture and Education at the European Parliament, January 2006)

European Capitals of Culture Programme as an incentive for strategic planning

The policy of European Capital of Culture included in the Culture 2000 framework has an impact beyond the local level, such as regional and international consequences. It allows regeneration within the chosen towns and emphasising European elements across the continent, since there is an obligation to emphasise Cultural Europe (rather than *the* culture of Europe).

This however, can create problems, as non European influences can be disregarded in the bid. For instance, the brochure about Mons 2015 puts the emphasis on European references while others receive hardly any attention. In the brochure explaining why it thinks it deserves to become European capital of Europe, the names of different artists are given who 'have brought a stone to European culture' (6).[6] The brochure repeatedly highlights European connections and obliterates, for instance, the different waves of migration that Mons witnessed over the past centuries.[7] Only at one point does the official prospectus mention that 'the project favours dialogue between cultures of Europe and other cultures

---

[6] From *Mons: capitale européenne de la culture en 2015*. All quotations in this paragraph come from this brochure unless otherwise mentioned.

[7] 'Mons 2015, an eminently European project' (9) or 'the project puts forwards cultural currents common to all Europeans' (10) or 'the project establishes long term cultural cooperations and favours circulation within the Union' (11).

of the world' (15), but this takes the form of musical festivals 'pretexts to discover culture, gastronomy or the communities of these countries implanted here' (15). On the one hand, this means reducing them to the "other", setting them on display as the exotic to be watched, tasted and discovered but never closes enough to be really part of the project and shaping it. On the other hand, surveys about quality of life and festivals carried out in the context of the PICTURE project evidence that this specific festival is hardly known within the population of Mons.

The jury deciding on the towns chosen for European Capital has to make sure that an equilibrium is reached between local, European and international influences, as well as between ambitious projects and local benefits. Capitals of Culture offer unique opportunities for cultural development on a large scale and bring benefits to the towns chosen. However, the procedure and criteria could be revised, first to make application and designation procedures easier, second to not allow political ambitions to overshadow the cultural dimension and integrate better long-term impacts (Palmer/RAE Associates, 2004). More guidance for candidate towns also proves necessary, as well as a system that would allow bidding towns to learn from past capitals and work in networks with good practices (Interview high official in the Committee for Culture and Education at the European Parliament, January 2006).

Research shows, however, that the bidding process itself and the fact that countries can only bid at a specific time, motivates towns to elaborate strategic cultural tourism plans that have benefits beyond the event, in terms of impact and their length. In Mons, for instance, the desire to bid has led to the development of a strategy (2004) for a new town project, auditing qualities and challenges and suggesting different axes of development for at least the coming decade. It is still unknown whether Mons will be successful in this enterprise. Belfast however offers us a good example of the importance of the bidding process. After failure, it was realised that the bidding process itself had major significance for the town, as it triggered many elements such as 'joint working, cross-community discussion and a coming together of the city's cultural resources' (Sutherland 2006:2). It was therefore decided to continue working in that direction (i.e. for the development of cultural tourism with local participation) and this gave way to the launch of a Cultural Tourism Strategy by Belfast city council in 2003. Capitals of culture play a significant role in sustainable development since they force towns to think in the long term and develop strategic plans. It is therefore very important to have specific criteria that foster sustainable development and make sure culture gets a prominent role alongside with political or economic factors.

Conclusion

Cultural diversity plays a central and unique role in EU cultural policies. This finds its most significant expression in the subsidiarity principle that prevents any general or centralised law or regulation about culture and leaves. The aim is to lead to a flowering of cultures rather than to globalisation and uniformity. Even though the construction of Europe started as an economic enterprise, culture now plays an increasing role. Its importance as a cohesive force, a vector of development has been realised, as well as the wealth constituted by the diversity of European cultures. This has given way to different actions such as European Capitals of Culture and the need to take culture into account for any action that will influence it. The specificity of EU policies then seems to lie, on the one hand, in the absence of rigid rules and on the other hand, in transversality

Even though this has the benefits of allowing freedom to the Member States, research on interdisciplinary questions such as cultural tourism shows that it can also mea that Member States or their components have to respond to a situation they do not always master, without the proper tools or guidance to face the challenges. Small and medium-sized towns in Europe often resort to tourism in the hope of economic revitalisation but lack the tools or resources to develop it in sustainable ways. They ask more than anything for guidance and funding from the European Union, rather than being left to their own devices. In the absence of support, the very cultural diversity that is aimed to be protected is actually endangered, as is evidenced in the cases mentioned.

At the moment, the European Union plays a role of global monitoring through diverted methods, such as keeping an eye on developments and reacting through resolutions, lobbying, negotiations or bilateral agreements. This article argues for more guidance and tools for development of tourism for the protection of cultural diversity. If such tools cannot be made compulsory, they can at least be made available and incentives could be provided for their use. That would mean, for instance, increasing the budget of culture.

Moreover, explicit and strong criteria in the different cultural actions are important in keeping in line with sustainable development. It also proves important to ensure that culture remains at the centre of such actions, not only economy or politics.

Admittedly, strict criteria and general guidelines can restrict freedom but guidelines can improve awareness, foster sustainability and lead to European integration and cooperation. This is more helpful than leaving members prey to the forces of globalisation or the survival of the fittest. In times of European expansion and the danger of a two-speed Europe this appears of utmost importance.

References

Ashworth, G.J. 2001. Conservation of the Built Environment in the Netherlands. In *the Construction of Built Heritage: A North European Perspective on Policies, Practices and Outcomes*, edited by Phelps & Johannson. London: Ashgate.

Batt, Judy. 2001. EU Citizenship and pan-Europeanism. In *Interlocking Dimensions of European Integration*, ed. Helen Wallace, 265-283. Basingstoke: Palgrave.

Commission of the European Communities (CEC). 1996 a. first report on the consideration of cultural aspects in european community action - com (96) 160, commission of the european communities, Brussels.

Commission of the European Communities (CEC). 1996 b. cohesion policy and culture. a contribution to employment - com (96) 512, commission of the european communities, Brussels.

Commission of the European Communities (CEC). 1996 c. environmental impact assessment – guidance on scoping, european commission, directorate general – environment, nuclear safety and civil protection, may 1996.

Commission of the European Communities (CEC). 1996 d. proposal for a council directive on the assessment of the effects of certain plans and programmes on the environment – com (1996) 511 final, Brussels.

Commission of the European Communities (CEC). 1998. First Framework Programme in support of Culture (2000-2004) - COM (1998) 266, Brussels.

Cia, Blanca. 2004. Los vecinos de los barrios de Diagonal Mar, Maresme y Besos piden compensaciones por el impacto del Forum. El Pais Catalunya. 27 May.

Cities and local governments for cultural development. 2004. Agenda 21 for culture; www.agenda21cultura.net [accessed 3/12/2004],

Delgado Ruiz, Manuel. 2000. Usos sociales y politicos del turismo cultural. In J. Larossa & C. Skliar (eds), *Habitantes de Babel. Politica y poéticas de la diferencia*. Barcelona: Laertes, 245-276.

Cram, Laura. 2001. European Identity and National Identity in Central and Eastern Europe. In *Interlocking Dimensions of European Integration*, ed. Helen Wallace, 248-265. Basingstoke: Palgrave.

Dumont, Elisabeth, Ruelle, Christine & Teller, Jacques. 2004. Multidimensional Matrix Gathering of Impacts, Methods and Policy Measures. Deliverable 3 of 'Picture Project,' www.picture-project.com/

Dumont Elisabeth, Teller Jacques, Origet du Clouzeau, Claude. 2005 'Pour une définition européenne du tourisme culturel' in *Espaces*, 231, novembre: 14-17.

Dumont Elisabeth, Teller Jacques, Origet du Clouzeau, Claude. 2004. 'Circum-scribing Cultural Tourism: Towards a Criteria-based Approach' Picture Position Paper to be downloaded on www.picture-project.com.

Forum Européen pour les Arts et le Patrimoine (FEAP). 2004. *Culture et Regions d'Europe. Premiers elements d'étude sur les politiques culturelles des Régions d'Europe.* Lille: Conseil Régional du Pas de Calais.

Gomez, Maria & Gonzalez, Sara.2001. A reply to Beatriz Plaza's 'The Guggenheim-Bilbao Museum Effect'. *International Journal of Urban and Regional Research*, 25(4), 898-900.

Guicheney, Jean-Claude & Rouzade, Gérard. 2003. *Le tourisme dans les programmes européens.* Paris: La Documentation française.

International Council of Museums and Sites (ICOMOS). 2002. *Inernational Cultural Tourism Charter. Principles and Guidelines for Managing Tourism at Places of Cultural and Heritage Significance.* ICOMOS International Cultural Tourism Committee.

Lask, Tomke. 2005. Protecting the Golden Goose Without Stuffing it or How to Create Efficient Policies to Protect Intangible Heritage. Draft of June 2005 keynote speech for UNESCO gathering on cultural tourism in Riga.

Massart, Guy (2004) Commentaries on D3 : Multidimensional Matrix Gathering of Impacts, Methods and Policy Measures. Unpublished commentaries.

Palmer/RAE Associates . 2004. 'European Cities and Capitals of Culture' Study Prepared for the European Commission, can be downloaded on europa.eu.int/comm/culture/eac/sources_info/studies/capitals_fr.html.

Pire, Jean-Miguel. 2002. Pour une politique culturelle européenne, Notes de la Fondation Robert Schuman, Note 1.

Richards, Greg. (ed.) 1996. *Cultural Tourism in Europe.* Wallingford: CAB International.

Sørensen, Henning & Vaever, Ole. 1992. State, Society and Democracy and the Effect of the EC. In *Denmark and EC membership evaluated*, ed Lise Lyck, 13-27. London: Pinter.

Sutherland, Margaret. 2006. 'Belfast – Unsuccessful Bidding Candidate for 2008' unpublished notes to be further included in Deliverable 16 of the PICTURE project, available on www.picture-project.com.

United Nations Development Programme (UNDP). 2004. Cultural Liberty in Today's Diverse World. Human Development Report. New York : UNDP.

United Nations Educational, Scientific and Cultural Organisation (UNESCO). 2002. Preliminary draft of a convention on the protection of the diversity of cultural contents and artistic expressions. CLT-2004/CONF.201/CLD.2.

United Nations Educational, Scientific and Cultural Organisation (UNESCO). 1994. *Tourism and Cities of Art : The Impact of Tourism and Visitors Flow Management in Aix-en-Provence, Amsterdam, Bruges, Florence, Oxford, Salzburg and Venice.* Venice: UNESCO regional office for Science and Technology for Europe.

United Nations Educational, Scientific and Cultural Organisation (UNESCO). 2000. Universal Declaration on Cultural Diversity.

Urry, John. 1990. *The Tourist Gaze: Leisure and Travel in Contemporary Societies.* London: Sage.

Ville de Mons. 2004. MONS : Capitale européenne de la culture en 2015.

World Tourism Organisation (WTO). 2004. Outbound Tourism – International Tourist Arrivals by generating region www.world-tourism.org/facts/trends/outbound.htm.

World Tourism Organisation (WTO). 2004. World Tourism Barometer, 2(3):1-3.

www.atlas-euro.org/ ; [accessed 25/01/2005].

www.mons.be ; [accessed 1/12/2004].

Zukin, Sharon. 1993. *Landscapes of Power: from Detroit to Disneyworld.* Berkeley: University of California Press.

EUROPEAN STUDIES 24 (2007): 65-90

MEDIATING SOCIAL COHESION:
MEDIA AND CULTURAL POLICY
IN THE EUROPEAN UNION AND CANADA[1]

Katharine Sarikakis

Abstract

The paper explores the ways in which audiovisual media policies articulate a particular agenda for cultural and political diversity in the European Union. It explores the approaches of Canada and EU to the question of social cohesion and problematises their respective agenda priorities. Locating media policy within the globalised context of market integration and supra-and-international policymaking, the article identifies not only perceptions – and realities – of concerns shared across two distinctive political and social contexts, Canada and the EU, but also a remarkable similarity in their approach to these problems. The article argues that globalisation provides a broader context within which the quest for diversity and the processes leading to the articulation of solutions and future policy is directly linked to the interaction between the pressures deriving from the conflict of representation of private interests and the social justice claims from diverse corners of societies.

Introduction

This article explores the ways in which media and cultural policy in the European Union is conceived as a tool for diversity and social cohesion.

[1] The author gratefully acknowledges the support of a British Academy Grant for conducting field work in Canada in 2004 which has formed part of this research. I am also grateful to Neil Blain who has offered the most constructive critique to earlier versions of this paper.

Through juxtaposition to the Canadian experience, it aims to demonstrate the similarity of claims and concerns that make up the political deliberation fabric of media and culture policy and the differences in their materialisation. Canada is seen as a proponent for the protection of culture, recognition of multiculturalism and diversity, and an advocate for progressive redistributive social policy, including the media and cultural industries. Therefore it is often approached as a useful and familiar example on which EU policymakers can draw, in order to design policy that addresses a similar range of issues. This article further locates the EU, and for that reason also Canada, within the broader spectrum of globalisation and brings attention to policy which, despite its significance for generalisable interests and therefore a broader category of actors, it remains outside the 'endgame' of policy output.

The policy experiences of the EU and Canada offer an interesting canvas that narrates the discursive and political economic frames of culture and media, cultural diversity and social cohesion in the two polities. Next to the more (or less) obvious differences between Canada and the EU, such as their political organisation, cultural makeup as well as proximity to economies of scale, there are common experiences and references that point to shared concerns and conceptions about the role of media and cultural policy. The debates surrounding the changes in the field and in particular in broadcasting de- and re-regulation are based on distinctive ideological underpinnings. These exemplify conflicting positions among free-market and interventionist approaches and are certainly neither apolitical nor neutral, as policy is often claimed to be. Moreover, in both polities, the structural reorganisation of the state as a consequence of globalisation determined the structural organisation of their respective media landscapes. Finally, in both cases, international structural determinants, ideological positions and the tensions between various interests underwrote the (supra)national approach to management of challenges in policy and their proposed solutions.

Next to these phenomena, which I am discussing later on, important struggles on the 'symbolic' immaterial level of culture have increasingly defined the quality and direction of media policy arguments. Overall, despite the hegemonic prevalence of neoliberal measures, the design and implementation of media and cultural policy proposals, especially when initiated by the European Parliament (EP) and the Canadian House of Commons, are driven by two overarching, distinct but interlinked, desires. On the one hand, proposed policies aim to counterbalance the cultural deficit by promoting 'domestic' cultural production vis a vis the Hollywood audiovisual (AV) industry and effects of cultural imperialism. On the other hand, both polities pursue a 'top down' approach to cultivate, through media and cultural policy, a common identity, whether in the sense of 'nationhood' as the Canadian case may articulate or in the broader sense of cultural belonging, as the European project may identify as a necessary condition for the legitimacy of the polity.

Within the framework of policymaking in these two constituencies, there comes to life a more global set of power dynamics, which is rooted in the tensions between the tendency of capital towards global expansion and the accompanying processes of social dispossession, economic polarisation and cultural fragmentation. The media and cultural industries are situated within the very core of these tensions and epitomize fundamental questions related to the role of culture for people's sense of place, identity and autonomy. In a world characterised by capital as well as human dis-and-relocation, the transformation of social institutions and institutional roles, and changing notions of citizenship, the question of social cohesion becomes a significant conceptual and strategic framework for public policy and social action.

Social cohesion, institutions and interests in the macro-level context

The relationship of social cohesion and cultural policy is an under-researched area in policy analysis. On the one hand, studies of EU media and cultural policy, but also the project of European integration in more general terms tend to concentrate on the particularities of the EU in its supranational institutional architecture, often neglecting the broader international environment within which the polity is called to operate. On the other hand, the question of social cohesion, which is addressed in a variety of ways by other disciplines, is not visibly linked to the European question in terms of media and cultural policy. Consequently, there is a lack in studies that address the impact of 'exogenous shocks' on the internal institutional organisation and the change in the ideological underpinnings of policy (Golob 2003) and the relationship of these dynamics to that of cultural policy and social cohesion. To better contextualise the changes in media and cultural policy, and in particular in appreciating the shift to a neo-liberal agenda, and their relation to the question of social cohesion, it is important to explore the ideas and basis of the legitimisation of policy, while taking into account a complex set of international exogenous factors, the internal institutional dynamics and the ways in which they provide a response to exogenous and domestic demands. These dynamics are expressed within the process and objects of policy, reflecting conflicts among positions, or 'stakeholders' as some of the recent international communications policy literature began to refer to, international and domestic periods of crisis and subsequent institutional changes.

The concept of social cohesion is explored in a variety of disciplines both from the perspective of causing certain outcomes, such as prosperity and economic productivity, political stability etc, and as an outcome itself, the degree of which results from factors such as globalisation, technology or cultural diversity (Beauvais & Jenson 2002). Although the causal relationship between social cohesion and these factors has not been empirically 'proven', their interrelationship and unilateral association is evident. Social cohesion is understood as the 'coming together' of communities, the fostering of partnerships and intercultural understanding, as well as the material and cultural sustainability of societies in cultural policy (Maloutas & Pantelidou Malouta 2004; Jeannote 2003; Beauvais & Jenson 2002). Kearns and Forrest (2000) break down 'social cohesion' into common values pattern, structured solidarity, social networks, group identification, and social capital, an approach that aims to make the concept more tangible for epistemological and policymaking purposes. Nevertheless, the problems associated with the use of the term social cohesion are not insignificant. Having become the antonym of 'social exclusion', itself a vague and problematic term that is used to redefine social inequality in terms of segregation from mainstream participation in the market, such as through consumption, social cohesion occupies a ubiquitous position among policy 'pragmatists', middle class groups, the New Labour as well as nationalists opposing multicultural agendas. The ambiguity of the concept is also related to the rise of conservative politics and its attempt to reconcile claims of social justice with neoliberal policies of the privatisation of solving social problems, something that until now and at least for the Left was considered irreconcilable (Maloutas & Pantelidou Malouta 2004).

In the EU context, the concept has been used to provide a counter-value to the overwhelmingly market-driven integrationism and to the projected US model of corporatist capitalism as one for the economic development of Europe. 'The content of social cohesion is therefore not a situation that can be unambiguously predefined following meticulous analysis but an issue at stake, and this is why it remains unclear and elusive' (Maloutas & Pantelidou Malouta 2004, 452). It is perhaps this level of ambiguity that reflects at the same time both the forces at play in the European project, as expressed through clusters representing conflicting interests and visions of the EU, and the multifaceted functions of media and culture in this specific field of policy. For Canada, the claim for social cohesion follows along similar lines of multifaceted aspects of the role of culture and media as well as the approaches to what cohesion, in this case national, may constitute in a globalised world. In both cases, ultimately social cohesion and media and cultural policy are related to the changing notions of citizenship and the lived experience of the citizen-subject[2], and her/his relationship to institutions as shaped through policy.

The normative function of institutions, such as the EP or the Canadian House of Commons, as parliamentary and therefore minimally representational expressions of citizens' interests, rests to a great extent on their ability to perform an ideological form of justification 'which either asserts or counterfactually supposes a generalisability of interests, that is dominant' (Habermas 2004 [1976] , 112). This 'generalisability of interests' constitutes also the 'test method' according to which the 'suppression of generalisable interests' can be compared discursively to the normative structures in a given society. Habermas argues that 'the specific achievement of such ideologies consists in the inconspicuous manner in which communication is systematically limited' (Habermas 2004, 113). The policy process as the site of political debate and deliberation between conflicting or interdependent sites operates to achieve both a normative justification of agendas and outcomes. That policy is itself embedded within the normative structures of the broader institutional

---

[2] A 'citizen' is a legally recognised entity entitled to rights before the state. The presumption of citizenship is − among others − based on the model of the male-subject, the sovereignty and legalised force of the state, and is territorial based (see the writings of Lister, Young, Benhabib). Citizenship rights coexist and depend upon Human Rights. However, an undocumented person in the EU is still entitled to Human Rights, simply by being human (Guild 2005). In this article, I do not distinguish between citizens with political rights and human beings without. I am fully aware of the analytical distinction. However, often this distinction is used to justify political or cultural, abusive treatment of 'non-citizens'. In this article the Human is also considered a citizen-at-large.

arrangement (of the European polity in this instance) *and* seeks to determine those of forthcoming value, presents an interesting dilemma: to
what extent is change, that is a departure away from the status quo,
possible and to what extent can such change be reflective of generalisable interests (in this case those deriving from social cohesion)?

As the historical development of media and cultural policies in the
EU shows, the road to including these areas in supranational jurisdiction
has paralleled the development of the EU's overall role in the inter-na-
tional relations of its member states. The emergence of media and culture questions is due to the EP's concerns in the early 1980s, as a jurisdictional area they became embodied in the EU treaties only after the
economic justification of such action had been presented. The rise of
neoliberal politics in the USA and UK in the early 1980s advocated the
rollback of the role of the state in addressing inequalities, providing
employment and mediating between market extremes and social and
economic polarisation. It also undermined the ideological and cultural
underpinnings of media and culture institutions up to that time in Europe, and in particular the near monopoly of the Public Service Broadcasting (PSB) system, as well as the public service remit of the few private broadcasters. It is important to note here that a series of exogenous
factors, or 'exogenous shocks' (as identified by the International Political
Economy literature) have contributed to the shift in policies and the re-
examination of the role of the state. The oil crisis in the late 1970s and
international economic recession in the 1980s have 'discredited the nationalist and statist economic policies of the 1970s and opened up a
period of disillusionment and uncertainty over each country's health and
international identity', writes Golob (2003, 374) referring to the experiences of Canada[3], the USA and Mexico. This certainly holds truth for
Europe, as governments sought to address the slipping trust in the ability
of the nation state to maintain levels of wealth and social security
through a set of policies, mainly focused around the privatisation of
public owned services, and their accompanying discursive justification
and ideological foundation, 'freedom from the nanny state' or 'consumer

---

[3] Townson writes 'Politicians continue to repeat that the United Nations rates
Canada as the best country in which to live [...] in fact, on the UN's Human Poverty
Index (IHPI) Canada ranks 9th [...] Canada's rate of poverty in 1997 was 12%. The
highest rate was 16.5% in the United States, closely followed by 15.3% in Ireland and
15.1% in the United Kingdom' (2000, 12).

choice' and neoliberalism. For Golob, critical junctures, generated by exogenous shocks and endogenous crisis (or 'crisis of state legitimacy') create the conditions for a paradigm shift in policy making. However, they do not determine the ways in which this may take place, as, here, the nation state has a protagonist role to play. Indeed, nation states on both sides of the Atlantic engaged in actively promoting a 'paradigm shift' in policy and most importantly the ideas that provide legitimacy to this shift, and by extension to their own role in dealing with crisis, before their citizenry[4].

In practice, and while deploying a 'liberalizing' discourse, many states – while seemingly retreating – play a key role in the process of transferring the oligopolistic power of the big groups into the new networks, in a close alliance between economic and political power which has expanded into the digital world and which seems to ignore the social and political dimensions of culture and communication while at the same time making use of these (Bustamante 2004, 804-5).

The institutional vacuum in this period, namely the lack of institutional, EU based jurisdiction to move towards a comprehensive policy framework for the development of the European media landscape, allowed for the dominance of a specific ideological framework that, spanning from public services, to the role of the nation and social relations underpinned not only national policies in Europe and across the Atlantic but also the EU approach in the years to come. Moreover, it was the lack of an alternative ideological basis upon which the emergence of new media would be shaped, one that could rid negative associations with

---

[4] At this point, it is important to note two things: legislative powers and legitimacy of force rest with nation states even in the era of globalisation, although for many scholars globalisation epitomises the contestation of state sovereignty; perhaps even more so, today, the nation state's legitimacy is more dependent on international integration, albeit of a neo-liberal, market-led nature. Indeed, as Moravscik argues (1992) reclaiming legitimacy and maintaining nation state sovereignty was one of the major reasons why European nation states participated in the construction of the EU. One can extend this to the numerous applications for accession to the EU by the former East European countries. Nevertheless, the power of nation states to design policy, although solid domestically, is unequal in the international terrain. As Hardt and Negri argue 'with the end of the Cold War, the United States was called to serve the role of guaranteeing and adding juridical efficacy to this complex process of the formation of a new supranational right' (2000, 181). Alongside the rise of the 'empire' a group of powerful states, working closely with some of the most powerful corporations headquartered in their territorial jurisdictions have significant negotiating power at the international 'round table'.

either state control (and therefore restriction of freedoms), 'communist' values (monodimensional cultural approach) and socialdemocratic or Keynesian derived models (public service sovereignty) that have 'proved' to be a failure[5]. It is within this context that the development of media and cultural policies in the EU and Canada has come to define the new era, characterised by the liberalisation of services and privatisation of functions of the public sector, the ideological construction of consumer sovereignty, the still in part 'fordist' way of (mass) production and distribution of media content, cross-ownership and concentration of media ownership to a media oligopoly, as well as the transnational networks of production and distribution of media products through a variety of platforms. To these new organisational and trade trends, we must add the parallel polarisation of the culture industries of small countries and linguistic or other 'minorities' towards production and consumption cycles of a shorter radius. The construction of new communications markets in the EU required the specific targeting of the PSB system with the aim to dismantle its financial stability on the basis of EU and national competition policy. Throughout this process, the interests of market-focused private interests superseded those of the public whose very role as a 'citizen-public' was reframed into the 'consumer-public'. Within this climate, the most significant EU piece of media legislation, the Television Without Frontiers Directive (TVWF), was drafted first and foremost as the European Single Market directive, as the *single* piece of EU legislation that actually set the ESM in motion in 1989. Technological issues were framed along the lines of individual consumption, state 'incapability' to keep up with change, and superiority of the competition of individual interests in the market as the regulator for media.

The contexts of policy claims

Political debate is the means through which 'personal aspirations that stem from experiences that individuals undergo' (Aglietta 2000, 403) within a system of economic organisation can be translated into goals for

---

[5] Numerous careful studies have shown the link between state withdrawal and decline of welfare state and increase in poverty, social polarisation, inequality and crime. Most importantly, for this paper, the decline of welfare support for women, the main wageless workers of the culture industries (through volunteer work among others) has detrimental effects for the continuation of community culture projects and the maintenance of a vibrant grassroots cultural creativity. See also Beale and van der Bosch 1998.

the wider population. In other words, political deliberation and state mediation transforms the individual quest for a better life into a social goal and thereby a matter of public policy. Through this process private interests reflect or are presented as reflecting generalisable interests. The mediation between private (capital) interests and those of the individuals, as situated within the larger social stratification and therefore become members of a stratum – or class or 'interest group' as women, minorities and disable people are often regarded – 'manages the tension between the expansive force of capital and the democratic principle' (402). Thereby, mutually exclusive or dependent interests are managed in the form of legislation or other agreement through the institutionalisation of these processes. However, even so, as Hardt and Negri (2000) point out:

> Today a notion of politics as an independent sphere of the determination of consensus and a sphere of mediation of mediation among conflicting social forces has very little room to exist. Consensus is determined more significantly by economic factors (307) .

Media are located within a broader cultural policy field, which is not limited to a static and archaic understanding of 'regulating museums' or a question of 'high arts' vs popular culture, but which is integral to the institutional organisation of the expression of 'national' culture and the legitimised version of the regulating polity (whether state as in the Canadian case or state-like as in the EU case). Against a background whereby increasing and intensified processes of communication and technologically enabled round-the-clock financial transactions are taking place, media policy is called to address the media as an economic factor. The institutional arrangements of the EU seek to accommodate, and further facilitate, changes in international relations that are increasingly shaped (beyond the nation-state) by the influence of transnational capital, expressed through the militancy of transnational corporations as these are represented by global corporate alliances, such as the European Roundtable of Industrialists (ERT), the Business Roundtable (BRT), Motion Picture Association of America (MPAA) or the Global Business Dialogue on electronic commerce (GBDe) or on the European level the European Publishers Council, the Association of Commercial Television in Europe and the Association Européenne des Radios[6]. Moreover, the

---

[6] See here for a discussion on the role of such alliances on global media policy Chakravartty and Sarikakis 2006 and for the role of private interests in the current

complex system of international integration of markets and the conspicu-
ous convergence of politics and business through the rise of the private
sector as an equal partner in public policy blurs the boundaries between
the jurisdiction and sovereignty of nation-states on the one hand, and
national and transnational, globally operating capital on the other. Indeed, one of the most significant actors in EU-USA bilateral relations is
the TransAtlantic Business Dialogue (TABD), which has the mandate 'to
boost transatlantic trade and investment through the removal of barriers
caused by regulatory differences' (European Commission 2004).

Especially in the field of media and communications and with the
advent of the commercialisation of culture, the pressures for a market-
led development (and use) of technologies is the strongest[7]. As communications technologies are enabling the management of financial capital
but also trade and the organisation of labour in other industries, they also
play a vital role in ensuring that consumption continues even when the
physical conditions – closure of shops, factories, banks – may dictate the
(temporary) cease of transactions. In the recent case of the review of the
TWVF Directive, the representation, and impact, of industrial interests in
the policy process through the close identification of national governments and national (and transnational) industries proves a hard opponent
for consumer organisations, NGOs and the EP (Williams 2006). For the
EU, the recent accession of nation states wherein PSB traditions are very
weak, or non existent, coupled with a knee-jerk affiliation to the US
model, weakens the foundations for a social market model[8]. With new

review of the Television Without Frontiers Directive Granville Williams 2004 Free
Press No 142

[7] See the work by Shore (2001) and Sarikakis (2004) for detailed accounts on the
trajectory of the development of media and cultural policy in the EU, and the distinctive 'phases' of integrating media and culture into the EU agenda, accompanied by a
mixture of market-oriented beliefs, populist sentiment, but also deep interest in the
role of culture in the democratisation of integration.

[8] For a detailed account of the role of lobbies in the ongoing TVWF directive see
also Williams 2006. In late (techno)capitalism the development of new markets also
maintains the manufacturing industry and therefore the still in-part fordist organisation
thereof, albeit organised in geographies of labour outsourcing to countries with lower
labour wages, weaker economies and higher vulnerability to corporations (Hardt and
Negri 2000). The role of communication technologies for international trade and
electronic commerce for the creation of new markets cannot be overstated. However,
beyond the buying and selling – and consuming – of products and services, it is mostly
in the domain of cultural goods, or the creative industries as have come to be known,
where the media and their technologies penetrate every waking moment in western

communications technology, new space opens up for the re-use of existing cultural goods and in particular of AV material, or material whose audio-or-visual properties can be digitalised and repackaged, and therefore the opportunity for new sources of revenue rises. The efforts to amend the TVWF directive, so that the use of new technologies also succumbs to a public interest ethos, are opposed by the projection of a set of private interests presented as generalisable. They are exemplified in the conflict about the protection of media as a cultural (not market) territory for free expression, creativity and political deliberation[9]. Moreover, the well explored 'clash' between the EU and the USA on the protection of AV industries in the GATT (GATS) and WTO rounds[10] is a struggle for the control over these spaces. As Venturelli argues:

> the cultural conflict over media and audiovisual content is not a superficial, high-diplomacy power play between the U.S. and France. It is, instead, about the fate of a set of enterprises that form the core, the socalled 'gold' of the Information Economy (13).

Transnational corporations are at the heart of this struggle: not only those upfront AV content producing industries such as the media giants AOL Time Warner or Bertelsmann are involved in the markets, and therefore directly interested in the policies that shape them, but also the electronics industries, some of which, such as General Electronics, own AV content producing industries and distributing networks. With the convergence of media platforms and digitisation of content, the issue of 'barrier free' trade becomes a major priority for transnational corporations. The policy agendas of global transindustrial alliances, focused around further liberalisation of markets, can be traced throughout the policy agendas and outcomes in supranational and international policy, such as the recent World Summit on Information Society (Chakravartty

---

societies. It is there, in the repeated use of cultural products, such as films and videos, music and electronic text and their relation to digital technologies, where the wealth of the new information society lies.

[9] That the neo-liberal agenda clearly favours private capital over public investment has been explored in macro-economic analyses and studies of the withdrawal of the public sector from areas crucial in the maintenance of basic service standards, such as postal services and telecommunications. It is within this spectrum of macro-level economic reregulation on the basis of 'pro-competitive' policy that 'transnational corporations gain access to publicly-financed infrastructures and service markets' (Grieshaber-Otto and Sinclair 2004; p, 8).

[10] See also Pauwels et al in this issue.

and Sarikakis 2006). Canada has shifted its long-held priorities, to respond to global pressures for the liberalisation of communications and the withdrawal of state aid from public services, including the public service broadcasting system, while leaving the building of the Information Society (IS) to the priorities set by private corporations. The institutional change following the Brussels GIS declaration in 1995 show the direct influence of the international policy regime and the particular set of agendas related to new communications (Abramson and Raboy 1999). Structural changes in ownership and operation of telecommunications, an industry central to the information age, have led to increased concentration and widespread privatisation. The industry has come under the jurisdiction of powerful or 'core' institutions such as the Industry Canada or the Telecommunications Commission DG or the current Information Society and Media DG, under which come now 'cultural' aspects that have digitised (ecommerce) potential, such as the production of digital films and digital content. To that, almost in a contrast, comes the separation of the 'soft' areas of cultural policy under Heritage Canada, responsible for broadcasting policy, or Education and Culture DG in the EU. Areas such as PSB, AV production training, film and the preservation of cinema and audiovisual 'heritage' and initiatives for the promotion of cultural diversity are, artificially, separated from the core activities of competition, (e)commerce and technology. Given that these three policy objects lead EU and Canadian approaches to domestic and international policy, it is significant that the very organisation of policy jurisdiction frames the question of diversity and expression along the 'soft' and disassociated lines of 'culture' vis a vis 'economy'.

The ideological and material underpinnings of media and cultural policy
In this broader paradigm shift of regulatory organisation of the media and cultural industries, the EU and Canada have according to Collins, 'embraced two determinisms' (Collins 1995, 4). *Technological* determinism supports that social and political change is shaped by technological development. *Cultural* determinism proposes that cultural and political identities are interdependent thereby axiomatically resulting in the creation of new political identities emerging from new cultural ones . Technological determinist discourses in media and cultural policy in Canada and the EU allowed space for only a limited range of regulatory decisions and a particular direction that redefined the relationship between

the state and corporate agency. Young (2003), exploring the discourses across dominant policy trajectories in these two polities identified the hegemonic discourse of the role of technology across claims for democratisation. These are associated for example with questions of access and 'choice' (technological democracy) and the creation of nationhood (technological nationalism) broadly related to the diverse ethnic and cultural fabric of Canadian and EU societies, in addition to the role of technology itself in providing the incentive for (specific) policy. Although not always or necessarily in the same timeframe, both Canadian and EU media policy frameworks have used 'technology' as a policy compass and cause in their approach to reregulation, blending in their rhetoric social policy questions, from broadcasting and the media as public goods to issues of cultural protection and promotion, to the prosperity of the nation(s). In Canada, these discourses can be traced back to the 1960s where the vision of nation-building together with issues of public access and community broadcasting became entangled with the spread of cable television (Raboy 1990; Young 2003). More recently, the same conversions of social values and deterministic framing are accompanying the emphasis on the IS policies for a policy that seeks to create the most 'wired' country in the world. On the EU front, as in the Canadian, these attestations can be found throughout the IS policy development, irrespectively of whether the 'visions' relate to the field of information technology or whether they address convergence of media platforms or digitalisation (Chakravartty and Sarikakis 2006; Mosco 2004; Murdock 2000; Winseck 1998). Within this context, questions of cultural diversity and social cohesion obtain a particular significance: As the digital divide debate gains momentum in the IS – technology bound discourse, which has come to enclose conventional as well as 'new' media, the illustration of lack of social cohesion through additional processes of division becomes even more profound.

This digital divide, often caricatured as a simple division between the connected and the non-connected (or more recently between those connected to broadband and those linked to obsolete networks), has acquired all its complexity and its impact in the world of communication and culture. This in turn affects the democratic society of the future. There is division by purchasing power, reinforced by cultural knowledge and codes; division between those who possess diverse types of information that have strategic and competitive value as opposed to the merely escapist and superficial. There is also a division between the producers and the consumers of knowledge, between nations that can exploit their cultures (and even the cultures of others) and nations destined to give up their cultures as raw material for free. And there is also a divide between countries, regions and within each society (including the richest and most industrialized). In both polities, these are not simply questions of a conceptual or symbolic nature, but are directly related to the materiality of the experience of citizenship – and therefore citizens' experience of the polity itself. They point to the legitimacy of the polity.

Social cohesion is closely linked to cultural diversity facilitated through the cultural production of the AV (traditional or new) media[11]. According to the UNESCO Convention 'Cultural diversity' refers to the manifold ways in which the cultures of groups and societies find expression. These expressions are passed on within and among groups and societies. Cultural diversity is made manifest not only through the varied ways in which the cultural heritage of humanity is expressed, augmented and transmitted through the variety of cultural expressions, but also through diverse modes of artistic creation, production, dissemination, distribution and enjoyment, whatever the means and technologies used.

Feigenbaum (2005) places a different 'kind' of significance upon diversity: he refers to the role of ideas and intellectual innovation being part of an environment rich in cultural stimuli, from language to symbols, perceptions and world views. These stimuli are further reflected upon the imagination and innovation of political and governing relations of a society. Ultimately the future is shaped by the richness or homogenisation of creativity[12]. Ironically, the homogenisation of cultural expression limits consumption and creativity, both seen as the global market driver, namely 'choice' (Feigenbaum 2005, 5). Venturelli, too, connects the necessity for diverse intellectual creativity to the market-led subversion of this same prerequisite:

---

[11] Recent global movements for the recognition of communication and cultural rights such as the CRIS campaign, and the democratisation of the media, such as the Union for Democratic Communications point to the centrality of the role of media and economic policies for determining the limits and possibilities of cultural expression and diversity, and its role in maintaining social cohesion.
[12] The detrimental role of economistic restrictions to the role of intellectual labour, vital for the functioning of participatory populi is identified by Lee (2005) and Park (2006) in their analyses of the labour conditions and market limitations exercised upon critical – non 'homogenised' – work

Every nation will need to have [...] a vibrant and diverse audiovisual industry, publishing industry, intellectual industry, and a dynamic arts community
if it is to 'grow' its other multimedia content and cultural sectors. In this
respect, nations which attempt effectively to prevent the total erosion of content
industries will have an advantage over those that simply give up the struggle to
diffuse and diversify knowledge and creative enterprises to the growing consolidation of international content producers and distributors (13).

It is in this terrain of debate that representational politics (EP, House of
Commons) have produced ideas that attempt to address the 'culture
drain' on the one hand, and the question of social cohesion, on the other,
through shared notions of and equitable access to cultural expression.
Social cohesion as an aim is emphasised by both polities in their cultural
and media policies. However public(s) claims for redistributive policies
and policies sensitive to claims for recognition and equitable representation, have not reached the policy implementation, as they largely clash
with the limited market-focused agenda[13]. Not only have both polities
struggled to define the question of cultural diversity pending between the
broad conception of culture as a 'way of life' and 'the Arts' loaded with
reminiscences of elitism and classism, but they have also had to face
their distinctive disarray. Cultural diversity as a requirement for social
cohesion presents a complex set of questions about the coexistence of
culturally heterogeneous groups, the apprehension of dislocation and
dispossession of migrant populations, the struggle of dealing with material polarisations across class, gender, age, and ethnicity[14] as well as the
particular framing of collective memory and experiences.

---

[13] In the EU TVWF review, attempts to subject new technologies to the same
universal ethics of cultural protection, limitation to advertising and product placement
methods, accountability of private media etc as represented by the EP and citizens and
cultural workers' organisations is in a colliding route with the demands of the media
and electronics industry.

[14] The decrease of real wages of the average worker across the NAFTA country
members, even in the USA, for example and the widening gap between the richest
20% of Canadians, the net loss of jobs, decline of stable full-time jobs, casualisation of
employment that hits women the hardest, as does poverty, through a policy of protection for investors and financiers undermines the very basic standards necessary for
minimum social cohesion across these societies. For detailed studies of the impact of
NAFTA and WTO on workers, poverty and employment see the following studies
from the Economic Policy Institute: Scott, Robert 2001 *NAFTA's hidden Costs. Trade
agreement results in job losses, growing inequality and wage suppression for the United States;* Salas,
Carlos 2001 *The Impact of NAFTA on wages and income in Mexico;* Campbell, Bruce 2001
False Promise. Canada in the Free trade Era all at http://epinet.org. For an overall study on
Women and Poverty in Canada see Townson, Monica 2000

The approaches of EU and Canadian policy are distinctive but are also based on similar experiences. Canadian cultural policy appears consolidatory and defensive, the European project (increasingly) aspirational and tendentious[15]. Europe's newly-found enthusiasm for culture is based on the intention of 'softening' the edges of – or tensions around – heterogeneity in the EU, not only with reference to the difference among nations but also those of migrant populations and diverse social and cultural groups. The expectation is to mediate a degree of social cohesion through culture in ways which will foster the growth of 'unity' among citizen subjects of the EU. However, there are three problems with the implementation of such a programme. First, the degree of structural imbalance across societies and media landscapes disallows processes of cohesion, as these may be based upon equitability in accessing and processing information among citizens. To that one needs to add the inequitable status of whole nations and regions in their media producing capability. Additionally, one has to deal with the ever-present perceived (or real) domination of US AV products. Second, often 'the eurocentrism and class bias inherent in conceptions of culture also promote exclusion and intolerance, particularly towards those who fall outside the boundaries of official European culture' (Shore 2001, 108). Third, internal processes of cultural fragmentation are the outcome of recent migration. As Schlesinger and Foret note 'The EU's expansion eastwards leaves us wondering how the additional ethnic, national, religious and culturo-linguistic diversity will be integrated and how this will change the EU's dynamics' (2006, 64). National and global media targeting specifically new constellations of ethnic, national or religious cultures are themselves becoming 'invasive others' from within, in the complex quest for the cultivation of a common identity. Finally, one must always keep in mind, that there is an alternative set of national drivers in Europe, such as diverse policy bodies and procedures, recognised values, socioeconomic contexts and other traditions that are active in policy making. In that respect, the great difference between Canada and the EU is one of the status of the nation state. The EU is clearly not one, but depends on a complex system of nation-states and supranational and

---

[15] I owe this idea to Neil Blain.

regional institutions. Nation states additionally are faced with internal cohesion questions[16]. Canada on the other hand *is* a national driver.

Indeed, the geographical boundaries of 'Europe' are themselves contested and inasmuch as the EU claims more and more to 'represent' Europe, its continual growth continually unsettles possible comprehensive identity-claims. Nor do cultural background or religious affiliation or ethnicity either individually or in combination settle the question of who is a European (Schlesinger & Foret 2006, 65).

The dependence of the Canadian broadcasting system on US originated AV material has been instrumental in the shaping of national broadcasting[17]. In a way, the US has 'forced' the development of a Canadian broadcasting approach to pursue the construction of nationhood. Canadian policymakers have sought to develop a definition of the country's cultural identity, understood as 'other than' American.[18] Broadcasting programming has been identified as the carrier of nationhood, which different from the US, would bring the nation together in much the same way or of the same significance as the great railways connected the diverse population of this vast territory. Europe's way to a supranational distinctly European identity is approached through the construction of citizenship *rights* introduced by the legal entity of European Citizenship.

[16] Not only the nation-states relation to the EU is included in this phenomenon, such as the vote for/against an EU constitution has shown, but also the 'need' felt within the boundaries of nation states to re-assert nationhood towards internal considered 'outsiders'.

[17] The global audiovisual sector, in particular, is controlled by seven Hollywood based transnational companies which dominate European and Canadian content distribution. Germann (2005, 95) argues that it is not the content that is responsible for the market success of cinema 'Blockbusters' but rather intensive marketing coupled by powerful distributing mechanisms that not only promote only certain audiovisual material to reach consumers but also disallow content originated 'elsewhere' from same levels of (widespread) distribution.

[18] Of course, it is important to acknowledge that not all media are colonised, as books, theatre and the arts, or even domestic television production demonstrate vibrant domestic modes of use. As far as mostly and broadly available AV content, as well as other digital internet material is concerned, the global AV industry is led by the Hollywood based cluster. Despite internal markets and productions that prefer or favour non-American content, the overall picture remains one whereby national or other domestic content is limited to consumption within national boundaries, is directly influenced by fluctuations in national or other (federal, supranational) subsidiaries and of limited multiplatform commercial use when compared to the elaborate merchandising industries associated with major film studios, television networks and internet portals.

Europe's own identity, historically based on the 'otherness' of defined outsiders (Hardt & Negri 2000; Shore 2001), and in this respect also of the 'invasive other' (the USA) relies on the complex system of media production and cultural creativity, folklore and tourism that seek to convey the feeling of common heritage and future. The emphasis on the 'invasive other' has led to a one-sided appreciation of the threats associated with concentration of media industries and internal signs of cultural domination, that ignore the significance of linguistic marginalisation, the impact of media content control by European media moguls, the uncomfortable fusion of politics and media business, and the restrictions of the single market imposing on small media, small national markets and their capacity for cultural expression (Sarikakis 2005). Furthermore, more careful attention upon the 'unknown' territories of recent EU members, as well as upon the consuming habits of recent migrants is missing. Moreover, for both polities, vis-à-vis the USA broadcasting industry, even the strongest fears and anxieties expressed in EU policy have only resulted in relatively small support for AV and film production.[19] At the same time, the homogenisation of culture exacerbated by the increasing media ownership concentration (in Europe and Canada) and the struggle over the role of PSBs are symptoms of the undermining of public interest policy towards cultural diversity. The well-rehearsed recipes for cultural products that guarantee profitability, and the expectation that they should, become an additional restriction to creativity but also on the 'acceptability' of forms of ways-of-life that may be ostracised in the process:

> Th[e] path to an authentic 'clone culture' which replicates past successes can only increasingly standardize the production for and consumption by majorities, punishing innovative or minority creativity, that of small and medium enterprises, and linguistic and cultural minorities, thereby jeopardizing the overall ecology of each sector' (Bustamante 2004, 804-5).

For Canada, the linguistic proximity with the USA exemplifies some of these problems, while admittedly the broadcasting of French language programming 'made in France' does also very little to enhance the cultural production of the country. On the other hand, of course, the de-

---

[19] For a discussion on the decline or stagnation of domestic production and success thereof see What's wrong with Canadian Broadcasting? in www.publicairwaves.ca; Canadian Broadcasting Corporation 2002 *Canadian Context in the 21st Century* (response to Heritage Canada).

bated 'two solitudes' only refer to the rather privileged majorities of English and French speakers, while problematically leaving out indigenous cultures and languages, as a rather folklorised 'other' in the debates over media and cultural policy. Canada is torn by cultural survival struggles, perhaps unhappily embodied in the 'linguistic' question or the 'two solitudes' that ignore the marginalisation of first nations. The folklorisation of their cultural heritage not only objectifies cultural expression as the distinctive internal 'other' in Canadian media and cultural policy but also, disallows the development of 'culture' as part of the country's policy and the populations' active involvement in culture-making. To that, questions surrounding the position of other minorities and especially those consisting of immigrant people began to resurface and point to the inadequacy of understanding Canada as the 'playground' of colonial residues, which is reflected in the minimalist attention given to indigenous and migrant media (Baeker 2002; Roth 1998).

In Europe, cultural policy has also been approached as part of the European structural funds, a major funding programme that began with the Delors administration, in an attempt to promote social cohesion in the EU. The structural funds continue to support ultra-and semi peripheral regions and are now directed to the new member states. In an attempt to invigorate the regions, cultural activities and programmes are envisioned primarily on the grounds of their economic benefits for regional development. Cultural policy in this context gains its credibility through its role in creating jobs and supporting local economies, but this 'adulteration' of purpose does not take place free of conflict. Delgado-Moreira (2000) argues that there is a conflicting view of the use of culture and cultural policy between the Commission and the Committee of the Regions, two institutional bodies with non identical views about social cohesion. These are epitomised in the 'supranational vs intergovernmental' approach to EU governance and consequently to the nature of the EU. Commission approaches culture – and within that the AV sector – as the means to better economic cohesion, which is expected to lead to better governability and therefore to a stronger EU (Commission 1996). The strengthening of the position of the polity is believed would consequently lead to better control of immigration flows and would strengthen the sense of citizenship and belonging to EU. The Committee of the Regions sees culture not as an 'asset' but as the watchdog of diversity; cultural policy for the COR is related to the integration of groups into local societies and not into the EU directly, as the Commission aims. Delgado-Moreira argues that this tension demonstrates a distinctive, not openly conflicting, view of the role of culture in the EU between Commission and COR based on the ideological dispositions of transnationalism and multiculturalism. Commission is interested in cultural heritage, high arts, cultural exchanges and audiovisual policies as part of cultural policy[20]. The fusion of cultural and tourism activities showcasing perceptions of current European cultures through symbolic festive events such as the European City of Culture demonstrates both confusion about the EU and an overtly economistic understanding of its role and of integration. The COR approaches cultural policy in its grassroots elements, through the experience of immigration and 'incoming' human flows. This multiculturalist approach focuses on the human rights approach and access to culture-making. Cultural policy despite intentions and despite the small accompanying funds becomes more than a strategic 'small' policy field through the impact it makes in the regional programmes (Delgado-Moreira 2000, 458).

Words will be words: concluding remarks

The diverse populations of Europe and Canada pose the question of social cohesion as a matter of identity and human survival, alongside the pressures exercised by increasing polarisation of materiality. In Europe, 'unity in diversity' is largely addressed by policies in terms of the diverse national cultures, themselves having undergone processes of homogenisation and 'cohesion' to enable (or construct) the emergence of national identities. Only secondarily, do internal transnational diasporas or third country ones are considered of a recognised diversity. In its struggle to move beyond its economistic remit, EU citizenship relies upon the conditions set out by attachment to a nation for recognition. In Canada, diversity has also been used to mask inequalities and 'culturalise' them, especially those, regarding populations that do not 'neatly' fit in the narrative of territorial based (space) claims or historical based (time) demands (Baeker 2002). Claims to the reality of the Canadian society are not without conflict when ethnic and visible minorities and aboriginals are considered. Europe is facing its own conflict in its process of turning

---

[20] Through the promotion of policy packages such as RAPHAEL, KALEIDO-SCOPE, MEDIA and later CULTURE 2000 and its continuation etc.

diversity into a process of culturally based social cohesion. Having been based largely on either national or regional perceived often stereotypified or folklorised characteristics, concentrated along the cultural 'lines' between for example the Mediterranean or Nordic countries, the internal divisions or fragmentations of national and religious cultures, coupled with increased migration, create a new, complex set of drivers not adequately or consciously enough addressed by existing media policy.

The EP emphasises a multicultural euro-politanism in political culture, cohesion among citizens and view to the world, as a 'European' way of life which is associated with public service, human rights and democracy. The concerns of parliamentary debates arising from the impact of the neoliberalist agenda for the media and cultural industry concentrate around the ways in which conditions of the production of expression, whether factual and journalistic or fictional, restrict the range of opinions, depth of aesthetic and analytic exploration and the range of narratives about the human condition. Editorial independence, long term support for PSB and investment in regional programming are areas of policy identified and advocated for by both the EP and the Canadian House of Commons, to which no satisfactory answers have been given. Underlying these aims is the attention given to the detrimental consequences of media ownership concentration, both for the richness of cultural creativity but also for democratic participation in the public sphere of Europe and Canada. Both institutions have repeatedly called for the establishment of an independent monitoring council that would monitor and intervene in the cases of power abuse, in terms of content, production and access to cultural sources. And both have shared the urgency for long-term support for cultural production, inclusive of, but also beyond, PSB, as in terms of training and education or in terms of subsidisation for distinctive works (the MEDIA programme in the EU or the Canadian Television Fund). However, despite the EP's numerous initiatives and calls for an overhaul of the TVWF and the design of anti-concentration policy and similarly despite the clear mandate the Lincoln Report gave the Canadian government (Standing Committee on Canadian Heritage 2003), these recommendations have not been taken up in regulatory provision. The issue of foreign ownership added to that of cross-ownership has become for the Canadian case one of cultural survival or oblivion, as 'once foreign companies are allowed to take control, the chances of Canadians ever reclaiming this vital space will be small indeed' (Raboy and Taras 2004, 64).

Not only that, but it seems that the US industry, as the archetype of the global media empire, is quickly finding ways to not only bypass the debate and actual policy obstacles on cultural diversity, but also to secure a strategic superiority vis-a-vis its problematic trade partners. Through bilateral agreements on digital content with third countries, it constructs a de facto environment that solves the problem of quotas and restrictions by moving digital content outside the jurisdiction of cultural exemption. Any digitalised form of content becomes automatically subject to market – not state – 'regul(aris)ation', through free trade agreements with countries as diverse as Australia and Morocco. This means that the liberalisation of ecommerce and digitalised content will bypass any culture protective measures. Moreover, it seems that the current policy status quo has reached its optimum impact, and new further proactive and comprehensive policies are required to address the range of unresolved issues within the two creative landscapes. This is evident by the fact that production of home grown works, in whatever form of Canadian or EU definition, has reached a plateau. In Canada broadcasting domestic content seems to be on a slightly downward cycle. Moreover, due to a chronic lack of funding for PBS[21] long term planning is unachievable. This means that PSB is less able to take risks and be innovative, which further condemns it to lower ratings and quality of output. On the other hand, both EU and Canada have effectively subsidised private broadcasters and the US industry through either direct subsidies for works commissioned but not funded by private broadcasters, tax credits and favourable investment conditions. Moreover, the EU's focus on the market-ability of culture reinforces the very material and symbolic conditions that are detrimental to social cohesion especially one based in part on the construction of a common European identity. '[B]y allowing the market to determine the nature of this identity, we become European consumers' This is 'doubly ironic' given that the EU project is moving beyond its narrow economistic remit (Harrison & Woods 2000, 490). Individualistic solutions to public policy problems such as those of access to media and culture, in terms not simply of consuming but also of

---

[21] Financial support for PBS in Canada is among the five lowest ones among OECD countries. For the decline in funding public services see also Grieshaber-Otto, Jim and Sinclair Scott 2004. Also for international cultural flows see UNESCO 2005

'handling' and processing, creating and actively 'making' culture, exacerbates social and economic polarisation.

As this article has tried to show, it is within the context of broader processes of market integration, human mobility and the development of global governance regimes that policy aiming at the re/construction of social cohesion can be best analysed. This contextualisation allows us to understand the reasons and ways in which different cultures and societies may face questions of the same magnitude. Although not developed in this article, the underlying assumption is that the location of *acting* upon solutions is the nation-state, the region or province, and ultimately the community. Indeed, the challenges facing today's enlarged Europe are twofold: they concern inasmuch its own constitutional sustenance as the constitution of its identity and that appropriated by its peoples on one level. On another level, questions of cultural pluralism within nation-states, and of contested national identity make the relationship between the citizen, the nation 'unit' and the polity significantly more complex than any policy has acknowledged. Moreover, the tensions between individualistic approaches, through an overall policy agenda that bears the symptoms of market-culture, and the aims for social cohesion through diversity, multi/cosmopolitanism, recognition of hitherto 'non-belonging' social groups and minimum material wealth defeat the proclaimed aim. Structured solidarity is poorly served by small funding pockets for cultural creativity across the two polities. The creation of a 'common values pattern' through symbolic expressions of identity such as flags, anthems and exhibitions can reinforce a feeling of belonging, but alone, not create it. The experience of citizenship through the construction of social networks, group identification, and social capital points to a changing notion of the role of citizens on the one hand, but also to the relationship of undocumented citizens with the state, through the mediation of culture. This is the intersection where the macro-level structural regimes meet the micro-level conditions of social and cultural existence.

References

Abramson, Bram Dov and Marc Raboy. 1999. Policy Globalization and the 'Information Society': A View from Canada. *Telecommunications Policy* 23: 775-791.

Aglietta, Michel. 2000 [1976]. *A Theory of Capitalist Regulation. The US Experience.*London: Verso.

Bustamante, Enrique. 2004. Cultural Industries in the Digital Age: Some Provisional Conclusions. *Media, Culture & Society.* 26(6): 803–820.

Beaker, Greg. 2002. Sharpening the Lens: Recent Research on Cultural Policy, Cultural Diversity and Social Cohesion. *Canadian Journal of Communication* 27 (2-3):179-196.

Beauvais, Caroline and Jane Jenson. 2002. *Social Cohesion: Updating the State of the Research.* Ottawa: Canadian Policy Research Networks (CPRN).

Bennett, Tony. 2001. *Differing diversities – Transversal Study on the Theme of Cultural Policy and Cultural Diversity, Followed by Seven Research Position Papers.* Strasbourg: Council of Europe Publishing.

Chakravartty, Paula and Katharine Sarikakis. 2006. *Globalization and Media Policy* Edinburgh: Edinburgh University Press.

Collins, Richard. 1995. Reflections Across the Atlantic: Contrasts and Complementarities in Broadcasting Policy in Canada and the European Community in the 1990s. *Canadian Journal of Communication* 20 (4) http://cjc-online.ca.

Delgado-Moreira, Juan M. 2000. Cohesion and Citizenship in EU Cultural Policy. *Journal of Common Market Studies* 38 (3) 449-70.

European Commission. 2005. External Relations http://ec.europa.eu/enterprise/enterprise_policy/business_dialogues/tabd/tabdoverw.htm.

Feigenbaum, Harvey B.2005. *Smart Practice and Innovation in Cultural Policy: Responses to Americanization.* The BMW Center for German and European Studies Edmund A. Walsh School of Foreign Service Georgetown University Working paper 14-05 http://georgetown.edu/sfs/cges/working_papers.html.

Gasher, Mike. 1995. The Audiovisual Locations Industry in Canada: Considering British Columbia as Hollywood North. *Canadian Journal of Communication* 20 (2) http://www.cjc-online.ca/viewarticle.php?id= 291&layout=html.

Germann, Christophe. 2005. Content Industries and Cultural Diversity: The Case of Motion Pictures. In *Cultural Imperialism. Essays on the Political Economy of Cultural Domination* eds. Hamm Bernd and Russell Smandych. Peterborough ON: Broadview Press.

Golob, Stephanie R. 2003. Beyond the Policy Frontier: Canada, Mexico, and the Ideological Origins of NAFTA. *World Politics* 55 (3): 361-398.

Grieshaber-Otto, Jim and Sinclair Scott. 2004. *Return to Sender: The impact of GATS 'Pro-competitive Regulation' on Postal and Other Public Services.* Ottawa: Canadian Centre for Policy Alternatives.

Harisson, Jackie and Lorna Woods. 2000. European Citizenship: Can Audio-Visual Policy Make a Difference? *Journal of Common Market Studies* 38(3): 471-495.

Habermas, Juergen. 2004 [1976]. *Legitimation Crisis.* Cambridge: Polity Press.

Hardt, Michael and Antonio Negri. 2000. *Empire*. Cambridge, MA: Harvard University Press.

Jeannotte, M. Sharon. 2003. Singing Alone? The Contribution of Cultural Capital to Social Cohesion and Sustainable Communities. *The International Journal of Cultural Policy*, 9 (1): 35–49.

Kearns, A. and R. Forrest. 2000. Social Cohesion and Multilevel Urban Governance. *Urban Studies*. 37(5-6): 995-1017.

Kofman, Eleanor and Gillian Youngs, eds. 2003. *Globalization: Theory and Practice*. 2nd edn. London: Continuum.

Maloutas, Thomas and Maro Pantelidou Malouta. 2004. The Glass Menagerie of Urban Governance and Social Cohesion: Concepts and Stakes/Concepts as Stakes. *International Journal of Urban and Regional Research* 28 (2): 449-465.

Mann, Michael. 1970. The Social Cohesion of Liberal Democracy. *American Sociological Review*, 35 (3): 423-439.

Murdock, Graham. 2000. Digital futures: European Television in the Age of Convergence. In *Television across Europe: a comparative introduction* eds. J. Wieten, G. Murdock and P. Dahlgren. London: Sage.

Raboy, Marc and David Taras. 2004. The Politics of Neglect of Canadian Broadcasting Policy. *Policy Options*. March, 63-68

Sarikakis, Katharine. 2004. *Powers in Media Policy. The Challenge of the European Parliament*. Oxford: Peter Lang.

Sarikakis, Katharine. 2005. Defending Communicative Spaces: The Remits and Limits of the European Parliament. *International Communication Gazette*. 67: 155-172.

Schlesinger, Philip and François Foret. 2006. Political Roof and Sacred Canopy? Religion and the EU Constitution. *European Journal of Social Theory* 9(1): 59-81.

Shore, Cris. 2001. The Cultural Policies of the European Union and Cultural Diversity Research Position Paper 3. In *Differing Diversities – Transversal Study on the Theme of Cultural Policy and Cultural Diversity, Followed by Seven Research Position Papers*. Ed. Bennett, Tony. Strasbourg: Council of Europe Publishing.

Tarschys, Daniel. 2002. Promoting Cohesion: The Role of the European Union. ARENA Conference, Oslo 4 March. www.arena.uio.no/ events/ Conference2002/documents/Paper%20Tarschys.doc.

The Standing Committee on Canadian Heritage Report *Our Cultural Sovereignty: the Second Century of Canadian Broadcasting* www.parl.gc.ca/ InfoComDoc/37/2/HERI/Studies/Reports/herirp02-e.htm.

Theiler, Tobias. 2001. Viewers into Europeans?: How the European Union Tried to Europeanize the Audiovisual Sector, and Why it Failed. *Canadian Journal of Communication* 24 (4) www.cjc-online.ca/ viewarticle.php?id=549.

Townson, Monica. 2000. *A Report Card on Women and Poverty*. Ottawa: The Canadian Centre for Policy Alternatives www.policyalternatives.ca.

UNESCO. 2005. *International Flows of Selected Cultural Goods and Services, 1994-200 Defining and Capturing the Flows of Global Cultural Trade.* Montreal. UNESCO Institute for Statistics.

UNESCO. 2005. *Convention on the Protection and Promotion of the Diversity of Cultural Expression* .Paris: UNESCO.

Venturelli, Shalini.Undated. *From the Information Economy to Creative Economy Moving Culture to the Center of International Public Policy.* www.culturalpolicy.org/pdf/venturelli.pdf

Williams, Grenville. 2006. Behind the Screens: Corporate Lobbying and the Media. In *Thinker, Faker, Spinner, Spy: Corporate PR and the Assault on Democracy.* Eds. Miller, D. and Dinan, W. London: Pluto Press.

Winseck, Dwayne. 1998. Pursuing the Holy Grail: Information Highways and Media Reconvergence in Britain and Canada. *European Journal of Communication* 13(3): 337-374.

Young, David. 2003. Discourses on Communication Technologies in Canadian and European Broadcasting Policy debates. *European Journal of Communication* 18(2): 209-240.

EUROPEAN STUDIES 24 (2007): 91-112

THE EU, COMMUNICATIONS LIBERALISATION AND THE FUTURE OF PUBLIC SERVICE BROADCASTING[1]

Peter Humphreys

Abstract

The article is concerned with the impact on public service broadcasting of the European Union (EU). It begins by explaining that, for various reasons, EU audiovisual policy is biased towards 'negative integration', namely market liberalisation and the direct exercise of extensive competition powers. This 'de-regulatory' bias has been seen by some as a threat to public service broadcasting. The paper examines the implications for public service broadcasting of two important lines of EU policy: 1) the EU's policy response to the digital 'convergence' of broadcasting, telecommunications and IT; and 2) the EU's handling of competition complaints from the commercial sector against public service broadcasters about their involvement in new media markets (including Internet).

Introduction

Since the 1980s broadcasting policy makers have sought to adapt to the challenge of globalization and dramatic technological change (satellite broadcasting, digital TV, 'convergence' with IT and telecoms). A key element of regulatory change has been the accumulation of influence in

[1] The impact of the EU's policies on cultural diversity and public service broadcasting is part of a current ESRC-funded project: 'Globalization, regulatory competition and audiovisual regulation in 5 countries', being conducted by Professor P. Humphreys, School of Social Sciences, University of Manchester, Professor T. Gibbons School of Law, University of Manchester and Dr. A. Harcourt Department of Politics, University of Exeter. ESRC Ref.No. RES-000-23-0966. Duration: 1 February 2005 – 31 January 2008.

the 'audiovisual' field by the European Union (EU). This paper explores the implications for public service broadcasting. The paper explains that, for various reasons, EU audiovisual policy has been biased towards 'negative integration', namely market liberalisation and the direct exercise of extensive competition powers. This de-regulatory bias has been seen by some as a threat to public service broadcasting. However, as environmental policy shows for example, the EU also has the potential to upwardly regulate or at least to moderate the strong de-regulatory pressures that arise from market competition. With this in mind, the paper examines the implications for public service broadcasting of two important lines of EU policy: 1) the EU's policy response to the digital 'convergence' of broadcasting, telecommunications and IT; and 2) the EU's handling of competition complaints from the commercial sector against public service broadcasters about their involvement in new media markets (including Internet).

Negative Integration and Public Service

As Scharpf (1996) has explained, EU governance is characterised by a structural asymmetry that makes negative integration (market making) far easier to achieve than positive integration (market correcting) measures.[2] Negative integration is far easier to achieve principally because the Commission and European Court of Justice wield very considerable powers of top-down direct intervention with regard to market making and competition enforcement. In the cases of action against infringement of Treaty rules or against violation of competition rules the Court and the Commission are unconstrained by the Council or Parliament. These direct powers of negative integration have a basis in the EU Treaties, but in their application they been significantly reinforced by the development by the EU institutions, accompanied by the acquiescence therein of the Member States, of the doctrines of 'direct effect' and the 'supremacy of EU law'. Scharpf describes this as having resulted in the 'constitutionalization' of European competition law, which he notes is primarily neo-

---

[2] It is important to note that market making is not exclusively related to negative integration, the removal of national legal and regulatory barriers to the European market. Market making may also require some positive integration, namely harmonization of rules. By the same token, positive integration is not solely about market correcting. Nonetheless, there is a predominant relationship between negative integration and market making, and positive integration and market correcting – and this is clearly the case in the field of audiovisual regulation.

liberal in its approach. In a series of *ad hoc* judgements and interventions the Court and Commission have steadily encroached on areas of policy and regulation that have customarily been regarded by the Member States as being exempt from the normal rules of the market and being more properly the scope of what the French call *service public*. Thus, Scharpf notes that, drawing on its direct competition powers, 'the Commission has been able to advance the liberalization of one area of 'service public' after another, from telecommunications, to air transport and airport operations, to road haulage, postal services, the energy market, and a number of other services …' (Scharpf 1996, 61).

By contrast, positive integration – market-correcting measures – has to be negotiated by the Member States within the Council of Ministers and requires the co-operation or co-decision of the Parliament. Given the diversity of Europe, its variety of models of capitalism and regulatory styles, and its patchwork of competing interests, this is not usually an easy task. Yet in many sectors there is plainly a need for positive integration in order to maintain adequate problem solving and regulatory capacity with regard to policy problems whose solutions are increasingly eluding national governments in the context of internationalising technologies and economic globalisation, the audiovisual sector being a very good example. However, the outcome of the EU's structural bias towards negative integration, according to Scharpf (1996, 28), is that 'the general constraints on national policy choices that have resulted from economic "globalization" are intensified and tightened through the legal force of negative integration.' Scharpf's *critique* relates to welfare state policies, yet an essentially similar argument has been made with regard to audiovisual policy.

Thus, Harcourt (2005) sees EU negative integration in the audiovisual field as having been characterised by top-down interventions by EU institutions with the potential to damage public service goals. In particular, Harcourt is critical of the major foundation-edifice of EU regulatory policy in the audiovisual sector, namely the market-making Television Without Frontiers (TWF) directive of 1989 (Council of the European Communities 1989 – revised in 1997, and currently being revised yet again). Notwithstanding a certain element of positive integration in the directive (a minimal amount of rule harmonisation regarding such matters as advertising, right of reply, child protection, etc.), the 1989 TWF directive was primarily concerned with removing national legal and regulatory barriers to the creation of a single European audiovisual market. The directive was based on the neo-liberal regulatory principles of 'mutual recognition' and 'country of origin' regulation. In Harcourt's view, once enacted and duly transposed into national laws (by 1992), TWF created a situation of 'regulatory arbitrage' whereby commercial broadcasting organizations have sought out the most favourable regulatory locations and some governments have made lax regulatory provision to cater to the new economic opportunities provided by TWF. Further, Harcourt notes that '[i]n numerous rulings the ECJ '… paid attention to TWF's provisions on market liberalisation (e.g. cross-border broadcasting), whilst ignoring those relating to public interest goals (e.g. restriction of advertising time, content quotas) and sometimes overriding them (e.g. protection of minors) (Harcourt 2005, 22). Essentially, Harcourt (2005) argues that European decision-making is eroding the national capacity to regulate for the public interest. Harcourt suggests that increased European coordination in public interest regulation – in other words positive integration – could be more conducive to growth and competitiveness than the dismantling of existing national laws. However, she notes that this would require changes to the political composition of the European Union. In similar vein, Venturelli (1998) has argued that European audiovisual policy has been driven primarily by an economic rationale and privileged the neo-liberal approach to regulation.

Ward (2002, 2003) dissents from such a negative evaluation. He does not see EU audiovisual policy 'as the destructive force it is too often perceived to be. It has evolved into a highly sophisticated regulatory framework that is driven by certain needs. These … are economic, but also cultural and political, and underpinned by … democratic values.' Ward is disappointed that the EU 'has achieved little towards attempting to approach the problem of the democratic deficit through its audiovisual policy'. In his view, 'it has, however, provided for the maintenance of democratic media within the terms of the EC Treaty and fully accepted the right of member states to support [media policy] instruments for the democratic needs of society' (Ward 2002, ix).

Between these two contrasting perspectives, there are those that take a more nuanced stance. Thus, Collins (1994, 1995) concedes on the one hand that the 'dirigistes' (as he refers to those seeking more interventionist, market-correcting positive integration) have exerted less influence on the European Union's audiovisual sector than the 'liberals', but points out that they have certainly registered some modest victories, such as establishing protectionist made in Europe programming quotas in the primarily market-making 1989 Television Without Frontiers (TWF) directive and the MEDIA support programme for European audiovisual production and defending the Europeans' right to maintain such culturally protectionist and interventionist policies against attempts by the USA to remove them in international trade negotiations (on this, see the paper by Pauwels et al in this special issue). Above all, Collins sees EU audiovisual policy in terms of a rather symbolic 'unity in diversity', which cloaks struggles between different interests and policy paradigms which can be broadly defined as 'dirigiste' and 'liberal'. Within the framework of the EU's institutions, policies emerging from one part of the Commission (DG Culture) will have more 'dirigiste' character than those emerging from other parts (DG Internal Market, DG Competition). Similarly, Verhulst and Goldberg 1998: 146) have explained how EU audiovisual policies 'must be regarded as the result of hard won compromise between both Member States and rival power centres within the institutions', with the struggle between 'liberals' and 'dirigistes' conducted beyond and within the Commission. Other studies that focus on the extraordinary complexity of the decision-making structures of the EU, with different policy paradigms being promoted in different EU-institutional 'venues' (i.e. different Commission DGs, the Council of Ministers, the European Parliament) and a strong tension between supranational and intergovernmental forces, are provided by very detailed analyses of the TWF process (Wagner 1994, Krebber 2001). Levy (1999) adopts a quite clear-cut position, arguing that despite powerful exogenous forces making for a convergent EU-level audiovisual policy, notably the regulatory implications of the 'digital revolution', the sheer diversity of Member States' traditional audiovisual policy approaches has set sharply defined and persistent limits to the development of a more comprehensive supranational EU audiovisual regulatory framework. Finally, Sarikakis (2004) argues that the EU certainly has a bias towards negative integration and market-led policies, but points out too that the supranational representation offered by the European Parliament has softened the harshest impacts and offered a significant line of defence for public service broadcasting.

Bearing in mind these various perspectives, the rest of the paper explores the implications of EU audiovisual policy for *service public*, through an examination of two specific lines of EU policy: namely the EU's policy response to the digital 'convergence' of broadcasting, tele-communications and the Internet; and the EU's handling of competition complaints from the commercial sector against public service broadcast-ers about their involvement in new media markets (including Internet). First, though, it is necessary to consider the concept 'public service broad-casting'. Herein it is argued that its general familiarity as an everyday term hides a diversity of different regulatory preoccupations and organi-sational approaches which vary considerably from country to country. It does, however, go to the heart of a country's sovereignty.

Public Service Broadcasting, a Vague and Diverse Concept

Public service broadcasting may be something the meaning of which everybody feels they understand, but nonetheless it does not lend itself easily to precise definition. A principal reason is the rich diversity of regulatory traditions within Europe (Humphreys 1996; Levy 1999). France has had a distinctive body of legal doctrine and an ostensibly very serious regulatory approach to *service public*, whereas public service broad-casting in the UK – the praxis of which has undoubtedly been of a com-paratively high quality – has only ever been relatively loosely defined (in the BBC's case in its Charter and Agreement rather than in statute as with the other terrestrial broadcasters with public services obligations). Only recently, with the establishment of the new Office of Communica-tions (Ofcom) has an attempt been made to spell out more clearly the precise nature of the public service remit (Prosser 2005). Successive broadcasting commissions have played an important role in fleshing out the concept, often inspirationally (as with the thinking that launched Channel 4), but it has taken the challenge of defending public service broadcasting from competition challenges to tighten up this traditional realm of discretion. In Germany, by contrast, the Federal Constitutional Court has played a key role in defining the nature of public service broadcasting in terms of constitutional legal precepts, laying a very spe-cial (historically conditioned) emphasis on broadcasting's democratic purposes. Thus, the Court explicitly declares broadcasting to be both a 'medium' and a 'factor' in the process of forming public opinion in a democracy. Public service broadcasters have a constitutional-legal duty – and guarantee of their existence and future development – to supply a diversity of programming; 'internal pluralism' is ensured through 'internal regulation' of public service broadcasting corporations by special 'broadcasting councils' which contain a range of representatives of 'socially significant groups', including political representatives (Humphreys 1994). In sum, the European countries' legal, regulatory and organisational arrangements for providing the staple core ingredients of public service broadcasting – namely, universality, pluralism, diversity, responsiveness, and accountability – have varied considerably. Furthermore, the public broadcasters' degree of political independence has varied notably, with some countries' systems being subject to government influence, others subject to multiparty or multiple group influences, and others relatively independent (see Humphreys 1996, 110-158).

Clearly, then, the organisation of public service broadcasting goes right to the heart of countries' democratic, social and cultural models. It has been natural therefore for the EU Member States jealously to guard their traditional primary control over broadcasting. It has been a key sovereignty issue, no less. Quite apart from this, the sheer diversity of national approaches would arguably render the formulation of any common European rules defining in detail the nature of public service broadcasting well nigh impossible. Moreover, as Harrison and Woods (2001) have noted, there is considerable uncertainty about the definition of public service broadcasting at the EU level. The competition Directorate-General of the European Commission (DG IV) is inclined to see public service broadcasters 'as economic operators subject to normal economic constraints', while the European Parliament, the Council and the Commission's Directorate-General for Education and Culture (DG X) are more concerned with public broadcasters' functions, such as promoting education, culture and democracy, and the means of achieving them, such as through the provision of a diverse range of high quality programming. The main question, then, is the degree to which the EU's market liberalisation initiatives and competition policies impinge on the Member States' particular models of public service broadcasting.

Broadcasting/Telecoms Convergence and Public Service Broadcasting

By the mid 1990s, the EU agenda concerning audiovisual regulation had progressed from market opening in the field of television (TWF) to a debate about the appropriate aims and methods of regulation given the 'convergence' of broadcasting, telecoms, and IT (Humphreys, 1999). There is general agreement that digital 'convergence' of electronic media, telecoms and computing produces compelling pressures for more flexible, 'technology neutral' regulation. However, the technological determinism of the proponents of far-reaching regulatory change has been resisted by those arguing the need to harness the new technologies to social and cultural goals. On the one side, stand those who consider that convergence will 'inevitably' lead to the complete and rapid collapse of traditional boundaries between the telecoms, IT and broadcasting industries and call for a lighter touch regulation, their technological determinism betraying a degree of vested interest on the part of the Information and Communications Technology (ICT) industry. On the other side are aligned those who argue that the specificity of existing separate sectors will continue to differentiate them and that broadcasting will retain a special role 'as the bearer of social, cultural and ethical values within our society, independent of the technology relied upon to reach the consumer' (CEC 1997: 5). The logic of the former position is that regulation will 'inevitably' have to converge, leading to a single 'horizontal' regulatory model for the entire 'converged' communications sector, whilst the logic of the latter position is that regulation of the economic conditions and infrastructure, on the one hand, and content of information services, on the other, should be kept distinct to safeguard non-economic public service goals.

The European Commission explored the regulatory implications of convergence in a Green Paper published in December 1997 (CEC 1997). The Green Paper reflected the fact that views and interests diverged, not least within the Commission itself, notably between DG X (cultural policy, broadcasting) and DG XIII (industrial policy, telecommunications and IT). The Green Paper presented three options. First, the existing sector-specific regulatory approach (i.e. for telecoms, IT, and broadcasting) might be built on and adapted to cater for the new services. Second, a separate 'horizontal' regulatory model for these new convergent activities could be developed alongside the continuing sector specific regulation of telecommunications and broadcasting. Third, there could occur a more radical regulatory overhaul involving the progressive introduction of a new 'horizontal' regulatory model to cover the whole range of existing and new ICT services. The Green Paper struggled to appear evenhanded about these options.

However, it can be argued that the Green Paper had an overall bias, that it was positing a shift towards 'horizontal' regulation (Humphreys

1999). Thus, Sauter (1998, 21) deemed the Green Paper 'an attempt to achieve a consensus around a coherent regulatory approach ... based on the third option of achieving a new comprehensive horizontal regulatory approach'. Similarly, Levy (1999, 132) detected 'a clear preference' for moving towards a converged 'horizontal' regulatory model for the entire communications sector, reflecting the position of DG XIII. In the view of Carole Tongue MEP (1998: 2) (at the time a very influential member of the European Parliament's culture committee) this was unsurprising: the Green Paper 'was largely the work of DG XIII together with consultants KPMG. The initiative was headed by Commissioner Bangemann, whose main brief [was] to create a liberalised environment for industry.' As Simpson (2000, 447-8) notes, DG XIII had developed a strong relationship with important players in the IT and telecommunications sectors and this had contributed to it having 'largely pro-market liberalisation sympathies'. However, the extent of opposition to this viewpoint emerged from the consultation and public debate that followed the Green Paper. While telecommunications and IT companies favoured a horizontal regulatory framework, some arguing for a distinctly light touch approach as well, there was little enthusiasm from other quarters. Public service broadcasters, broadcasting regulators and Member State governments emphasised the specificity of broadcasting and its special role in ensuring democratic pluralism and promoting culture. Obviously, this distinguished broadcasting from telecoms and IT and provided a justification for its continued sector-specific regulation, and for public interest measures designed to promote pluralism and diversity, the European production industry, and public service broadcasting. In the face of the strong opposition from national governments, European parliamentarians (such as Carole Tongue), and public service broadcasters, the ambitious project of DG XIII to create a light touch horizontal regulatory regime had to be significantly modified when the Commission set about drafting the new regulatory model (Levy 1999: 138-40; Simpson 2000; Ward 2002: 111-124; CEC 1998).

The EU's 2002 Electronic Communications Regulatory Framework (ECRF) streamlines and extends the EU's essentially neo-liberal, pro-competitive telecommunications regulatory framework, developed in a whole series of market-opening and accompanying regulatory harmonization directives over the course of the 1990s, to all electronic communication networks and associated services (Humphreys and Simpson 2005,

93-142). Broadcasting content, however, would continue to be regulated according to Member States' preferred socio-cultural models. Recital 5 of the Framework Directive (European Parliament and Council 2002) states that the new regulatory framework:

> does not therefore cover the content of services delivered over electronic telecommunications networks using electronic telecommunications services such as broadcasting content, financial services and certain information society services, and is therefore without prejudice to measures taken at Community or national level in respect of such services, in compliance with Community law, in order to promote cultural and linguistic diversity and to ensure the defence of media pluralism (See also Framework Directive Article 1 [3]).

The special role and distinctiveness of broadcasting was explicitly recognised in the Recital 6, noting that:

> audiovisual policy and content regulation are undertaken in pursuit of general interest objectives, such as freedom of expression, media pluralism, impartiality, cultural and linguistic diversity, social inclusion, consumer protection, and the protection of minors (European Parliament and Council, 2002, 5-6).

Adequate network access for public service broadcasters in the de-regulated, multi-channel, and converged communications landscape could not simply be assumed, without positive protection. The Universal Services Directive, a key element of the new EU package, therefore allowed Member States to impose 'reasonable "must carry" obligations', for the transmission of public service channels (services that meet 'general interest' objectives), on providers of electronic communication networks used for the distribution of radio or television broadcasts (Article 31).

The EU's convergence regulatory framework thus leaves enduring scope for very considerable national diversity regarding audiovisual policy making and public service broadcasting in the digital era. As David Levy (1999) has described, the French approach has been characterised by *service public*, economic *dirigisme* and cultural protectionism. In Germany, regulatory reform has been preoccupied by the constitutional issue of which new media services should fall under the regulatory jurisdiction of the federation and which under the *Länder*, with new media laws produced at each level. The UK has sought to maintain a commitment to public service broadcasting in the context of an open-ness to market forces and regulatory convergence with telecommunications. Of these three cases, only the UK has opted for a converged regulator for the entire electronic communications sector (Ofcom). Although Ofcom has had an important say in defining public service broadcasting more closely than in the past, its powers over the BBC reside mainly in the field of competition-related assessment of the market impact new BBC services.

Competition Policy and Public Service Broadcasting

Following the 1989 TWF Directive, the European Commission Competition Authority became very involved in making media decisions, over a range of matters from the acquisition and sale of programme rights to media mergers (Pauwels 1998; Levy 1999; Harcourt 2005). Until the 1990s, the Commission's competition policy principally affected the private sector and had little impact on the public sector. However, the institutionalisation of the 1992 European single market programme accompanied – and to an important extent reinforced the pressure for – the dismantling of state monopolies in many areas of the economy. It led to a questioning of the scope of public funding for the provision of services and it saw the mobilisation of firms and business associations demanding that the EC take regulatory action to open the market and prevent anti-competitive practices (Smith 2001, 219). The broadcasting sector has been no exception. The future scope of the public-service remit in the digital age quickly became the key competition policy issue bearing on public service broadcasting. Public broadcasters continue to see their mission in the most comprehensive terms. Commercial operators, however, seek a narrower definition of the public service remit and the confinement of the public broadcasters to compensating for market failure, leaving new media markets to the private sector. In recent years, national regulators and the EC competition authorities have received a significant number of complaints from the private sector about alleged distortion of the media market by public service broadcasters. The Commission has therefore had to consider the future scope of public-service broadcasting. Some have stressed the threat that this presents to public service broadcasting. Thus, Wheeler (2004, 350) has suggested that '… as public service broadcasters (PSBs) have been understood as constraining the internal market, a number of EU institutions, most especially the Competition and Information Society Directorates have become hostile to them.' Harrison and Woods (2001: 498-9) suggest that '[t]he operation of state aid rules unfortunately has a limiting effect on what might be felt properly to be funded by the state, with consequent adverse effects on the likely provision of PSB.'

In the EU Treaty, public undertakings to which Member States grant special or exclusive rights are covered by Articles 86 and 87, both of which provide for derogations from competition rules under certain conditions. To take the latter first, Article 87 empowers the Commission to take action if a scheme 1) is granted aid by the state or through state resources; 2) provides an economic advantage; 3) is capable of distorting competition; and 4) affects trade between Member States. Article 87 (3) allows the Commission to permit state aid granted specifically to promote culture. However, this has been much less relevant that might have been expected, the problem being that 'culture' has been interpreted narrowly. Article 86 (2), however, provides for a derogation for 'services of general economic interest' (i.e public services) in order to allow them to perform the particular tasks assigned to them.

The Treaty of Amsterdam (EU 1997) marked a turning point in the EU's extension of neo-liberalism into the public sector, by explicitly recognising the importance of public services. It introduced a new provision in its Article 16 which emphasises the importance of public services generally and the ability of Member States to provide these services as they see fit, subject to competition provisions. Prosser (2005: 121) sees this new Treaty Article, as well as the later inclusion of a right of access to services of general interest in the EU's Charter of Fundamental Rights and the subsequent incorporation of these provisions into the (now stalled) Constitutional Treaty, as having introduced a 'partial constitutionalisation' of the value of public services, marking a significant turning away from a predisposition, associated with the earlier development of the single internal market, to see public services as an 'unwelcome impediment to the task of market creation'.

For our purposes even more significantly, reflecting the particular sensitivities of the Member States in the media field, public service broadcasting has received special consideration as a service of general interest. Within the EU there exists a strong commitment on the part of the Member States (in the Council) and the Parliament to protect a comprehensive 'European-style' concept of public service broadcasting, as more than a 'US-style' marginal concept. Following an EP resolution on public service broadcasting drafted by Carole Tongue MEP, a Protocol on this subject was attached to the 1997 Treaty of Amsterdam. It notes that the contracting parties (the Member States) have taken into consideration that:

> the system of public service broadcasting in the Member States is directly related to the democratic, social and cultural needs of each society and to the need to preserve media pluralism

And goes to note that they have therefore agreed that:

> The provisions of the Treaty establishing the European Community shall be without prejudice to the competence of the Member States to provide for the funding of public service broadcasting insofar as such funding is granted to broadcasting organisations for the fulfilment of the public service remit as conferred, defined and organised by each Member State, and insofar as such funding does not affect trading conditions and competition in the Community to an extent which would be contrary to the common interest, while the realisation of that public service shall be taken into account (EU 1997, 87).

In Prosser's (2005, 213) view, the Protocol appears '... to have influenced the Commission in favour of an approach which affords a considerable degree of discretion to national authorities in conferring a public service broadcasting remit so long as that remit is properly defined'. On the other hand, Harrison and Woods (2001: 479) note that, in the Competition's interpretation, the Protocol leaves it 'the power to review the scope of PSB in the interest of the common good and, in particular , in the light of competition policy.'

How, then, have competition cases against public service broadcasters actually been handled? As Ward (2002, 97-110; 2003) has explained, the complaints fell into two categories: complaints against the launch by public service broadcasters of new thematic services; and complaints against public service broadcasters deriving funding from a mixture of state aid and advertising.

Into the first category fell the complaints raised by the satellite broadcaster BSkyB in the UK against the launch of BBC News 24 and by the German private broadcasters' interest association, the *Verband Privater Rundfunk und Telekommunikation* (VPRT), against the launch by the ARD and ZDF of a children's channel, the *Kinderkanal*, and also an information and documentary channel called *Phoenix*. The introduction of these new services by publicly funded broadcasters was held to amount to unfair competition for private broadcasters operating these same kinds of service without the benefit of state aid. In both of these cases, in the late 1990s, the European Commission upheld the public service broadcasters against their challengers. The Commission accepted that such services might distort the market, but found that this was an acceptable cost of their fulfilment of a public service remit.

In these cases, the Commission deemed licence fee funding to constitute state aid, thereby empowering it to adjudicate them. In the BBC News 24 case, the British government had tried to argue that the fee was simply reimbursement for expenditure for carrying out PSB obligations. This argument had simply not washed. The Commission clearly reserved for itself the right to review the cases on the grounds of competition objectives. However, in these cases, the Commission based its favourable ruling to the public services on the exception from competition rules that Article 86 (2) gave to services of general interest. In doing so, the Commision clearly acknowledged the principle of member State competence for defining public service broadcasting, enshrined in the Amsterdam Protocol. The Commission saw itself as competent only to judge whether or not trade and competition had been affected in such a way as to be 'contrary to the interests of the Community'. As Ward (2002, 2003) concludes, the Commission clearly looked favourably on these public service undertakings. It limited itself to judging whether or not their funding was commensurate with their remits as defined by their national authorities and found that they were not disproportionate in meeting these objectives. The cases demonstrated that the Commission was plainly alert to the politically sensitive nature of broadcasting and the strong interest of Member States to retain primary responsibility for it. This was underlined when, in May 2002, the Commission approved the launch by the BBC of no fewer than nine new BBC digital services – four TV and five radio – because they are subject to public service obligations and the state financing was not deemed disproportionate to the net costs of running the services. In approving all these cases, the Commission demonstrated that it recognised that public service broadcasting could develop and diversify their activities in the digital era so long as the new services met fulfilled the 'service of general interest' derogation requirements of Article 86 (2).

The second category raised issues that were more difficult to handle. The Commission's slow response clearly reflected its reluctance to make judgements about state aid in such a politically sensitive field as public service broadcasting (Smith 2001, 230). In September 1998, the Court of First Instance ruled that DG IV had delayed for too long in resolving complaints against the Spanish public broadcaster RTVE lodged over five years before by the private company Telecinco.[3] One result of this ruling was the codification in a 1999 Commission regulation of time limits for state aid decisions. Specifically with regard to broadcasting, the ruling spurred DG IV to explore ways of dealing with the back-log of private sector complaints against those public broadcasters that received a mix of advertising and public funding.

With this in mind, DG IV officials circulated a discussion paper in October 1998 floating a series of guidelines that might be employed in making rulings on the issue (Humphreys 1999: 12-14). These guidelines appeared to recognise the right of Member States to decide on the funding and remit of their public service broadcasters. However, as Levy (1999, 97) notes: 'in fact, they challenged this principle with the assertion that PSBs in receipt of advertising and licence-fee funding could not justify the showing of films, entertainment programmes or most sports coverage as part of their public service remit'. This signified clearly a 'minimalist' definition of public service broadcasting – at least for those public service broadcasters with mixed financing – whereby public funding would be justified for informational, educational, cultural services but not for other genres of programming that had hitherto been accepted as part of their legitimate remit (Michalis 1999, 161). However, Competition Commissioner Karel van Miert immediately distanced himself from this controversial suggestion, which had antagonised the Member States. Led by Germany, they were quick to re-assert the basic principle that underlined their right to define public service broadcasting (*European Voice*, Vol: 4, No: 40, 05/11/1998 and No: 41, 12/11/1998). In November 1998 the Culture and Audiovisual Ministers of the Member States agreed a resolution on public service broadcasting that reaffirmed the Amsterdam Protocol. It emphasised the need for PSBs to offer a wide range of programming to a wide audience, stating explicitly that: 'public service broadcasting must be able to continue to provide a wide range of programming in accordance with its remit as defined by the Member States ...' (Council of the European Communities 1999, 1).

---

[3] Court of First Instance Judgement of 15 September 1998 in Case T-95/96 Gestevision Telecinco SA.

In November 2001 the Commission released a Communication on the application of State aid rules to public service broadcasting (CEC 2001). Citing the report of the High-Level Group on Audiovisual Policy, the Protocol of the Amsterdam treaty, and the Council Resolution on public service broadcasting, the Commission's 2001 Communication concluded: 'a public service mandate encompassing a wide range of programming in accordance with its remit can be considered as legitimate, as aiming at a balanced and varied programming capable of preserving a certain level of audience for public service broadcasters and, thus, of ensuring the accomplishment of their mandate' (CEC 2001, Para 13). The Communication confirms that state support for public service broadcasters does indeed amount to state aid in the terms of the EC treaty and therefore 'will have to be assessed on a case by case basis' (CEC 2001, Para 17). But it is clear that, *so long as the remit is clearly defined by the Member State* (my emphasis), the Commission has to confine itself to evaluating the proportionality of that aid. The Communication states that Article 86 (2) of the EC Treaty provides for a derogation from competition rules for 'services of general economic interest' (such as public service broadcasting) so long as three tests are met: namely, the service must be a service of general economic interest and clearly defined as such by the Member State (definition); the undertaking in question must be explicitly entrusted by the Member State with the provision of that service (entrustment); the application of the competition rules of the Treaty (in this case, the ban on State aid) must obstruct the performance of the particular tasks assigned to the undertaking and the exemption from such rules must not affect the development of trade to an extent that would be contrary to the interests of the Community (proportionality test) (CEC 2001, Para 29).

The Commission Communication stressed the need for transparency. In the first place, there should be a 'clear and precise definition of the public service remit'. Secondly, the Communication guidelines make clear that in order to allow the Commission to carry out its 'proportionality test' for funding, a separation of accounts between public service activities and non-public service activities must be maintained to 'provide the Commission with a tool for examining alleged cross-subsidisation and for defending justified compensation for general economic interest tasks'.

In nearly all cases, approval of state aid to public service broadcasters has been granted by the Commission. However, in 2004 the Commission ordered Danish public service broadcaster TV2 to pay back 'excess compensation for public service tasks' and launched a probe into Dutch state financing of public service broadcasters based on a preliminary conclusion that it was more generous than necessary (CEC 2005, 18), indicating how seriously the Commission viewed 'proportionality'.

Finally, on this theme of the implications of competition policy for public service broadcasting, there is the issue of the expansion of public service broadcasting into 'information society' services. The BBC provided the test case when in 2003 the BBC's Digital Curriculum project was given the green light by government, aiming to use TV licence fee payers' money to make large parts of the school syllabus available online and to provide interactive e-learning services to schools and students free of charge. Commercial providers expressed the fear that the BBC might end up dominating the market for online educational resources. In February 2003, a private company called Research Machines plc filed a complaint with the European Commission on behalf of itself and other complainant companies. Having first determined that the case did indeed fulfil the conditions making for a case to be adjudicated under EU state aid rules under Article 87, the Commission examined whether the venture could simply be seen as an ancillary service within the BBC's established educational provision. It was acknowledged 'that education had been an element of the BBC's public service throughout its existence'. Further, 'provision of educational material over the internet may be considered to be within the [established scope of the BBC's licence fee funded service] 'to the extent that it remains closely associated with the BBC's "television and radio services"'. However, the Commission also observed that 'the use of public funding to enter markets that are already developed and where the commercial players have had little or no exposure to the BBC as a competitor cannot be considered as maintaining the status quo' (CEC 2003, paras 35-36). The Commission therefore went on to assess whether the new service merited a derogation as a 'service of general economic interest' under Article 86. Here it noted that the UK government's had legitimately defined a free educational service for schools and students as such. It acknowledged that the government had clearly defined and entrusted the new service to the BBC. Significantly, the Commission noted that, in specifying the nature of the service, the

Secretary of State had imposed no fewer than eighteen conditions, one of which was that 'the service, taken as a whole, should be distinctive from and complementary to services provided by the commercial sector' (CEC 2003, para 41). Otherwise, the Commission judged the funding to be necessary and proportionate, and the accounting mechanism transparent (CEC 2003, paras 50-58). Observing that according to the EU Treaty 'quality education is one of the objectives of the Community', the Commission concluded that it did 'not consider that the State financing of the services in question would affect the development of trade within the Community to an extent contrary to the common interest'(CEC 2003, para 62-63). Therefore, Digital Curriculum was deemed to fulfil all the conditions for an Article 86 (2) derogation. However, as a precedent for dealing with cases of public service broadcasters' involvement in information society services – and future cases can be expected – it is perhaps of most significance that the Commission highlighted the principle of the *distinctiveness from and complementarity to* (my emphasis) services provided by the commercial sector.

Concluding Remarks

The EU has acquired much influence concerning the creation of a European audiovisual internal market and in enforcing competition, these being areas where Commission and the Court exercise direct powers. Negative integration, the removal of legal and regulatory (if not the surmounting of cultural and linguistic) barriers to the internal market, has been the EU's main achievement to date. The long-term implications for public service broadcasting of the two lines of EU policy discussed herein remain uncertain. It is possible to make the following observations:

The politics surrounding the enactment of a new Electronic Communications Regulatory Framework, intended to cater for technological convergence, has resulted in the creation of a horizontal regulatory framework only for communications carriage (and related services). The Member States have defended audiovisual *content* as a field of regulation lying in the field of their competence, so long as they observe the internal market requirements of the TWF directive. Indeed, the Draft treaty on the Establishment of a European Constitution defines it as an area where the EU can only take 'supporting, coordinating or complementary action'. Thus, whatever kind of public service broadcasting they want largely resides in the Member States' own field of discretion and political choice. This is not to ignore that the new converged broadcasting environment presents a tremendous challenge to public service broadcasters. Audience fragmentation, new means of viewing (Internet, on-demand services), uncertainty over the future of licence-fee funding, the difficulty of providing equal and universal access in the digital era, all pose very serious questions, along with the need to maintain the public's and politicians' support for a well-funded and comprehensive service.

With regard to competition policy, where the Commission and the Court exercise direct power, there is certainly the potential for a negative EU impact on public service broadcasting. The European competition authorities have assumed the right to act on the basis that it is 'appropriate' to apply state aid rules to public service broadcasters, even if the justification may be open to question (Harrison and Woods 2001: 490-91). Yet, in its decision making so far, the Commission has plainly been generally supportive of public service broadcasting and acknowledged the Member States' right, underlined in the Amsterdam Protocol, to define its scope. Nonetheless, as Collins (2002, 10) has argued, the 'structural conflict between the competition principles of the European treaty and the status and practice of PSB is both inescapable and likely to become more salient.' The Commission and Court wield considerable discretionary power in making their competition judgements. The private commercial sector will hardly give up in attempting to invoke competition law to delimit public service broadcasters' activities. To the extent that public service broadcasters diversify into areas of new media where the distinctiveness and complementarity of their services from commercial services is not very clear, and possibly obtain commercial funding for some services (e.g. on-demand programmes), the competition issues become much more salient. Should public service broadcasters fail to convince that their services fulfil a clearly defined public service remit, or should the Member States be deemed to have been disproportionally supportive or their regulatory provisions too lax, they may well fall foul of the EU's competition authority. It has already showed itself prepared to act on the proportionality issue.

References

Collins, Richard. 1994a. *Broadcasting and Audio-Visual Policy in the European Single Market.* London: John Libbey.

Collins, Richard. 1994b. Unity in Diversity. The European Single Market in Broadcasting and the Audiovisual, 1982-92. *Journal of Common Market Studies* 32 (1): 89-102.

Collins, Richard. 2002. The Future of Public Service Broadcasting in the United Kingdom. Paper presented at the conference *The Future of Public Broadcasting in a Changing Media Society*, Institute of Mass Communication and Media Research, University of Zurich, 27-29 September 2002.

Commission of the European Communities (CEC). 1997. *Green Paper on the the Convergence of the Telecommunications, Audiovisual and Information Technology Sectors and the Implications for Regulation. Towards an Information Society Approach.* Brussels: COM (97)623, 03.12.98.

Commission of the European Commission (CEC). 1998). *Summary of the Results of the Public Consultation on the Green Paper on the Convergence of the Telecommunications, Media and Information Technology Sectors: Areas for Further Reflection*, Brussels: SEC (98) 1284 29.09.1998.

Commission of the European Communities (CEC). 1999a. *State Aid to Public Service Broadcasting Channels 'Kinderkanal and Phoenix'*, OJ C 238, 21.8.

Commission of the European Communities (CEC). 1999b. *State Aid No NN 88/98 – UNITED KINGDOM. Financing of a 24-Hour Advertising-Free News Channel out of the Licence Fee by the BBC.* Brussels: SG(99) D/10201, 14.12.1999.

Commission of the European Communities (CEC). 2001. *Communication from the Commission on the Application of State Aid Rules to Public Service Broadcasting*, OJ, C 320/04.

Commission of the European Communities (CEC). 2003. *State Aid No N 37/2003- United Kingdom BBC Digital Curriculum*, Brussels, C (2003)3371fin, 01.10.2003.

Commission of the European Communities (CEC). 2005. *EU Competition Policy in the Media Sector. Commission Decisions (Compilation 2004)*, Brussels: Competition DG, March 2005. http://europa.eu.int/comm/competition/ publications/studies/ecompilation_2005.pdf

Commission of the European Communities (CEC). 2005. *Proposal for a Council Decision on the Conclusion of the UNESCO Convention on the Protection and Promotion of the Diversity of Cultural Expressions*, Brussels, COM (2005).

Council of the European Communities. 1989. *Directive on the Coordination of Certain Provisions Laid Down by Law, Regulation or Administrative Action in Member States Concerning the Pursuit of Television Broadcasting Activities*, 89/552/EEC. OJ, L 298/23, 17.10.89.

Council of the European Communities. 1999. *Resolution of the Council and of the Representatives of the Governments of the Member States, Meeting within the Council of 25 January 1999 concerning public service broadcasting*, OJ, C 30, 05.02.1999.

European Parliament and Council. 2002. *Directive of the European Parliament and Council on a Common Regulatory Framework for Electronic Communications Networks and Services (Framework Directive)*. Brussels: PE-CONS 3672/01, 04.02.2002.

European Union. 1997. *Treaty of Amsterdam Amending the Treaty on European Union, the Treaties Establishing the European Communities and Related Acts.* OJ, C 340, 10.11.1997

Harcourt, Alison. 2005. *The European Union and the Regulation of Media Markets.* Manchester: Manchester University Press.

Harrison, Jackie, and Lorna Woods. 2001. Defining European Public Service Broadcasting. *European Journal of Communication* 16 (4): 477-504.

Humphreys, Peter. 1994. *Media and Media Policy in Germany. The Press and Broadcasting since 1945.* Oxford, UK, and Providence, RI, USA: Berg.

Humphreys, Peter. 1996. *Mass Media and Media Policy in Western Europe.* Manchester: Manchester University Press.

Humphreys, Peter. 1999. Regulating for Pluralism in the Age of Digital Convergence. Paper presented to the *Joint Research Sessions of the European Consortium for Political Research (ECPR)*, Mannheim, Germany, 26-32 March. Workshop 24: 'Regulating Communications in the Multimedia Age'. www.essex.ac.uk/ECPR/events/jointsessions/paperarchive/mannheim/w 24/Humphreys.PDF

Humphreys, Peter, and Seamus Simpson. 2005. *Globalisation, Convergence and European Telecommunications Regulation.* Cheltenham, UK, and Northampton, MA, USA: Edward Elgar.

Krebber, Daniel. 2002. *Europeanisation of Regulatory Television Policy. The Decision-Making Process of the Television Without Frontiers Directives from 1987 & 1997.* Baden-Baden: Nomos Verlagsgesellschaft.

Levy, David. 1999. *Europe's Digital Revolution. Broadcasting Regulation, the EU and the Nation State.* London and New York: Routledge.

Michalis, Maria. 1999. European Union Broadcasting and Telecoms: Towards a Convergent Regulatory Regime? *European Journal of Communication* 14, (2): 147-171.

Pauwels, Caroline. 1998). Integrating Economies, Integrating Policies: The Importance of Anttrust and Competition Policies within the Global Audiovisual Order. *Communications and Strategies*, 30: 103-132.

Prosser, Tony. 2005. *The Limits of Competition Law. Markets and Public Services*, Oxford: Oxford University Press.

Sarikakis, Katharine. 2004. *Powers in Media Policy: The Challenge of the European Parliament.* Oxford/Bern/Berlin/Brussels/Frankfurt am Main: Peter Lang.

Sauter, Wolf. 1998. EU Regulation for the Convergence of Media, Telecommunication, and Information Technology: Arguments for a Constitutional Approach. *ZERP-Diskussionspapier1/98, Zentrum für Europäische Rechtspolitik an der Universität Bremen*: 12-26.

Scharpf, Fritz. 1999. *Governing in Europe: Effective and Democratic?* Oxford: Oxford University Press.

Simpson, Seamus. 2000. Intra-institutional Rivalry and Policy Entrepreneurship in the European Union. *New Media and Society* 2 (4): 445-466.

Smith, Mitchell. 2001. How Adaptable is the European Commission? The Case of State Aid Regulation. *Journal of Public Policy* 21 (3): 219-238.

Tongue, Carole. 1998. Submission on the Commission's Green Paper on Convergence of the Telecommunications, Media and Information Technology Sectors and the Implications for Regulation. Accessed at: www.poptel.org.uk/carole-tongue/index2.html, on 20/06/03.

Venturelli, Shalini. 1998. *Liberalizing the European Media: Politics, Regulation, and the Public Sphere.* Oxford: Oxford University Press.

Verhulst, Stefaan, and David Goldberg. 1998. The European Institutions. In *Regulating the Changing Media: A Comparative Study*, eds. David Goldberg, Tony Prosser and Stefaan Verhulst, 145-176. Oxford: Clarendon Press.

Wagner, Jürgen. 1994. *Policy-Analyse: Grenzenlos Fernsehen in der EG.* Frankfurt am Main: Peter Lang.

Ward, David. 2002. *The European Union Democratic Deficit and the Public Sphere. An Evaluation of EU Media Policy.* Amsterdam: IOS Press.

Ward, David. 2003. State Aid or Band Aid? An Evaluation of the European Commission's Approach to Public Service Broadcasting. *Media, Culture and Society* 25: 233-250.

Wheeler, Mark. 2004. Supranational Regulation. Television and the European Union. *European Journal of Communication* 19 (3): 349-369.

EUROPEAN STUDIES 24 (2007): 113-134

MORE EUROPE: MORE UNITY, MORE DIVERSITY?
THE ENLARGEMENT OF THE EUROPEAN
AUDIOVISUAL SPACE

Hedwig de Smaele

Abstract

This article studies the link between the Eastern enlargement of the European Union and issues of audiovisual policy and audiovisual markets. The main link between audiovisual policy and EU enlargement is through alignment with the Community *acquis*, in particular the Television Without Frontiers Directive. Legislative alignment has been achieved in all Central and Eastern European countries by adopting new media laws. This process can be described one of (neutrally defined) Europeanization. EU enlargement offers opportunities for Central and Eastern European audiovisual industries such as increased investments and funding, cooperation partners, and enhanced export possibilities, but also bears the threat of Europeanization as a process of cultural diffusion or cultural dominance. Both Eastern and Western Europe, however, are culturally and linguistically fragmented. Enlargement, it is argued, basically enlarges the characteristics of the European audiovisual market. Enlargement adds to Europe 'more of the same': more diversity, more languages, and more (audiovisual) cultures.

Introduction

This article will study the link between the Eastern enlargement of the European Union (EU) on the one hand, and issues of audiovisual policy and audiovisual markets on the other hand. What are the implications of EU accession for the audiovisual policy/market of the new Member States of Central and Eastern Europe? And what are the implications of the 'Eastern enlargement' for the audiovisual policy/market of the European Union? In general, discussion of the enlargement is largely focused on the most sensitive chapters of agricultural policy, regional policy, and the common budget. And the vast amount of literature on European enlargement only sparsely mentions the issue of audiovisual policy and media. Likewise, a discussion of the European audiovisual and media policies often goes by without even mentioning the enlargement. At the same time, however, the audiovisual world is probably the world that connects the largest numbers of citizens throughout Europe, both old and new, and has a daily impact on the lives of millions of citizens. The audiovisual sector carries both economic and cultural importance, and touches upon questions of identity and citizenship. Therefore it is at the heart of Europe.

In what follows we will discuss briefly the process of EU enlargement and the nature of EU audiovisual policy before turning our attention to harmonisation of audiovisual legislation in Central and Eastern Europe, participation of Central and Eastern European countries in community programs and integration of Western and Eastern audiovisual markets.

The battleground of Europe

The breakdown of the communist system in Eastern Europe at the end of the 1980s – beginning of the 1990s caused some analysts to proclaim 'the end of history', as the ideological battle was fought and won by Western (political and economic) liberalism. Leaving aside the core idea of Fukuyama's thesis, it has been obvious that 'the Western model' can take on many forms. And 'the battle of models' has not enjoyed a long cease-fire. In the Eastern European audiovisual field, many models were involved in the process of shaping an indigenous media system: the old communist model, to name one, but also the idealist model of former dissidents and writers, or the materialist model of new businessmen (see for example Jakubowicz 1999; Sparks & Reading 1998). Foreign troops were present too, and very influential. Alison Harcourt (2003b) distinguishes two main camps in the audiovisual battlefield of the 1990s: the adherents of the European model, with the promotion of public service broadcasting and European content in programming, versus the American model, characterised by the promotion of private broadcasters and against European content laws. The European model was (and is) promoted mainly by the European Union and the Council of Europe and the American model by, of course, the USA, but mainly via the World Trade Organisation (WTO) and to a lesser extent the Organisation for Economic Co-operation and Development (OECD). As the Eastern European countries aspired membership of both EU and WTO, they saw themselves confronted with walking a tight rope. Some accession states were particularly prone to US pressure before they joined the WTO because the USA opposed their WTO membership precisely on the issue of audiovisual markets. This was particularly felt when the Baltic States joined in 1999-2001 (Harcourt 2003b, 319) but also Poland experienced difficulties compromising both views. In the eyes of Europe, Poland was considered too nationalist and protectionist on occasions but at the same time also 'too Americanized' and even named the 'Trojan horse' for American audiovisual interests (Cirtautas 2000). Since all the accession states have been admitted to the WTO this pressure has largely been relieved (Harcourt 2003b, 319). And the outcome of the battle? While the American model has triumphed largely in the world of the print media, broadcasting has mainly been the domain of the European model, partly due to the own historical and cultural traditions of the Eastern European countries but also due to EU pressure with regard to harmonisation of broadcasting policy.

EU Enlargement

Since its inception with six countries, nineteen further states have joined the European Union in successive waves of enlargement. The fifth (and, for the time being, last) round of enlargement appeared as somehow different from the previous ones because of its size (not one, two, or three, but ten countries joined the EU at the same time – among them eight Central and Eastern European countries) but also because a couple of new principles were put to the fore. A look at these principles, and at the way the process of enlargement was taken care off, can tell us something about the actual result of enlargement.

Asymmetry is probably the word that pops up most in describing both the process and the outcome of enlargement. The EU had all the benefits to offer (principally accession, trade, and aid). The Central and Eastern European countries, by contrast, had much to ask and little to offer the EU, given their tiny economic size, and little to bargain with because the desire of their political elites to join was generally much greater than

that of the Member States to let them in (Grabbe 2003, 315). The EU
candidacy of Central and Eastern European countries, though largely
inspired by political, economic, and military interests (stability, prosperity, and peace in the region), carried an important cultural, emotional,
even moral dimension as well. The 'return to Europe' had to do away
with the 'mistake of Yalta' and symbolised the definitive break with the
Soviet past. Acceptance by international organisations, such as the European Union, appeared to the young Eastern European states as the con-
firmation of their independence and the proof of their successful transition (Grabbe and Hughes 1998). The European Union, on the other
hand, agreed on enlargement in principle, but showed less enthusiasm in
considering enlargement a priority. Bideleux (1996, 241) calls it significant that the EU dealt with the enlargement issue as an aspect of foreign
policy. Enlargement, in the view of the EU, was not allowed to disturb
the already far reaching European integration process (internal market,
economical and monetary union, etc.). Starting point for the European
Union therefore was the necessary adaptation of Central and Eastern
European prospective members *prior* to membership. As a consequence
asymmetry and rigidity of the EU were far greater in the last eastward
enlargement than in previous enlargements.[1]

At the Copenhagen Council (European Parliament 1993) the EU set
forth in broad terms the *conditions* for Union membership. Prospective
members need to have a 'functioning market economy' and 'the capacity
to cope with competitive pressure and market forces within the Union',
as well as 'stability of institutions guaranteeing democracy, the rule of
law, human rights, and respect for and protection of minorities'. Next to
this political and economic conditions, candidate member states have to
take on the 'obligations of membership' – i.e. they have to take on the
80.000 pages of legislation, directives, regulations and judgements which
constitute the *acquis communautaire*. An additional condition for enlarge-

---

[1] Membership of the Council of Europe was easier to obtain for the Central and
Eastern European countries. Created in 1949 as an intergovernmental organisation
aimed to protect human rights, pluralist democracy and the rule of law, the Council of
Europe united until 1989 twenty-three Western European states. In contrast to the
European Union, the Council of Europe has almost denied its values by making them
not the *condition* but rather the *aim* of membership. Through the massive inflow of
Central and Eastern European member states – not only Poland, Hungary, and the
Czech Republic but also Russia, Albania, and Macedonia – the Council of Europe
evolved towards a 'school for democracy' with 45 members.

ment is, from the EU perspective, the capacity of the EU to absorb new members. The Madrid Council Conclusions (European Parliament 1995) also mentioned the adjustment of administrative structures as important as preparation for accession though not as a condition.

Notwithstanding the qualifying conditions of market economy, democracy, and the rule of law, the stress was laid almost entirely on *'taking on the acquis'*. This is not, as it may seem, self-evident. The adoption of the *acquis* is a condition that existing EU Member States have achieved mostly only after a long period of life within the EU. Only Austria, Finland and Sweden, all advanced industrial countries, adopted most of the *acquis* in advance of accession to the EU in 1995. Moreover, in all previous enlargements, the scale of the *acquis* and necessary adaptation was much smaller. Central and Eastern Europe started from a much lower starting-point and with a very limited scope for negotiation transitional periods. Besides, in Central and Eastern Europe the EU alignment process occurred almost simultaneously with the massive political and economic transformations which have been underway since the collapse of communist regimes across the region. Focusing exclusively on the adoption of the *acquis* 'as a scoreboard in the accession process' – as the Bulgarian Deputy Foreign Minister and chief negotiator for the EU, Meglena Kuneva (2001), properly observed – carries the risk of making the *acquis* a goal in itself and thus of 'isolating the society from the process' (Kuneva 2001). The exclusive focus on the *acquis* contributed to the rigidity of the process and led to basically *non-negotiable negotiations*. Although the enlargement procedure was essentially a process of negotiations, the *acquis* (which forms the basis of every negotiation) appeared as nonnegotiable. The East European applicants could at best hope to influence the pace, but not the content.

In addition, an extensive system of *verification* (monitoring the process of harmonisation) was set up that did not exist in previous enlargements. Mayhew (2000) considers this symptomatic for the lack of trust between Member States and the Union. It is significant that the monitoring of the Central and Eastern European countries did not disappear once the countries were accepted as Member States. The Regular Reports were replaced in 2003 by Country Monitoring Reports of the acceding states. 'In doing so [monitoring progress], the Commission has given further guidance to the acceding states in their efforts to assume the responsibilities of membership *and has given the necessary assurance to current Member*

States.' (European Commission 2003a). Mayhew (2000, 9) describes the verification process as an attempt to create 'perfect Member States' in that higher levels of compliance are required from the candidates than from the existing Member States.

The 'logic of control', used in the 2004 EU enlargement, made the enlargement an on-way process with 'domestic concerns of the candidate countries not reflected in the process', Maniokas (2004, 32) convincingly argues. Is this true for the audiovisual field? What, then, are the domestic concerns with respect to audiovisual policy? And what, in the first place, does the audiovisual policy of the EU consist of?

EU Audiovisual policy

Media policy of the European Union (EU) is principally understood to mean *audiovisual* policy or indeed audiovisual *broadcasting* policy, partly as a result of the strong lobbying of broadcasting associations such as the European Broadcasting Union (EBU) (Goldberg, Prosser and Verhulst 1998, 8) but also because of the important strategic economic, cultural and social role of television and video as they dominate the entertainment scene in Europe. Strictly speaking, broadcasting policy in the EU does not constitute a policy area in itself but it expands into other policy fields such as competition and industrial policy, cultural policy, consumers and internal affairs. Consequently, it affects a large number of (competing) departments and regulatory bodies within the EU as well as within the Member States which makes it difficult to reach a consensus even over the key priorities of broadcasting policy.

The predominant conflict is that between broadcasting as a commercial industry or as a cultural product – or, indeed, as both such as the concept of 'cultural industry' indicates. Initially, to make broadcasting a competence of the EU in the first place, broadcasting was mainly considered in economic terms. The EU had no cultural competence whatsoever until the Maastricht Treaty came into force in 1993 (cf. Article 128 of the Treaty establishing the European Community, renumbered to Article 151). The new article 128/151 permitted the development of cultural actions as well as the taking into account of the cultural dimensions in other community policies, such as industrial policy. The advance of the cultural argument parallels the growing power of the European Parliament (Sarikakis 2004), which always emphasized the cultural values of broadcasting more than did the European Commission. The European

Commission, on the other hand, has never been univocal. The Directorate-General for Education and Culture, and the Audiovisual Directorate often find themselves positioned against those DGs who are responsible for Competition, the Internal Market or the Information Society (formerly the DG for Telecommunications), not to mention the internal divisions within the Directorate-General for Competition (Levy 1999, 40-41; Collins 1994, 17-20). Each side has its supporters within the broadcasting industry too. The economic approach is favoured, for instance, by commercial broadcasters, advertisers, and new entrants to the cable and satellite market while the film industry, new independent producers, and most public service broadcasters lean toward the cultural camp. The division can be found as well between the Member States of the European Council with some members (e.g. France, Italy, Belgium, Spain) on the cultural side and other members (e.g. the UK, Germany, Luxembourg, Denmark) on the economic side of the duality. Central and Eastern European Member States tend to stress the cultural dimension as well, in line with the 'traditional definition of the media as political, cultural, and educational institutions, with almost total disregard – at least at the beginning – for their economic and technological dimensions' (Jakubowicz 2004, 160). Jakubowicz does even detect a conflict of opinion here between the 'new' EU members and the 'old' EU: 'We [Central and Eastern Europe] still treat the media as meaning-making machines. We have the impression that the EU treats the media as money-making machines.'

The constant tension between economic and (semi-)cultural priorities is reflected in the contrasting principles of *liberalisation* and *protectionism*, or *deregulation* and *reregulation*, that are at work in EU audiovisual policy. The most important single piece of legislation in the audiovisual field, the Television Without Frontiers Directive (1989/1997), incorporates these contrasting tendencies by encouraging both the free flow of television programmes within the EU by eliminating national barriers (liberalisation) and the protection of European audiovisual industry against the dominant US programme industry (e.g. European content quotas, proactive reregulation). How are the new Central and Eastern Member States of the EU coping with both these demands?

Harmonisation of audiovisual legislation

The principle of harmonisation of legislation occurred already in the first (pre-accession) Association Agreements or *Europe Agreements*. Ten countries of Central and Eastern Europe concluded *Europe Agreements* with the European Community and its Member States between 1991 and 1996 (Hungary and Poland in 1991, the Czech Republic, Slovak Republic, Bulgaria and Romania in 1993, the Baltic states Estonia, Latvia and Lithuania in 1995 and Slovenia in 1996). Under the agreements, the partner countries committed themselves to approximating their legislation to that of the European Union, particularly in areas relevant to the internal market including audiovisual legislation:

> The Parties shall coordinate and, where appropriate, harmonize their policies regarding the regulation of cross-border broadcasting, technical norms in the audiovisual field and the promotion of European audiovisual technology. (Europe Agreement with Bulgaria: Art. 92, the Czech Republic: Art. 97, Estonia: Art. 93, Hungary: Art. 91, Latvia: Art. 94, Lithuania: Art. 95, Poland: Art. 90, Romania: Art. 99, Slovakia: Art. 97 and Slovenia: Art. 92)

Audiovisual legislation is subsumed under Chapter 20 of the *acquis* under the heading of 'Culture and Audiovisual Policy'. The focus, and the sole legal requirement, of Chapter 20 was alignment by the candidate countries with the Television Without Frontiers (TWF) Directive (1989, replaced in 1997, and again under revision). Negotiations concerning Chapter 20 have been opened with the Central and Eastern European countries in two waves: in October-November 1998 with the first group of the relatively advanced Czech Republic, Estonia, Slovenia, Poland and Hungary and in May-October 2000 with Bulgaria, Latvia, Lithuania, the Slovak Republic and Romania. On the basis of progress achieved in the legislative alignment process (as monitored by the EC on a yearly basis between 1998 and 2003), negotiations have been closed with all the Central and Eastern European candidate Member States in December 2002 – *provisionally* closed with Bulgaria and Romania and *definitely* closed with the eight others. There are no transitional arrangements in this area.

Harmonisation of national media laws in Central and Eastern Europe took place at almost the same time as shaping the national media laws in the first place. Between 1991 and 1996, following the transformation of the political, economical and societal system, all Central and Eastern European countries passed new media laws, putting an end to the state monopolisation of press, radio, television and film industry and giving a start to the moulding of an indigenous media system. As Harcourt (2003b) observed, all these laws reflect hybridisation and adaptive borrowing from different Western (American, French, German, ...) models. Complete alignment with EU law, however, caused 'a second wave' of media legislation in Central and Eastern Europe, following 'the first wave' in the first half of the 1990s. From 1998 onward, but mainly in the years 2000-2002 all the national laws in Central and Eastern Europe became the subject of numerous amendments and/or replacements by new laws. The changes and replacements were dictated by the 'need' to adapt the different national legislations to the European legislation, in particular the Directive TWF.

Bulgaria replaced its 1996 Law on Radio and Television with a new law in 1998, amended in October 2000 and again in November 2001. The *Czech* Broadcasting Act of 1991 was replaced in July 2001 by a new Act on Radio and Television Broadcasting. *Estonian* legislation is largely in line with the TWF Directive since the adoption in 2000, and again in 2001 and 2002, of amendments to the Broadcasting Act of 1999 (in substitution for the Broadcasting Act of 1994). In *Hungary* the 1996 Act on Radio and Televison Broadcasting (= Act 1) was replaced by a new Media Act in July 2002 which aimed to align with the *acquis*. In *Latvia,* amendments to the 1995 Radio and Television Law with a view to further alignment with the TWF Directive were adopted in February 2001 and again in May 2003. In 2000 and 2001, the *Lithuanian* Parliament adopted amendments to the 1996 Lithuanian Law on National Radio and Television which, together with the 1996 Law on Provision of Information to the Public (amended in 2000 and 2002), makes up Lithuania's legal corpus in this domain. The *Polish* Broadcasting Act of 1992 was made largely conform EU legislation via the 2000 amendment. The audiovisual sector in the *Slovak* Republic has been considerably reshaped since adoption of the Act on Radio and Television Broadcasting in 1993. A new Act on Broadcasting and Retransmission, which entered into force in October 2000 and was slightly amended in April 2001, has brought Slovakia's legislation largely into line with the Television Without Frontiers Directive. In *Slovenia*, the new Mass Media Act, which sets the legal framework for Slovenian media in general, was adopted in April 2001 in substitution for the Law of 1994. The act brings Slovenia's legislation largely into line with the TWF Directive. In addition, amendments to the 1994 Law on Radio and Television of Slovenia were adopted in

September 2001 to ensure compliance with the Mass Media Act and to bring it in line with the Directive. Slovenia's 2001 Mass Media Act established a joint authority for both media and telecommunications. Slovenia therefore is one of the first European countries to embrace EU's convergence initiative, following Italy (1997), Spain (1997) and Switzerland (2000) and even proceeding the United Kingdom (2002) (Harcourt 2003a, 199-200). As for *Romania*, a new audiovisual framework law that fully covers all aspects of the *acquis* was adopted in July 2002 in substitution for the law of 1992. This law was amended again in 2003 and 2005.

Focus 1: Freedom of reception and retransmission of programmes (Article 2)

An important aim of the TWF Directive is liberalisation of ownership and freedom from national restrictions. Or, in other words, access of all EU residents to all EU broadcasts. Central and Eastern Europe was no exception in disliking this idea as conflictuous with national interests. In addition, the legacy of the norms under the former communist regime added another dimension to this. Hence, under communist regime programmes were screened prior to transmission and foreign programmes were largely blocked or disturbed.

In the new broadcasting laws of the early 1990s the *principle* of freedom of reception and retransmission was recognised explicitly in the laws of Poland (1992), Hungary (1996), Estonia (1994), Slovakia (1993) and Slovenia (1994) but only for the own, national programmes. Nowhere the distinction was made between *European* and *other* foreign programmes. Registration and/or licensing procedures for all broadcasting channels, including foreign channels, which favoured national programmes and used criteria such as the interest of the national culture stood in the way of European-wide freedom of (re)transmission. The European Commission also rejected the (discriminating) prohibition on transmitting programmes other than in the language of the state (e.g. Slovenia).

Bulgaria was the first candidate Member State to conform itself to the Directive in 1998 (Art. 9.3 of the new Bulgarian Law on Radio and Television). The others followed only hesitantly in 2000 and later. The concept of a European market appeared as a difficult concept for countries that only recently regained national markets that, in their view, deserved protection from European expansion.

Focus 2: The promotion of European works (Articles 4 and 5)

The other important aim of the Television Without Frontiers Directive is the creation of a strong European audiovisual industry that can resist the dominant US one. Underlying the economic rationale is the political rationale that television can create and foster a sense of being European and thus European unity although it was quickly realised to be a 'unity in diversity'.

The Directive TWF asks the EU Member States that broadcasters reserve a majority proportion of their transmission time, excluding the time appointed to news, sports events, games, advertising, teletext services and teleshopping for 'European works, within the meaning of Article 6'. Article 6 defines European works broader than just works originating from Member States. Also works originating from European third States party to the European Convention on Transfrontier Television of the Council of Europe, or from contracting partners, as well as co-productions are considered European. This brings authors as Fabris (1995, 230) or Trappel and Mahon (1996, 19) to the conclusion that the European enlargement was already foreseen in the 1989 Directive. Works originating in Central and Eastern Europe were considered from the very start as 'European works'.

European quotas were largely absent in the 'first wave' of media laws in Central and Eastern Europe. Only the laws of Latvia (1995) and Hungary (for public broadcasters) (1996) contained *European* production quotas – both countries which were rather late in shaping new postcommunist media legislation. In other countries, namely in Poland (1992), Hungary (for private channels), Lithuania (public channels) (1996), Estonia (public channels) (1994) and Slovenia (public channels) (1994) only *domestic* quotas were imposed. In still other countries (Czech Republic, private channels in Estonia, Lithuania and Slovenia) the promotion of the European and/or national audiovisual industry was only indirectly promoted. Promotion/protection of the national culture is very often one of the assessment criteria to obtain a license (e.g. Czech Republic, Slovakia, Bulgaria, Romania, Slovenia, Estonia, Lithuania) or a task or recommendation for particular channels (e.g. Nova TV in Czech Republic or MTV in Hungary).

The 'second wave' of media legislation, starting with Bulgaria, Romania and Slovakia in 1998, lead in all countries to conformity with the European criteria. Member States, however, maintain the right to establish more detailed and stricter rules (read: national quotas) for broadcasters falling under their jurisdiction. This right is used in many Central and Eastern European countries, such as Hungary, Poland, Latvia, Estonia and Slovenia. Two criteria of the 'own production' are hereby in use: the location of the producer (eg. Estonia, Slovakia, Slovenia) and the language of the production (eg. Hungary, Latvia, Poland). Or, what Jakubowicz and Fansten (2003, 11) have called, the 'business logic' and the 'cultural logic'.

The conflict between national and European interests (identities, culture) was felt more strongly in countries with a strong national identity and/or a strong audiovisual policy tradition prior to EU accession. Poland, for instance, has long had an active and efficiently managed audiovisual policy. In the accession negotiations, however, this appeared an obstacle rather than an advantage. Hence, the comprehensive Polish quota system in support of *national* (and even regional) audiovisual productions (outlined in the 1992 Act but also in a number of decrees passed by the National Broadcasting Council) appeared incompatible with the demand for protection of *European* works. Notwithstanding the fact that Poland considers itself part of the European culture and European heritage, the strong national consciousness hindered the implementation of the European directives. The European 'laggard' Bulgaria, in contrast, was a front runner in harmonising its Radio and Television Law with European standards. Negotiations about Chapter 20 (cultural and audiovisual policy) opened in May 2000 to be closed already a few months later, in November 2000. The lack of an existing comprehensive legislative framework made possible a fast adoption of the European directives in the field.

A 2003 survey conducted among media experts from 'acceding, candidate and transition countries' (Shein and Rajaleid 2003) shows the ongoing difference of opinion among Central and Eastern European countries on the efficiency of articles 4 and 5 of the TWF Directive in order to protect national interests and national culture. Poland, for instance, remains of the opinion that the Directive aims to protect pan-European interests, not the national ones. The Czech Republic calls Directive art. 4 and 5 not particularly efficient but better than nothing. While Estonia, Latvia, and Lithuania, call the articles 'efficient', and even 'vitally significant'. Poland is also the most critical about the neglect of the 'legitimate interests of small countries' with restricted language areas and not fully developed advertising markets. Estonia and Hungary, and to a lesser degree Lithuania and Slovenia follow this statement, stressing before all the limited advertising market (Shein and Rajaleid 2003).

Participation in Community programs

In addition to legislation, other means such as the European funding programs, are equally (or even more) important for promoting national audiovisual industries. Funding programmes are the central means of European support for cultural activity (Owen-Vandersluis 2003, 155). In addition to the general Culture 2000 Programme, the eContent Programme specifically aims at the multimedia industries while the MEDIA Programme supports the audiovisual media, including the cinema. The current MEDIA Plus Programme (2001-2006), following the original MEDIA Programme (1991-1995) and the MEDIA II Programme (1996-2000), aims at strengthening the competitiveness of the European audiovisual industry with a series support measures dealing with the training of professionals, development of production projects, distribution and promotion of cinematographic works and audiovisual programmes. Although the MEDIA programme is justified primarily in terms of promoting industrial competitiveness, it obviously has additional effects in terms of promoting European cultural goods (Owen-Vandersluis 2003, 158). Per 1 January 2004 the participating countries of Central and Eastern Europe in MEDIA are Bulgaria, the Czech Republic, Estonia, Latvia, Lithuania, Poland, Slovakia, Slovenia and Hungary. Participation in the MEDIA Programme, in its turn, requires prior alignment with the audiovisual *acquis*.

In the Central and Eastern European countries, the MEDIA programme has been an essential player in the development of the young audiovisual industries. But on the whole, evaluation of the MEDIA programme has shown that the programme has been most effective in countries with a high production capacity (Commission of the European Communities 2004). Both EU media policy and funding programmes are protecting the interests of the big audiovisual players which are, until now, located within Western Europe (notably France and the UK). In addition, the MEDIA budget (453,6 million euro for Media Plus + 59,4 million euro for Media Training) is far too small to really make a difference and the few successes cannot compensate for the general policy in advantage of the bigger players. The new, forthcoming programme ME-

DIA 2007 (for the period 2007-2013) has the ambitions to correct this situation. MEDIA 2007 will substantially increase the modest spending budget to 1055 million euro. The programme will make priority of reducing, within the European audiovisual market, the imbalances between countries with a high production capacity and countries with a low production capacity and/or a restricted language area (Commission of the European Communities 2004). If this comes true, the new Programme will be more advantageous to Central and Eastern European countries.

More Europe, more markets?

Accession to the EU not only resulted in harmonisation of audiovisual legislation but also in being part of the common European (audiovisual) market. The main characteristic – and at the same time the main weakness – of the European audiovisual market is its *fragmentation* into numerous small, national markets with consequently small financial means for national productions and small survival chances for small producers. The new countries of Central and Eastern Europe fit into this picture with only Poland, and in the second place Hungary and the Czech Republic, as countries with sizeable markets.

The smallness of the national markets would not be a problem if not of the *limited cross-border distribution*. Productions from small states are often not of an exportable nature because they are too culturally specific. In addition, there are extra costs for dubbing or subtitling (see for a discussion of the structural handicaps of small countries: Burgelman and Pauwels 1992, 172-173). The European Commission has calculated that 80 percent of the films made in the 'EU of the 15' never leave the country of origin. The same goes for television programmes (De Bens and de Smaele 2001). Again, Central and Eastern Europe follows this trend. A study by the European Audiovisual Observatory showed that between 1996 and 2001 only 42 films from the countries of Central and Eastern Europe were distributed commercially in at least one 'old' Member State of the European Union, seen by a total of 2.2 million people in the Union, making a market share of 0.054 percent (European Commission 2003b). On Western European television, Eastern European films are broadcast only sporadically and outside prime-time (De Bens and de Smaele 2001, 61). At the same time, exchange programmes within the region of Central and Eastern Europe (e.g. OIRT) disappeared causing a halt to the cross-border circulation within the Central and Eastern European region as well (de Smaele 2000). As Iordanova (2002, 33) notices : 'In their drive to get themselves out of the economic ghetto of the Soviet sphere (which they believe also extends over culture), Eastern European countries end up in isolation from each other'.

The low rate of intra-European distribution contrasts with the large market share of *US productions*, both in cinema and on television. The audiovisual trade between the EU and US over the last decade shows a year upon year rising trade deficit, mounting to 8 EUR billion in 2000 or a trade deficit of 14.1% (European Audiovisual Observatory 2002, 1: 36-37). US fiction mounts to 63.4% on average on Western European television channels (De Bens and de Smaele 2001, 57) and even higher on Central and Eastern European channels (de Smaele 2000, 100). Smaller countries have the greatest difficulties in resisting cheap import, which is predominantly US originated.

Smaller countries are also more confronted with the presence of *foreign channels*. Not surprisingly, the European Audiovisual Observatory (2004, 12) observes that the market share of foreign channels is only marginal in the major European markets (Germany, the UK, Italy, France, Spain) but on the contrary very significant in smaller countries, which in general are also those with a high level of cable penetration. Levy (1999, 161) holds the opinion that the EU policy to open up the European TV market to cross-frontier services primarily benefited the US-controlled and UK-registered channels such as CNN, MTV and TNT Cartoon network, together with national channels seeking to escape domestic licensing constraints. These channels were also the first to make use of the newly opened Eastern European market. This 'move to the east', however, was not always welcomed by Eastern European citizens and politicians as the use of the concept of 'colonisation' suggests (Petrić and Tomić-Koludrović 2006).

An enlarged market offers enlarged possibilities for *co-operation*, mainly via co-productions. European co-productions are, indeed, on the increase. European-American co-productions, however, grow even faster (Esser 2006) with European co-productions mainly replacing single-country productions and thus not contributing to an increase in total European production (De Bens and de Smaele 2001, p. 68). This might be true *a fortiori* for the Central and Eastern European countries where national film production collapsed in the late 1980s to recover only slowly throughout the 1990s. Infrastructure, institutions, and funding mechanisms had to be renewed and a new culture of managing the audiovisual sector had to be given shape.[2] Participation in the MEDIA programme, funding by Eurimages (a pan-European funding body which many of the Central and Eastern European countries joined in the course of the 1990s) and partnership in European co-productions all contributed to the recovering of the Eastern European film industries. International financing for film increasingly became the major component in every East European film production industry (Iordanova 1999), especially as the new national funding mechanisms of some Eastern European countries made national subsidies dependent on foreign participation: 'if a production can show it has been granted funding from abroad, it becomes automatically eligible for domestic support' (Iordanova 2002, 518).

Regular cooperation patterns stand out, in which geographical, cultural or linguistic proximity plays its part. France appears as the main partner for Hungary, Romania, and the Czech Republic; Germany is Poland's primary co-production partner, while in the Balkan region one observes a number of regional co-productions involving Greece (Iordanova 1999). Eastern European partners, however, are much more likely to appear as minority producers (Iordanova 2002, 34). In addition, Iordanova (2002, 31) shows that the wider distribution of co-productions is not self-evident either as 'many films never go into distribution in all their co-production partner countries. This is particularly true for the minority co-producers'. Next to (minority) co-producers, Central and Eastern European countries became regular 'guest countries' for so called *cross-border productions* – foreign initiatives using (cheaper) local facilities and extras, from landscapes to actors (Steven Spielberg's Schindler's List, filmed in Poland, is a classic example). Although cross-border productions are essentially foreign productions, they can bring in money resulting indirectly in more national audiovisual productions. At last, full membership of the EU may result in less migration of Eastern European film talent to Western Europe (see Iordanova 2002, 26-27).

[2] A report by order of the European Commission describes the Central and Eastern European countries as 'young' audiovisual industries, characterised by a proportional overweight of television (from 60% in the Baltic states to 92% in Romania), an underdeveloped advertising market and a low share of private investment in audiovisual media (IMCA 2004, 17-27). According to these criteria, Poland, the Czech Republic and Hungary stand out in positive sense. Not surprisingly, they are also the three largest audiovisual markets.

As the discussion of the opportunities offered by the EU enlargement (financing, coproductions, markets) shows, there is a drawback to everything and every opportunity appears to be a potential threat. In the worst case scenario Eastern European countries end up as minority partners, suppliers of cheap facilities, and additional markets for large European players while the own national production stagnates, is replaced by coproductions or, at the least, is not distributed outside the national borders. Iordanova (2002, 31-33), for example, convincingly shows how European support mechanisms such as Eurimages favour the distribution of Western European productions (in particular the French cinema) to Eastern Europe, but not the reverse. The main threat, then, that stands out for Central and Eastern European countries is, next to *Americanisation*, also Europeanisation.

Europeanisation of Europe?

The concept of Europeanisation takes many forms. Europeanisation as a neutrally defined process of 'domestic adaptation to the pressures emanating directly or indirectly from EU membership' (Featherstone 2003, 7) did indeed occur in Central and Eastern Europe for the obvious reason that the implementation of the European directives (particularly the Television Without Frontiers Directive) prompted overhauls of national laws. This process of institutional adaptation also took place in Western Europe. Harcourt (2003a), for example, detected substantial convergence at the national levels of the 15 old Member States in policy paradigms, domestic laws, and policy instruments. Europeanisation, according to Harcourt, took place both via vertical mechanisms (directives and competition decisions of the European Commission, decisions of the European Court of Justice) and via horizontal mechanisms (suggestion of best practice through European level policy forums). According to Grabbe (2003, 306-307) there are some reasons to expect that policy convergence in Central and Eastern Europe is even greater (similar, but wider and deeper in scope) than in Western Europe. In the first place, there is the speed of adjustment, the fast adaptation prior to membership, and from a much lower starting point. In the second place, Grabbe points at the openness of Central and Eastern Europe to EU influence owing to the process of post-communist transformation: 'This process has made them more receptive to regulatory paradigms than the EU's member-states were, because EU models were being presented at the same time as

Central and Eastern European policy-makers were seeking a model to implement' (Grabbe 2003, 306-307). Thirdly, Grabbe names the breadth of the EU agenda in Central and Eastern Europe, including also economical and political conditions: 'that gives the EU a license to involve itself in domestic policy making to an degree unprecedented in the current member states' (Grabbe 2003, 307). Also Dimitrova and Steunenberg (2004, 185) observe, on the one hand, effects that are 'farther reaching than Europeanisation effects in the current member states'. On the other hand, they also point at the danger of 'symbolic' or 'instrumental' adaptations due to conflicting sets of values in Central and Eastern European countries and the European Union coupled to the necessity to comply with some of the EU's wishes in order to become full members (Dimitrova and Steunenberg 2004, 190). 'Pressures from the EU promote these sorts of Potemkin-stillage organizational structures', writes Wade (1999, 64).

While Europeanisation as a process of institutional adaptation clearly is present, the prospect (threat or opportunity?) of Europeanisation as 'transnational cultural diffusion' – that is 'the diffusion of cultural norms, ideas, identities, and patterns of behaviour on a cross-national basis within Europe' (Featherstone 2003, 7) – is less well-evident. Despite a decade of policy measures to enhance European cross-national distribution, little has changed in this respect. European productions remain nationally produced and nationally distributed productions. The inflow of US films and series has not been stopped at all, whereas the internal European circulation of fiction remains stagnant (De Bens and de Smaele 2001). European habits of film consumption reveal that audiences watch either domestic productions or American ones, but not those of other European countries (IMCA 2004, 30). A pan-European audiovisual culture does not come to existence. Attempts to make films that reflect a cross-cultural European content (as some Euro-funded initiatives are bound to) remain artificial and end up as weak 'Europuddings' (Iordanova 1999) failing even more in cross-national distribution as they even lack a 'home market'. 'Television rhymes with nation' writes Semelin (1993, 58). In the same sense Schlesinger (1993, 11) refers to the 'continuing importance of the national level and the resistance it offers to *Europeanisation*'.

Although the conflict between national and European identity and interests is by no means an exclusively new Member States affair as 'Member States are always tempted to put short-term national interest before medium-term strategic European interest' (Mayhew 2000, 11), the very specific situation of the new Central and Eastern European Member States gives this conflict an extra dimension. The concepts of a European market, European identity, and European culture are difficult concepts for countries that only recently regained national markets, national identity, and national culture. The asymmetry, felt by Central and Eastern European countries, between the old EU and the new EU fuels the idea that 'European' is mainly referring to 'the interests of others' in contrast to the own, national interests.

Despite many differences, though, Eastern and Western European audiovisual landscapes have a lot in common and are growing nearer. In the 1980s Western European countries massively changed the monopoly of public service broadcasting for dual systems comprising both public service television and commercial television. In the 1990s Eastern European countries switched from communism to post-communism and from monopolism in broadcasting to dual systems as well comprising both state (public service) and private television. In January 1993 the Western *European Broadcasting Union* (EBU) and its Eastern counterpart, the *International Radio and Television Organization* (OIRT), did merge. The audiovisual industry is characterized in most European countries (both West and East) by a large amount of independent production and distribution companies whereas the government preserves an important regulatory and supportive (financing) role. Both East and West do experience the same problems as well as the same ideas. More Europe, therefore, basically adds more of the same: more diversity but also 'unity in diversity'.

References

Bideleux, Robert. 1996. Bringing the East Back In. In *European Integration and Disintegration. East and West,* eds. Robert Bideleux and Richard Taylor, 225-251. Londen: Routledge.

Burgelman, Jean-Claude and Caroline Pauwels. 1992. Audiovisual Policy and Cultural Identity in Small European States: The Challenge of a Unified Market. *Media, Culture and Society* 14: 169-183.

Cirtautas, Arista Maria. 2000. Poland. *East European Constitutional Review* 9. www.law.nyu .edu/eecr/vol9num4/features/Euarticle2.html.

Collins, Richard. 1994. *Broadcasting and Audio-visual Policy in the European Single Market*. London: John Libbey.

Commission of the European Communities. 2004 (14 July). Proposal for a Decision of the European Parliament and the Council. Concerning the Implementation of a Programme of Support for the European Audiovisual Sector (MEDIA 2007). http://europa.eu.int/comm/avpolicy/media/pdffiles/com470_en.pdf.

De Bens, Els and Hedwig de Smaele. 2001. The Inflow of American Television Fiction on European Broadcasting Channels Revisited. *European Journal of Communication* 16: 51-76.

de Smaele, Hedwig. 2000. Oost- en West-Europa: naar een eengemaakt audio-visueel beleid? In *Transformatie en continuïteit van de Europese televisie*, eds. Daniël Biltereyst and Hedwig de Smaele, 79-107. Gent: Academia Press.

Dimitrova, Antonaneta L. and Bernard Steunenberg. 2004. Conclusions: The 'End of History' of Enlargement or the Beginning of a New Research Agenda? In *Driven to Change. The European Union's Enlargement Viewed From the East*, ed. Antonaneta L. Dimitrova, 179-193. Manchester: Manchester University Press.

European Audiovisual Observatory. 2002. *Yearbook 2002. Film, Television, Video and Multimedia in Europe*. Vol. 1, 5. Strasbourg: European Audiovisual Observatory.

European Audiovisual Observatory. 2004. *Transfrontier Television in the European Union: Market Impact and Selected Legal Aspects*. Background paper prepared by the EAO for a Ministerial Conference on Broadcasting organised by the Irish Presidency of the EU. www.obs.coe.int/online_publications/transfrontier_tv.pdf.en.

Esser, Andrea. 2006. *Audio-Visual Content in Europe: Transnationalisation and approximation*. Paper presented at the International Conference 'Media in the Enlarged Europe', University of Luton, 5-6 May.

European Commission. 2003a. Comprehensive Country Monitoring Reports. Background. http://europa.eu.int/comm/enlargement/report_2003/index.htm

European Commission. 2003b. Enlargement soon to be a reality. 9 candidate countries admitted to MEDIA programme. (http://europa.eu.int/comm/avpolicy/media/enlarg_en.html).

European Parliament. 1993. *European Council in Copenhagen, 21-22 June 1993. Conclusions of the Presidency*. www.europarl.eu.int/summits/copenhagen/co_en.pdf.

European Parliament. 1995. *Madrid European Council, 15-16 December 1995. Presidency conclusions*. www.europarl.eu.int/summits/mad1_en.htm.

Fabris, Hanz Heinz. 1995. Westification? In *Glasnost and After. Media and Change in Central and Eastern Europe*, eds. David L. Paletz, Karol Jakubowicz and Pavao Novosel, 221-231. Cresskill, N.J.: Hampton Press.

Featherstone, Kevin. 2003. Introduction: In the Name of 'Europe'. In *The Politics of Europeanization*, eds. Kevin Featherstone and Claudio. M. Radaelli, 3-26. Oxford: Oxford University Press.

Goldberg, David, Tony Prosser and Stefaan Verhulst. 1998. *EC Media Law and Policy*. London, New York: Longman.

Grabbe, Heather. 2003. Europeanization Goes East: Power and Uncertainty in the EU Accession Process. In *The Politics of Europeanization*, eds. Kevin Featherstone and Claudio M. Radaelli, 303-327. Oxford: Oxford University Press.

Grabbe, Heather and K. Hughes. 1998. *Enlarging the EU Eastwards*. Londen: Pinter.

Harcourt, Alison. 2003a. Europeanization as Convergence: The Regulation of Media Markets in the European Union. In *The Politics of Europeanization*, eds. Kevin Featherstone and Claude M. Radaelli, 179-202. Oxford: Oxford University Press.

Harcourt, Alison. 2003b. The Regulation of Media Markets in selected EU Accession States in Central and Eastern Europe. *European Law Journal* 9: 316-340.

High Level Group on Audiovisual Policy. 1998. *The Digital Age: European Audiovisual Policy. Report from the High Level Group on Audiovisual Policy*. Brussels, Luxemburg: Office for official publications of the European Communities.

IMCA [International Media Consultants Associés]. 2004. *Etude du paysage audiovisuel et des politiques publiques des pays candidates dans le secteur audiovisuel. Rapport transversal*. Pour la Commission européenne – DG EAC/59/02. europa.eu.int/comm/avpolicy/stat/2002/5886_imca/59-02-finalreport.pdf.

Iordanova, Dina. 1999. East Europe's cinema industries since 1989. *Media Development* 3. www.wacc.org.uk/publications/md/md1999-3/iordanova.htm.

Iordanova, Dina. 2002. Feature Filmmaking Within the New Europe: Moving Funds and Images Across the East-west Divide. *Media, Culture & Society* 24: 517-536.

Jakubowicz, Karol. 1999. Normative Models of Media and Journalism and Broadcasting Regulation in Central and Eastern Europe. *International Journal of Communications Law and Policy* 2. www.digital-law.net/IJCLP/2_1999/ijclp_webdoc_12_2_1999.html.

Jakubowicz, Karol. 2004. We Need an EU With a Heart, a Social Conscience, and Courage. *Trends in Communication* 12: 157-161.

Jakubowicz, Karol and Michel Fansten. 2003. Enlargement: Grounds for Enthusiasm or worry? *Diffusion* 1: 10-11.

Jones, Clifford A. 2004. Transfrontier Media, Law, and Cultural Policy in the European Union. In *New Frontiers in International Communication Theory*, ed. Mehdi Semati, 157-177. Lanham: Rowman & Littlefield.

Kuneva, Meglena. 2001. The Acquis is not Enough. Speech at the Federal Trust's Conference on European Union Enlargement: Linking Civil Society, the Citizen, and the State, 21-24 November, Berlin. *Transitions Online* (12 December 2001).

Levy, David A. 1999. *Europe's Digital Revolution. Broadcasting regulation, the EU and the nation state*. London: Routledge.

Maniokas, Klaudijus. 2004. The Method of the European Union's Enlargement to the East: A Critical Appraisal. In *Driven to Change. The European Union's Enlargement Viewed from the East*, ed. Antoaneta L. Dimitrova, 17-37. Manchester: Manchester University Press.

Mayhew, Alan. 2000. *Enlargement of the European Union: an analysis of the negotiations with the Central and Eastern European candidate countries*. Brighton: University of Sussex, European Research Centre. (SEI working paper no. 39).

Owen-Vandersluis, Sarah. 2003. *Ethics and Cultural Policy in a Global Economy*. Houndmills, Basingstoke, Hampshire: Palgrave.

Petrić, Mirko and Inga Tomić-Koludrović. 2006. Changing Media Ecologies: Croatia Approaching the EU. Paper Presented at the International Conference 'Media in the Enlarged Europe'. University of Luton, 5-6 May.

Sarikakis, Katherine. 2004. *Powers in Media Policy. The Challenge of the European Parliament*. Oxford: Peter Lang.

Schlesinger, Philippe. 1993. Wishful Thinking: Cultural Politics, Media, and Collective Identities in Europe. *Journal of Communication* 43: 6-17.

Semelin, Jacques. 1993. The reshaping of East-West Communication Flows in Europe. In *Europe Speaks to Europe. Telecommunications in a Common European House*, eds. Jörg Becker and Aleksander Butrimenko, 53-60. Frankfurt: Haag+Herchen Verlag, Moscow: ICSTI.

Shein, Hagi, and Tarmo Rajaleid. 2003. Implementation of European Union Media Policy Standards and Television without Frontiers Directive Requirements into Broadcasting Practices in Acceding, Candidate and Transition Countries. www.epra.org/content/english/press/papers/Final%20Report_Plenary_Hagi%20Shein.pdf

Sparks, Colin and Anna Reading. 1998. *Communism, Capitalism and the Mass Media*. Londen, Thousand Oaks, New Delhi: Sage.

Trappel, Josef and David Mahon. 1996. Television in the Enlarged European Audiovisual Area – a Community perspective. In *The Development of the Audiovisual Landscape in Central Europe since 1989*, ed. Audiovisual Eureka, 13-22. London: John Libbey.

Verhulst, Stefaan and David Goldberg. 1998. The European Institutions. In *Regulating the changing media: a comparative study,* eds. David Goldberg, Tony Prosser and Stefaan Verhulst, 145-176. Oxford: Clarendon Press.

Wade, Jacoby. 1999. Priest and Penitent: the European Union as a Force in the Domestic Politics of Eastern Europe. *East European Constitutional Review* 8: 62-67.

EUROPEAN STUDIES 24 (2007): 135-156

UNDERMINING MEDIA DIVERSITY:
INACTION ON MEDIA CONCENTRATIONS
AND PLURALISM IN THE EU

Gillian Doyle

Abstract

In the context of European media and cultural policy-making, the impetus to protect diversity is at least partly a reflection of recurrent concerns about concentrations of media and cross-media ownership across Europe. Such concerns have regularly spurred the European Parliament into calling on the Commission to take action. For example, in Parliament's recent response to the UNESCO initiative on Cultural Diversity, it again urged the Commission to take steps to counter concentrations of media ownership that may pose a threat to pluralism (EP, 2003). But a range of serious practical and political obstacles stand in the way of any possible harmonising initiative in this area. This article examines the European Union's efforts to work towards a pan-European policy on media ownership and the many difficulties and conflicts that have accompanied this process. It concludes that the Commission's long-standing record of inaction on the question of media concentrations and pluralism is unlikely to change any time soon.

As part of Britain's recent presidency of the European Union, the Department of Culture, Media and Sport and the European Commission hosted a major conference on Audiovisual Policy in Liverpool in September 2005 at which the main topic under debate was revisions to the TWF Directive and, in particular, the possibility of extending the scope of the Directive to cover 'non'-linear' services. However, also on the agenda was media pluralism. Ahead of the Liverpool conference, six discussion papers dealing with different aspects of the future legislative framework for audiovisual were published by the Information Society and Media Directorate-General of the EC.[1] One of these highlighted recurrent concerns expressed by Parliament about concentrations of media ownership in Europe and it resurrected a familiar question: what role should the EU should play in promoting and maintaining media pluralism across Europe (CEC, 2005)?

Parliament's desire to curb concentrations of media power stems from a perceived need to maintain plurality – a concept closely associ-ated with diversity – within systems of media provision across Europe. In the context of media, pluralism is generally taken to embrace notions of diverse content and also diverse ownership. As discussed below, pluralism is about having a number of different and independent voices in the media that offer different opinions and perspectives and that pro-vide a range of representations of culture. A diversity or plurality of sources and voices and diverse ownership of media are generally seen as necessary to the achievement of broader socio-political and cultural goals such as promoting democracy and building social cohesiveness.

That concerns about pluralism keep re-surfacing on the European Commission's agenda is not surprising. Over the years, numerous bodies such as the European Audiovisual Observatory and the Council of Eu-rope have been active in observing and monitoring levels of media and cross-media ownership across Europe. Their findings confirm the gen-eral prevalence of trends towards enlargement, diversification and con-centrated ownership within and across European media and communica-tions industries (Council of Europe, 1997). Such trends persist today (Bruck et al, 2004; Ward, Fueg and D'Armo, 2004; Terazona, 2006), notwithstanding disappointing returns from Internet investments in the late 1990s and the impact of recession in many advertising markets in the early 21st century.

Concentrations of ownership are a widespread phenomenon despite the fact that most member states of the EU have some forms of domes-tic regulation which, in theory, are supposed to prevent the development of undesirable concentrations of media ownership. The approaches used to curb concentrations and support pluralism vary from one European

---

[1] Retrieved at www.europa.eu.int/comm/avpolicy/revision-tvwf2005/ consult.en.htm.

country to the next, reflecting the specific history and circumstances of each national market (Kevin et al, 2005, 216-22). Upper restrictions over ownership of broadcasting (as measured by, say, audience or revenue share) have been widely adopted but some countries prefer the approach of using a special public interest test where mergers and acquisitions involve media interests.

Although many European countries have relaxed their restrictions over media ownership in recent years, the general notion that diversity or plurality of media requires special protection has not been abandoned insofar as that a majority of countries still have enshrined within domestic legislation some or other special policy measures over and above safeguards provided by domestic or EU competition law designed to promote pluralism as an objective (ibid; Doyle, 2002b: 148-153). But ongoing evidence that ownership of media tends to be highly concentrated at national level right across Europe raises obvious questions about how well national policies are coping, perhaps particularly so in the context of Italy, which Parliament keeps on returning to (EP, 2004).

Transnational media empire-building has emerged as a related concern over recent years. Whereas up until the 1990s, European media concentrations tended to occur predominantly at national level, more recently the strategic expansion of dominant players for example from Germany and Scandinavia into Central and Eastern Europe has resulted in transnational conglomerations too (Bruck et al, 2004: 7-8). A pattern of large media companies extending their activities into these newly competitive markets has in many cases resulted in extensive foreign ownership of national press and broadcasting. For example, the Estonian daily newspaper market is now wholly owned and dominated by Norwegian company Schibsted and the Swedish Bonnier Group (ibid: 9).

Policy Concerns surrounding Media Ownership
Wherever they occur, patterns of concentrated media ownership tend to raise at least two different sorts of public policy concerns. Pluralism is the main one. Many scholars have focused attention on the risks and harms for culture, society and democracy that may result from concentrated media ownership, including the abuse of political power by media owners or under-representation of some important viewpoints (Demers, 1999; Humphreys, 1997; Lange and Van Loon, 1991; MacLeod, 1996; Meier and Trappel, 1998; Murdoch and Golding, 1997; Sánchez-

Tabernero and Carvajal, 2002; Tunstall and Palmer, 1991). It is widely acknowledged that individuals and societies need a system of media provision that supplies a range of ideas, viewpoints and different forms of cultural expression. Concentrations of media ownership narrow the range of voices that predominate in the media and consequently pose a threat to pluralism and to the interests of society.

Recognition of the need to safeguard pluralism has historically been the main impetus behind the special regulations alluded to above that exist in most European countries in order to curb media empire building (Harcourt, 2005). However, ownership patterns are also viewed as important by policy-makers because of their potential impact on the economic and financial performance of media and communication industries. Doubts about the desirability of regulatory interventions in this area are often framed in terms of the economic ability of indigenous players to 'compete in the global market' while curtailed by domestic media concentration restrictions (DCMS, 2005: 25).

Looking purely at economic policy goals, concentrations of media ownership are liable to impact on broadly two sorts of economic policy objectives: the desire to maximize efficiency and also the need to sustain competition (Doyle, 2002a: 166-167). These goals are related insofar as that fair and plentiful competition is seen as a general prerequisite to efficiency. In other words, the detrimental economic effects (in terms of anti-competitive behaviour, waste etc) which may accompany excessive concentration of ownership are as much a concern in the media as any other sector and this underlines the case against permitting monopolization to occur. At the same time though, a media industry which is too fragmented and does not allow firms achieve the scale and corporate configuration needed to exploit all available economies is also prone to inefficiency. Media industries are characterized by the widespread availability of economies of scale and scope and therefore media firms' ability to maximise their efficiency depends partly on being allowed grow and achieve the corporate size and structure most conducive to exploiting these economies (Doyle, 2002b: 45-82). So, the two broad economic policy objectives associated with concentration can pull in opposite directions, thus requiring policy-makers to make a trade-off between (with tighter restrictions) greater competition and (with looser controls) maximised efficiency.

But concentrations within the European media sector and the con-comitant accumulation of power and influence on the part of individuals and corporations have implications that go well beyond the realm of economics. The European Parliament's persistent calls for action on this issue are unambiguously based on concerns about pluralism. Pluralism is also the underlying reason why the Council of Europe, which is respon-sible for ensuring compliance with the European Convention on Human Rights, has long taken an interest in the development of media concen-trations across Europe. From the Council of Europe's point of view, the need for diversity and pluralism is associated with the fundamental right to freedom of expression as set out in Article 10 of the Convention (Lange and Van Loon, 1991: 13-26). The main concern is that without an open and pluralistic system of media provision, the right to receive and to impart information for some individuals or groups within society may well be curtailed.

To assist its work in this area, the Council established a Committee of Experts on Media Concentrations and Pluralism (MM-CM) and through-out the 1990s this Committee gathered information about patterns of media ownership in Europe and about the implications for pluralism. Since 2000, an Advisory Panel on Media Diversity (AP-MD) has supple-mented this work by monitoring levels of transnational media concentra-tions. MM-CM has defined pluralism in the following terms:
media pluralism should be understood as diversity of media supply, reflected, for example, in the existence of a plurality of independent and autonomous media and a diversity of media contents available to the public.

So, as indicated earlier, the concept of pluralism is generally under-stood to involve both diversity of media ownership and diverse content. And the need to sustain pluralism (with a view towards protecting de-mocracy, preserving languages, promoting cultural diversity and strength-ening social cohesion) is, to a greater or lesser extent, accorded recogni-tion within most national approaches to media regulation across Europe (Kevin et al, 2005: 222). However, where the policy instrument to be used in order to secure pluralism involves curbing concentrations of media ownership, policy-makers will face countervailing industrial con-cerns related to the perceived economic opportunity costs of restricting indigenous media enterprises. A further problem for policy-making is

that the nature of the relationship between concentrated media ownership and pluralism is complicated and at times appears contradictory.

Preserving diverse ownership – ensuring the existence of a range of
separate and autonomous voices in the media – seems in many ways an
obvious and central aspect of protecting pluralism. But, for example,
because different media suppliers sometimes share editorial resources
between them, diverse ownership cannot necessarily be equated with
different voices (Doyle, 2002a: 18-22). Direct and unambiguous links
between media concentrations, diversity of content and pluralism are
difficult to establish (Ward, 2006: 4). And because concentrations of
ownership are but one of a range of variables with potential to impact on
the availability of pluralism (Mortensen, 1993), a regulatory framework
intended to promote pluralism needs to incorporate and draw upon a
wider array of policy interventions than simply restricting ownership of
media.

Nonetheless, recent evidence of transnational as well as national
corporate expansion within Europe by European and US media suppliers
is plentiful and this has contributed to a re-opening of concerns about
whether the EU is playing an effective enough role in protecting and
developing media pluralism in member states (CEC, 2005). Newly
emerging patterns of transnational and cross-sectoral domination, partly
accommodated by regulatory change in several European member states,
appear to provide a more compelling case than ever for action at the EU
level. But the Report of the Working Group on Media Pluralism at the
recent Liverpool Audiovisual conference suggests that there remain very
serious doubts about whether concentrated media ownership is a European rather than a national policy question (DCMS, 2005: 25). As is
discussed below, the legality of any European intervention on this issue
is open to question. Added to this, many influential industrial voices are
firmly opposed to 'interference' from Brussels in the design of media and
cross-media ownership regulations and, as the Commission is only too
aware, a range of practical obstacles stand in the way of harmonization
of policy in this area.

Media Ownership within the context of EU law
One of the major problems besetting any possible move by the Commission to address Parliament's concerns about the effect of media concentrations on pluralism is that it does not have a clear legal remit to tackle

this problem. The primary source of European law is the Treaties – the Treaty of Rome (1957) as amended by the Single European Act (1986), the Maastricht Treaty (1991) and more recently the Amsterdam Treaty (1999) and Nice Treaty (2003). These set out the legal framework of the European Union and the Commission may take action to create or harmonise European laws only if and when a remit for such action has been established through these Treaties. The main problem with trying to instigate a policy at the European level to promote pluralism is that there does not appear to be a sufficient legal basis for doing so contained in any one of these Treaties.

Other than the Amsterdam Treaty which introduced a short but significant Protocol allowing member states to support public service broadcasting, there is little or no direct reference to the media or to policies for the media in any of the European Treaties. A new collective Constitution for Europe, if ratified by all member states, could alter the basis for regulatory interventions but is unlikely to proceed, given that voters in France and Holland rejected the initiative in 2005.[2]

So, the Treaties continue to dictate what can and cannot be done. And because they say little about media, European policy in this area – especially audiovisual policy – tends to be founded on broad EU objectives or more general Articles within the Treaties applied in the specific context of the media sector (Goldberg, Prosser and Verhulst, 1998). For example, the EC Directive 'Television Without Frontiers', which at the time of its introduction in 1989 was mainly concerned with establishing a single borderless market for any European television service, reflected aims set out in 1957 Treaty of Rome, such as the free exchange of services between member states.[3]

As recently confirmed by Fabio Colasanti, Director-General for Information Society and Media, the competence of the European Commission to initiate policies concerning pluralism and media ownership is very far from certain (DCMS, 2005: 25). The EU's general rules on competition apply to the media as any other economic sector but, while serving to restrict dominant market positions or anti-competitive behaviour, these are not specifically designed to promote pluralism (Iosifides, 1996:

---

[2] Article II-71 enshrines the right to freedom of expression and Part 2 of this Article states that 'freedom and pluralism of the media shall be respected'.

[3] Articles 59-66

24). The Maastricht Treaty[4] introduced competence for Community intervention in pursuit of cultural objectives, but this is limited to support measures and it explicitly excludes the possibility of harmonisation of legislation (Weatherill and Beaumont, 1995: 477). So, although concerns about national and transnational media concentrations have been on the 'pan-European' policy agenda, on and off, for some time, it seems that the European Commission does not actually have the ability to promote pluralism and diversity within the media.

Instead, the promotion of pluralism has traditionally been undertaken at member state level. But because each member state has established a different set of domestic media ownership regulations to safeguard pluralism, an alternative justification may be called upon to justify Community intervention. The EU's wider objectives involve eliminating possible obstructions to the single internal European market, i.e. obstructions to the free movement of goods, persons, services and capital.[5] Divergences in national media ownership legislation could, it has been argued, serve to obstruct the internal market, by impeding cross-border investment in European media. So, quite separately from the issue of pluralism, this 'internal market' argument can be seen as providing the Commission with competence to tackle regulation of media ownership throughout the member states.

The European Parliament's long-standing wish for action to tackle media concentrations is not couched in terms of completing the single market. According to Beltrame (1996: 4), the main protagonists for more effective measures to protect pluralism, both within Parliament and at the Commission, have been Italian MEPs who are particularly concerned about the situation in their own country and especially the position of Mediaset. Their concerns have persistently been expressed in terms of the need for pluralism, and without any acknowledgement of limitations over the EU's competence in this area.

The Commission took the first major step towards a pan-European policy approach to media ownership with the publication of a Green Paper on Pluralism and Concentrations (CEC, 1992). This document emerged as a response to the concerns expressed by Parliament about the

---

[4] Article 128.
[5] Free movement of capital is governed by Articles 67-73 of the Treaty of Rome and Articles 73b and 73g of the Treaty on European Union.

need to safeguard pluralism[6] but, at the same time, the Green paper emphasised that the main justification for European-level intervention would be completion of the single market (an area where the Commission clearly has competence) rather than pluralism (which, at least officially, is supposed to be a matter for member states). This dichotomy, according to Hitchens (1994: 587), 'produces a tension which pervades the whole of the Green Paper'.

The 1992 Green Paper reviewed existing levels on media concentration in Europe and suggested three possible policy options: first, no action at the pan-European level; second, action to improve levels of transparency, or; third, positive intervention – via a Regulation or a Directive – to harmonise media ownership rules throughout the member states. By default, Option I has prevailed. The failure to move forward with some form of positive intervention may be attributed, in large measure, to the range of conflicting opinions within Europe about what the aims and the substance of a collective policy on media ownership ought to be.

Competing Policy Objectives: A Dilemma for the Commission

The path towards a harmonised approach to media ownership policy became progressively more tortuous following the publication of the 1992 Green Paper because of diverging ideas about which goals such a policy ought to strive towards. In part, this reflected the fundamental question of whether the Commission has any legal right to pursue policies aimed at safeguarding pluralism (Beltrame, 1996; Hitchens, 1994). Parliament appears to believe so and, throughout the early 1990s, was pressing hard for action to address the many worrying examples of concentrations which could readily be observed in national and transnational European media markets.[7] The Council of Europe also evidently believes that pluralism is integral to the principle of freedom of speech and, as such, should be protected under the European legal order. However, the 1992 Green Paper concluded that EU intervention in media ownership legislation may be justified only on the basis of securing the proper functioning of the internal market and *not* on the basis of protection of pluralism (CEC, 1992: 99).

---

[6] *OJ* No. C 68/137-138.
[7] A comprehensive analysis of the role played by the European Parliament in the formation of policies affecting media can be found in Sarikakis (2004).

Because concerns about competition and promoting the single market are different from concerns about pluralism, the implied aims for harmonising media ownership restrictions under these different approaches will immediately diverge (Iosifides, 1996: 24). Safeguarding pluralism implies a need for European-wide restrictions which would eliminate undesirable concentrations of media power, whereas promoting competition implies equalisation of ownership restrictions purely by reference to the economic needs of industry. Some mergers which do not threaten competition might pose a threat to plurality. Since media pluralism is a special concern in its own right, 'reliance on a competitive environment to foster pluralism may be to adopt a too simplistic approach' (Hitchens, 1994: 591).

From the outset, the Commission's approach to harmonisation of media ownership was characterised by uncertainty about aims and means. Rifts were apparent even within the Commission, and, according to Beltrame (1996: 4), these particularly reflected rivalry between the competition directorate and DG15 which was then responsible for the Internal Market. After DG15 took charge of advancing a pan-European media ownership policy in 1993, the Commission attempted 'to inscribe Parliament's quest for pluralism in the logic of the Internal Market' (1996: 4).

But contention about the appropriate legal basis for intervention was not the only obstacle thrown into the Commission's path (Harcourt, 1996). The 1992 Green Paper set in motion a prolonged period of public consultation concerning which of the options set out at its conclusion would represent the best course of action. The responses to this consultation served to introduce an additional layer of complexity and contention to the issue of what objectives a harmonised European media ownership policy regime ought to be pursuing (Kaitatzi-Whitlock, 1996).

In summary, these responses indicated widespread agreement about the need, in principle, for action to harmonise European media ownership legislation. But, while some groups (especially, the European Parliament) believed that the purpose of a harmonised regime should be to crack down on undesirable concentrations of media power that represent a threat to pluralism within Europe, others (especially, industry participants in the larger member states) took the opposite view; that harmonisation should aim to provide a more liberal media ownership regime, conducive to greater cross-border investment.

Such divergences of opinion between important interest groups made it difficult for the Commission to move forward. Conflicting objectives were highlighted when, for example, the follow-up Communication to the 1992 Green Paper spoke of 'facilitat(ing) the exercise of freedom of establishment for media companies and the free movement of media services in the Union, while maintaining pluralism in the face of certain concentrations' (CEC, 1994: 6). Contradictory policy agendas were also apparent in the contrast between objectives simultaneously being pursued in other Directorates of the Commission. While the drive towards a European 'Information Society' was characterised by the theme of 'liberalisation' (espoused by Commissioner Bangemann of DG13 and others), this did not sit altogether comfortably with the wish to protect indigenous cultures and to accommodate safeguards for pluralism, expressed by DG15 (Schlesinger and Doyle, 1995).

So, rather than proceeding directly to formal proposals for a draft Directive in 1994, DG15 instead embarked on a second round of consultation. But responses to this second round only appeared to reaffirm the lack of consensus between opposing ideological camps as to what the aims should be for a harmonised European media ownership policy (CEC, 1997). Again, the European Parliament and the Economic and Social Committee confirmed their support for harmonisation aimed at safeguarding pluralism. But, again, the majority of responses to the Commission came from large media firms expressing the view that harmonisation ought to provide a more liberal media ownership regime, conducive to greater cross-border investment.

In addition, the Commission was faced with practical problems associated with the enormous discrepancies in national market sizes across Europe. An absolute ceiling on media ownership capable of preventing undesirable concentrations in smaller countries would clearly place a very tight leash on media companies operating in large markets. On the other hand, if thresholds were set by reference to a certain proportion or percentage of national audiences (say, at 10 percent of the national media market), then operators in large member states would be allowed to grow considerably larger than rivals in smaller countries.

Such difficulties deterred most European member states from firmly supporting the need for a harmonised media ownership regime, and others (especially, the UK) felt compelled to speak out in favour of the principle of subsidiarity. The UK's submission to DG15 pointed out that, even on the grounds of promoting the Internal Market, there was little to be gained from harmonising media ownership rules, since the main obstructions to cross-border expansion by European media companies were cultural and linguistic barriers, not disparities in national regulations (DNH, 1996). This point was echoed by many industry players who were opposed to any involvement by the Commission in the determination of media ownership rules for Europe (Tucker, 1997).

But, quite apart from the potential for the *status quo* to disrupt the Commission's wider objectives of completing the Internal Market, a range of other arguments could potentially be articulated in favour of action on media ownership at the European rather than the national level. The most compelling of these might be that dominant media operators in Europe wield such significant political power in their domestic markets as to impede national regulators from making pluralism the key priority in the design of media ownership policy (Humphreys, 1997: 9). Clearly, pan-European policy-makers cannot overlook the needs of industry. EU policy-making is not immune to industrial lobbying but, because of the diversity of national interests represented at the European level, there may arguably be less opportunity for any individual media player to superimpose its own requirements on the policy formulation process.

Against a background of increasing concerns about the competitiveness of domestic industries, the system of allegiances between national political parties and media industry participants, evident in many member states, has made it virtually impossible for national regulators in the large European markets to buck the general trend towards deregulation. Industrial participants in these markets have been amongst the most vociferous opponents of a pan-European policy aimed at protecting pluralism (or, as some would have it, unnecessary 'Brussels bureaucracy'), and it is difficult to escape the conclusion that this reflects the potential dilution of their own influence at the pan-European level.

Efforts to bring forward an EU Directive on Media Ownership
Despite the many obstacles to progress on a pan-European media ownership policy, a tentative step forward was taken by DG15 in Autumn

1996 with the first draft of a possible EU Directive on Media Pluralism.[8] The Commission's proposals involved a 30 percent upper limit on monomedia ownership for radio and television broadcasters in their own transmission areas and, also, an upper limit for 'total' media ownership – i.e. ownership of television, radio and/or newspapers – of 10 percent of the market in which a supplier is operating. All market shares would be based on audience measures – i.e. calculated as a proportion of total television viewing, radio listenership or newspaper readership within the area in question – with consumption of each single type of media (television, radio or newspapers) divided by one-third for the purposes of assessing a supplier's overall share of the total market. The proposed derogations would allow member states to exclude public service broadcasters from these upper limits, if they so wished.

Although the definition of precise upper limits for media ownership moved the policy debate onto a more practical footing, it also inevitably provided a locus for major controversies about what level of diversity of ownership was appropriate for markets of different sizes. The approach taken in DG15 involved setting identical fixed limits which would apply in any member state and either at the local, regional or national level, depending on which constitutes the appropriate market for the media supplier in question. Crucially, the Commission took the view that what counts is market share within the specific transmission area for a broadcasting service. This contrasted with the approach taken at that time, say, in the UK, where what counted is a broadcaster's share of the national market, irrespective of what areas its service is transmitting in. From a point of view of achieving equality of pluralism for all European media consumers, the Commission's approach seemed entirely defensible. The problem was that it seems to disregard the fact that different market sizes – whether national or sub-national – can support different levels of diversity of ownership.

It could be argued that, in principle, the imposition of a 30 percent upper limit on monomedia radio, television or newspaper ownership plus a 10 percent upper limit on total media ownership, is not unreasonable. If pluralism is to exist, then a minimum of four suppliers each in the radio, television and newspaper sectors or ten different suppliers in the

---

[8] The history of efforts to introduce a directive on media ownership and pluralism is discussed more fully in earlier work by the author which is drawn upon here (Doyle 1997; 1998; 2002b).

market as a whole may well seem like an appropriate requirement. But in practice, because of different histories and rules and differing levels of resources available for media provision in each country, some of the member states of Europe would already fall foul of these proposals, even in terms of diversity of ownership at the *national* level. For example, some smaller European countries had only two national broadcasters, each with a market share in excess of 30 percent (Barnard et al, 1996). The number of observable transgressions throughout Europe multiplied as the focus shifted down to smaller regional and local levels. At the same time, the proposed upper monomedia ownership limit of 30 percent paved the way for even higher levels of concentration in some larger national markets than was allowed under existing national rules.

DG15's proposals addressed the problem of diverging national regulations and they also seemed well-suited to the task of establishing and protecting minimum levels of pluralism, in equal measure, for all citizens of the EU. But opponents of a pan-European policy initiative were quick to seize upon the distinction between promoting pluralism and completing the Internal Market, and to question which of these objectives DG 15's proposals were really aimed at. The Corporate Affairs Director of one of the UK's largest newspaper publishers[9] expressed the following views on the 1996 draft Directive:

> You have to keep saying to them [the Commission], where is the problem? And they say 'single market' – they need to tidy up disparities. But they are *not* looking at it as a single market; they are talking about pluralism and diversity and saying they have competence in this area. Then, it's not a single market issue. Is it about tidying up the rules to increase cross-border sales or about preventing one person from owning too much? These are two completely different things. And they have tried to address both in one single document and they have fallen over themselves really, really badly …'

Whether member states wanted and could afford to resource equal levels of diversity of ownership at the sub-national as well as national level was an additional matter. It was not at all clear how member states or the EU at large would find the economic means to redress shortfalls in diversity of ownership in some sub-national or smaller national markets.

DG15's response to objections raised (in particular, from the UK and Germany) was to promise a more flexible approach to the upper ceilings suggested in the July 1996 draft, indicating that the 30 percent thresholds

---

[9] Interviewed by the author in April 1997.

could be varied if national circumstances so demanded. But the Commission's negotiating position on upper ceilings was constrained by Parliament's consistent support for robust measures to counteract concentrations. Clearly, the greater the discretionary power left to member states in setting their own upper limits on media and cross-media ownership, the less effective any new Directive would be, whatever its objectives.

A revised set of proposals put forward by DG15 in Spring 1997 introduced two small but significant modifications (Gabara, 1997). First, the title of the proposed Directive was changed from 'Concentrations and Pluralism' to 'Media Ownership' in the Internal Market. This signalled a move to deflect the focus away from pluralism (where the Commission's competence would be in question) towards the aim of removing obstacles to the Internal Market.

Secondly, a 'flexibility clause' was introduced. This added, to the proposed derogations, the flexibility for individual member states to exclude any broadcaster they wished from the (unchanged) upper limits, provided that the broadcaster in question was not simultaneously infringing these upper thresholds in more than one member state and, also, provided that other 'appropriate measures' were used to secure pluralism. 'Appropriate measures' might include establishing, within any organisation that breached the limits, 'windows for independent programme suppliers' or a 'representative programming committee' (CEC, 1997).

These modifications represented an unambiguous withdrawal from the original ambition of imposing a fixed minimum level of diversity of ownership for all European markets. Instead, member states could decide for themselves (at least in the short term) whether or not the ownership thresholds set out in the Directive should apply to organisations operating within their own national territories. According to the revised proposals, there would be no absolute requirement for member states to enforce the upper thresholds set out in the Directive, but the new measures would prevent any member state from adopting *more* restrictive domestic media ownership rules (which, arguably, could obstruct cross-border investments or distort competition).

In effect then, as the switch of title suggested, the Directive was no longer about guaranteeing an equal right to pluralism (as represented by diversity of media ownership) for all EU citizens, irrespective which European markets they happened to live in. Although, in theory, the proposed Directive introduced a uniform set of media ownership restrictions throughout the EU, it was clear that, in practice, the 'flexibility clause' would allow member states to maintain whatever upper restrictions on ownership were affordable – either economically or politically – in their own territories. What, then, was the point of introducing a harmonising initiative?

Such back-tracking was intended to boost support for a new Directive but, at the same time, it made it difficult to see how a harmonised approach could appease long-standing concerns (especially, in the European Parliament) about national and transnational concentrations of media ownership in Europe. And, in spite of this 'legalistic subterfuge', opposition to the idea of any pan-European policy initiative was not extinguished (Gabara, 1997). The problem remained that *regional* media suppliers (e.g. UK broadcasters ITV), whose local market share exceeded 30 percent but whose share of the national market was relatively small, were to be caught out by the proposed European-wide rules in exactly the same way as what are perceived as genuine 'media moguls'; i.e. *national* media suppliers whose market share exceeded 30 percent (e.g. Mediaset in Italy, or TF1 in France, or News International in the UK). But if member states used the 'flexibility clause' to exempt domestic operators from the proposed upper thresholds, then the new Directive would be meaningless. For some commentators, the legal uncertainty which the exemption clause would create 'would be worse than not having a common Directive at all. In the absence of an EU law, potential investors at least have the certainty that the national legislation applies' (Gabara, 1997).

Debate about the revised EU initiative had to be postponed in March 1997 'in the face of ferocious lobbying against it' (Tucker, 1997). The European Publishers Council again publicly espoused its view that a pan-European media ownership initiative was unnecessary and would only hinder the development of European media companies (McEvoy, 1997; Tucker, 1997). ITV also expressed strong concern about how the UK's regional television system could be jeopardised under the new draft Directive, unless a 'cast-iron guarantee' of exemption were given to regional broadcasters (ITVA, 1997).

A uniform set of media ownership restrictions imposed rigidly throughout all European markets seemed unfeasible, both economically and politically. But, if the solution was to adopt a flexible approach, then it was open to question whether the Commission should get involved at all, given that member states themselves were better placed than DG15 to take account of and directly legislate for the particular characteristics of their own markets.

If a Directive on media ownership was to convey any useful benefits over and above the *status quo*, something more visionary than a 'flexible' approach would be needed. But DG15 found itself unable to build a supporting consensus around any proposals for a new Directive on media ownership. So in the end the initiative had to be quietly abandoned.

From pluralism to competition policy and beyond

The range and complexity of seemingly insurmountable legal, practical and political obstacles which overwhelmed efforts to bring forward a pan-European Directive on media ownership in the late 1990s seem to rule out any possibility of the Commission returning to the task of introducing a harmonising initiative in this area any time soon. The Information Society & Media Directorate-General, in its discussion paper on Media Pluralism of July 2005, acknowledged Parliament's ongoing concerns about the need to tackle media concentrations but, in bold letters, pointed to the difficulty of proposing 'any kind of harmonisation of rules between the EU member States' (CEC, 2005: 6). In a similar vein, the Information Society & Media website emphasizes that promotion of pluralism is 'primarily a matter for member states'.[10]

The European Parliament, however, is not reconciled to this position. Parliament initially revisited the question of media concentration when, in November 2002, it passed a Resolution proposing that, in the light of new technological developments and the impact of additional media mergers, the time was ripe for a new consultation process and Green Paper. It called again on the Commission to take action to strengthen and harmonise curbs on concentrations of media ownership across Europe in order to protect pluralism (EP, 2002). A position of support for action on the part of the Commission to curb media concentrations was reiterated in a European Parliament Report of December 2003 responding to and endorsing the UNESCO Convention on Cultural Diversity (EP, 2003). This was followed by a further Resolution concerning 'the risks of violation, in the EU and especially in Italy, of freedom of expres-

---

[10] See www.europa.eu.int/comm/avpolicy/info_centre/a_z/index_en.htm#p

sion and information' which, in April 2004, again called on the Commission to review the state of media pluralism in the EU and to act on the Resolution of November 2002 by submitting a proposal for a draft directive to safeguard pluralism (EP, 2004).

It is difficult to envisage the circumstances under which action to harmonise media concentration measures might successfully be taken forward. Even were the legal basis for an initiative in this area to be improved by, for example, the ratification of a new European Constitution incorporating specific protections for the citizens' rights to pluralism, the Commission would still be liable to face very significant conflict on the question of exactly what objectives a harmonised framework ought to serve. And the ongoing process of EU enlargement has done little to ameliorate practical problems surrounding the implementation of a common approach for countries of different sizes and very different national circumstances.

Although harmonised rules on media and cross-media ownership are probably out of the question for the foreseeable future, the Commission still retains some interest in regulating concentrations in the media industry. The EU's general rules on competition apply to the media as any other economic sector and the Competition Directorate General has intervened on several occasions to deal with proposed mergers or allegations of anti-competitive conduct involving large European media players.[11] Of course, while European competition law serves to restrict dominant market positions or anti-competitive behaviour, it is not specifically designed to encourage or safeguard pluralism.

Even so, the Commission's recent competition-based interventions in the media and communications industries have undoubtedly served to encourage wider market access and therefore to promote greater diversity and pluralism. The useful role played by competition law in safeguarding against abuses of excessive market power across the converging media and communications sectors has led some, particularly large industry players, to ask whether regulation of media ownership can now be left entirely to competition law.

The promotion of competition in the media sector is clearly a vital starting point for ensuring pluralism. But there are two main problems with relying solely on competition law. First, competition law is not

---

[11] Fuller discussion of recent competition investigations and interventions can be found at Doyle, 2002b (pp166-170) and Wheeler, 2004.

particularly effective at national level in some European countries (Gold-berg, Prosser and Verhulst, 1998: 18) and, at the collective EU level, it is evident that many media mergers and alliances are also ignored by DG Competition because they fall below the high revenue thresholds set out in the 1989 Merger Control Regulation. So, it is questionable whether existing competition laws in Europe are sufficiently well-attuned to pick up on all significant media mergers and acquisitions or whether, without additional sector-specific regulations, many would fall through the regu-latory loop.

Second, as discussed earlier, safeguarding competition and promoting pluralism are different objectives. The need to ensure plurality in the media on democratic, social and cultural grounds is a separate and dis-tinct policy objective from ensuring market efficiency through competi-tion. As acknowledged in a recent UK White Paper on Communications, '[a] competitive market is likely to be one with many voices and diverse content, though there is no guarantee that this will be the case' (DTI/DCMS, 2000: 36). Sometimes, media markets that raise no con-cerns in terms of competition may nonetheless lack the range and diver-sity of voices needed to safeguard pluralism.

To maintain pluralism and avoid the risk of an unhealthy domination of the media within and across member states of the EU, policy instru-ments other than competition law must come into play. Notwithstanding the apparent unfeasibility of a harmonizing initiative to curb concentra-tions of media ownership, the Commission can and, to some extent, is active in supporting pluralism through alternative means. Measures such as, for example, regulations to encourage open access, diverse content, subsidies for minority language media, special protections for journalistic independence or support measures for public service broadcasters also have a useful role to play in promoting pluralism and diversity. But it remains to be seen how long Parliament's persistent reminders of the dangers that accompany the unfettered growth of concentrations of media ownership across Europe can be ignored.

References

Beltrame, F. 1996. Lawmaking in the European Union. Paper prepared for the *W G Hart Legal Workshop*. Institute of Advanced Legal Studies.

Bruck, P. Dorr, D. Cole, M. Favre, J. Gramstad, S. Monaco, M. and Culek, Z. 2004. *Transnational Media Concentrations in Europe.* Report prepared by Advisory Panel on Media Concentrations, Pluralism and Diversity (AP-MD). Media Directorate. Strasbourg: Council of Europe, November 2004.

Council of Europe (CoE). 1997. *Report on Media Concentrations and Pluralism in Europe.* MM-CM (97). January.

CEC (European Commission). 1992. *Pluralism and Media Concentration in the Internal Market: An Assessment of the Need for Community Action.* COM(92) 480 Final. Brussels. 23 December.

CEC (European Commission). 1994. *Communication to Parliament and Council: Follow-up to the Consultation Process Relating to the Green paper on 'Pluralism and Media Concentration in the Internal Market – An Assessment of the Need for Community Action'.* (COM [94] 353 final). 5 October.

CEC (European Commission). 1997. *Explanatory Memorandum,* (Media Ownership in the Internal Market). DG XV. February.

CEC (European Commission). 2005. *Media Pluralism – What should be the European Union's role?* Issues Paper for the Liverpool Audiovisual Conference. Information Society and Media Directorate-General. July 2005. Posted at www.europa.eu.int/comm/avpolicy/revision-tvwf2005/consult.en.htm.

Council of Europe (CoE). 1997. *Compilation of National Reports on Media Concentrations,* Secretariat memorandum prepared by the Directorate of Human Rights. MM-CM (97) 10. Strasbourg: Council of Europe, July.

Demers, D. 1999. *Global Media: Menace or Messiah?* Creskill, NJ: Hampton Press.

Department for Culture, Media and Sport (DCMS). 2005. *Liverpool Audiovisual Conference: Between Culture and Commerce* (Conference Report). Department for Culture, Media and Sport. September 2005.

Department of National Heritage (DNH). 1996. *United Kingdom Submission to DG XV on a possible EC Directive on Media Pluralism.* December 1996.

Doyle, G. 1997. From 'Pluralism' to 'Media Ownership': Europe's Emergent Policy on Media Concentrations Navigates the Doldrums. *Journal of Information Law and Technology.* http://elj.strath.ac.uk/jilt/commsreg/ 97_3doyl/, October.

Doyle, G. 1998. Towards a pan-European Directive? From 'Concentrations and Pluralism' to 'Media Ownership'. *Journal of Communications Law.* 3 (1): 11-15.

Doyle, G. 2002a. *Understanding Media Economics.* London: Sage.

Doyle, G. 2002b. *Media Ownership: The Economics and Politics of Convergence and Concentration in the UK and European Media.* London: Sage.

DTI/DCMS. 2000. *A New Future for Communications.* Cm 5010. London: HMSO.

European Parliament (EP). 2002. *European Parliament Resolution on Media Concentration.* P5_TA(2002)0552. November 20 2002.

European Parliament (EP). 2003. *Report on Preserving and Promoting Cultural Diversity: The Role of the European Regions and International Organizations such as UNESCO and the Council of Europe (2002/2269(INI)).* Committee on Culture,

Youth, Education, the Media and Sport. Rapporteur: Christa Prets. A5-04777/2003. 15 December 2003.

European Parliament (EP). 2004. *European Parliament Resolution on the Risks of Violation, in the Eu and Especially in Italy, of Freedom of Expression and Information (Article 11(2) of the Charter of Fundamental Rights) (2003/2237(INI))*. P5_TA(2004)0373. April 22 2004.

Gabara, I. 1997. 'The EU Should Leave Media Rules to Member States', *The Wall Street Journal*. March 25: 7.

Goldberg, D. Prosser, T. and Verhuslt, S. 1998. *Regulating the Changing Media: A comparative study*. Oxford: Clarendon Press.

Harcourt, A. 1996. Regulating for Media Concentration: The Emerging policy of the European Union. *Utilities Law Review*. 7 (5): 202-210.

Harcourt, A. 2005. *The European Union and the Regulation of Media Markets*. Manchester University Press.

Hitchens, L. 1994. Media Ownership and Control: A European Approach, *The Modern Law Review*, 57 (4): 585-601.

Humphreys, P. 1997. Power and Control in the New Media. Paper presented at the ECPR-Workshop *New Media and Political Communication*. University of Manchester.

Iosifides, P. 1996. Merger Control and Media Pluralism in the European Union. *Communications Law*. 1(6): 247-9.

ITVA. 1997. 'ITV concerned about proposed EU Media Ownership Directive', Press Release. ITV Association. March 17.

Kaitatzi-Whitlock, S. 1996. Pluralism and Media Concentration in Europe: Media Policy as Industrial Policy. *European Journal of Communication*. 11 (4): 453-83.

Kevin, D. Thorsten, Fueg, O. Pertzinidou, E. Schoenthal, M. 2004. *The Information of the Citizen in the EU: Obligations for the Media and the Institutions Concerning the Citizen's Right to Be Fully and Objectively Informed* (Final Report). Prepared on behalf of the European Parliament by the European Institute for the Media. Dusseldorf: EIM.

Lange, A. and Van Loon, A. 1991. *Pluralism, Concentration and Competition in the Media Sector*. IDATE/IVIR. December.

MacLeod, V. ed. 1996. *Media Ownership and Control in the Age of Convergence*. London: International Institute of Communications.

McEvoy J. 1997. 'EU angers publishers by pushing on with media law'. Reuters Press Release. March 11.

Meier, W. and Trappel, J. 1998. Media Concentration and the Public Interest. In McQuail D and Siune K. eds. *Media Policy: Convergence, Concentration and Commerce*. 38-59. Euromedia Research Group.

Mortensen, F. 1993. *Study by a Consultant on the Notion of Access to the Market*. Council of Europe. Committee of Experts on Media Concentrations and Pluralism (MM-CM). MM-CM (93) 21. Strasbourg.

Murdock, G and Golding, P. 1977. Capitalism, Communication and Class Relations. In Curran J, Gurevitch M and Woollacott J. eds, *Mass Communication and Society*, London: Edward Arnold.

Sánchez-Tabernero, A. and Carvajal, M. 2002. *Media Concentrations in the European Market, New Trends and Challenges, Media Markets Monograph*. Pamplona, Spain: Servicio de Publiciones de la Universidad de Navarra.

Sarikakis, K. 2004. *Powers in Media Policy: The Challenge of the European Parliament*. Oxford: Peter Lang.

Schlesinger, P. and Doyle, G. 1995. Contradictions of Economy and Culture: The European Union and the Information Society. *Journal of European Cultural Policy*. 2 (1): 25-42.

Terazono, E. 2006. Convergence Requires the Complete Vision, *Financial Times*, 16 February: 21.

Tucker, E. 1997. 'EU Media Initiative Bogged Down'. *Financial Times*. 13 March: 23.

Tunstall, J. and Palmer, M. 1991. *Media Moguls*. London: Routledge.

Ward, D. Fueg, O. and D'Armo, A. 2004. *A Mapping Study of Media Concentration and Ownership in Ten European Countries*. Commissariaat voor de Media. Hilversum: Netherlands Media Authority.

Ward, D. 2006. *The Assessment of Content Diversity in Newspapers and Television in the context of Increasing Trends towards Concentrations of Media Markets*. Consultant Study for Group of Specialists on Media Diversity (MC-S-MD). Strasbourg: Council of Europe, 26 February 2006.

Weatherill S and Beaumont P (1995), *EC Law: The Essential Guide to the Legal Workings of the European Community* (2nd Ed), Penguin.

Wheeler, M. 2004. Supranational Regulation: Television and the European Union. *European Journal of Communication*. 19 (3): 349-369.

EUROPEAN STUDIES 24 (2007): 157-182

THE CONSTRUCTION OF EUROPEAN IDENTITY AND CITIZENSHIP THROUGH CULTURAL POLICY[1]

Liza Tsaliki

Abstract

Developing a 'European' citizenship and identity has become a major priority for the EU in order to address the democratic deficit it is faced with and legitimize itself. As a result, it would be interesting to examine how exactly is this objective operationalised and materialised within EU cultural policy. Hence, this article discusses the patterns of construction of European culture and citizenship through cultural policy-making. What does culture mean for the European Union? What kind of citizenship does the EU envisage for its peoples, and what kind of action does the Union take towards this goal? In order to frame and better illustrate this discussion, I will be using a number of European cultural policy initiatives as examples of the way in which Europe tries to construct its citizens. These examples, I argue, encapsulate the Commission's quest of a new common European identity and articulate 'a new politics of cultural belonging'.

The construction of European culture

The geo-political enlargement of the EU has altered how we debate questions of national and supranational identity and has prompted intense questions about the nature, reality and source of such a Europeanness. Forging a European identity has since become an explicit target of EU policy. The drive to forge such an identity has accelerated

[1] I would like to thank Henry Scott at the National Documentation Centre in Athens for the data and charts provided.

since 1980, if only at the mundane administrative level of driving li-
censes, flag, anthem, and such initiatives as the European Cities of Culture. These all seek, as demanded by the Maastricht Treaty, to bring 'the
common cultural heritage to the fore'. In initiatives supported by the
World Commission on Culture and Development (WCCD) (UNESCO
1996, *Our Creative Diversity*), the Council of Europe has also produced a
series of policy documents (i.e. ETCD 1997, *In from the Margins: A Contribution to the Debate on Culture and Development in Europe*) that aim to define
Europe through a 'common European culture'. Accounts perceive a
cultural heritage wherein democracy, Enlightenment values, reason,
individualism, and a Greco-Roman historical tradition are infused to
produce a unique European flavour. This heritage not only describes a
common European culture, but concurrently prescribes its protection
and advancement as a proper policy (Bondebjerg and Golding 2004,
introduction).

Increasingly, EU policy recognises that culture is at the heart of the
European project, and has identified the audiovisual and communications industries as key instruments in creating a sense of European cultural identity. The creation of a pan-European market in the audiovisual
sector is largely motivated by the Commission's ambition to promote a
'European audiovisual space'. In fact, through initiatives such as the
MEDIA programme, European Cinema and Television Year – 1988, the
RACE and EUREKA programmes, and by means of legislative and
regulatory liberalisation and harmonisation, the Commission has clearly
sought to lay the foundations of what Morley and Robins dubbed 'a
post-national audiovisual territory' (1995, 3). On the basis of a 'Europe
without frontiers', European media interests can become global players
alongside their American and Japanese counterparts. The European
audiovisual agenda had a significant cultural dimension as well, though:
improving mutual knowledge among European peoples and increasing
their awareness of what they share in common. The Commission has
hitherto encouraged programme-makers to appeal to a broad European
audience in order to help develop a sense of cultural belonging to the
EU.

Gradually, due to developments related to the enlargement process as
well as to globalisation, the structural position of art and entertainment
has changed, and, within the EU, member states have realised that in
order to maintain or strengthen European cultural production, products

need to be commercially competitive and attract large audiences. Indeed, the Union has realised that cultural production must become part of a European industrial policy; in that respect, the EU recognises that 'culture' has a special status, as its works are both economic goods, creating jobs and producing wealth, and vehicles for the construction of cultural identities. 'Culture' has taken centre stage in official EU discourse as stated in Article 128 of the 1992 Maastricht Treaty (now 151 in the amended Treaty of Amsterdam): 'the Community shall contribute to the flowering of the cultures of the Member States, while respecting their national and regional diversity and at the same time bringing the common cultural heritage to the fore'. Culture, in this respect, is seen by the Commission to lie at the basis of the formation of identity – without however being exclusively connected to a particular community. It transpires that according to this discourse, if the corpus of European culture is sufficiently promoted and protected, a European consciousness will eventually emerge – in other words, using culture as a legitimising tool while claiming that culture deserves to be safeguarded as the highest product of human activity becomes an end in itself. Additionally, the EU has to manage the fostering of this common heritage without challenging national or local cultures (Sassatelli 2002, 440). Without the construction of this 'imagined [European] community' in Benedict Anderson's words (1983), Europe will be at risk of being reduced to a purely economic entity – something the EU has been trying vividly to avoid.

Elsewhere, the EU takes a more informed view of 'culture'. In the Council of Europe's *In From the Margins* report (ETCD), a follow-up report to UNESCO's deliberations on culture and development (WCCD, *Our Creative Diversity*), cultural policy and the socially excluded were brought 'in from the margins' of political and economic governance. Both reports are considered to have initiated a 'paradigm shift' in the theory and practice of cultural policy where 'a wide anthropological definition of culture' is employed (Kleberg 2000, 49). *Our Creative Diversity* places culture at the centre of global political, social and economic development, arguing that cultural development should broaden its previously narrow remit of arts and high culture, and encompass the promotion of 'human development', defined as diversity, creativity and self-expression. The report emphasises the common space of the global and the specificity of place, and interprets culture as both high and popular culture wherein each national and regional culture can discover their particular identity and their global commonality. Attempting to define European identity, *In from the Margins* combines definitions of culture as a shared system of cultural production and as a signifying or symbolic system. 'Culture with a capital C', defined as what is artistic or creative, is considered alongside the 'anthropological' idea of culture as 'the values and practices that underlie all forms of human behaviour'. The report argues that 'culture is a powerful promoter of identity' with a potential for empowerment and entitlement. This report aims to define a common European identity through a cultural heritage of 'civilization' and a common mass culture disseminated through an integrated European media space (Cronin 2002, 313). Although it celebrates the political, cultural and linguistic heterogeneity within Europe, *In from the Margins* also posits the specificity of Europeans as bearers of the legacy of civilization and democracy – a common European cultural bond. As a result, the report, and European cultural policy, propagates the co-existence of a common cultural identity and cultural diversity in Europe.

One can hardly disagree with this new paradigm of cultural develop-ment and diversity, exemplified in both reports, though they tend to a certain opacity when it comes to the object of their critique, says McGuigan. Instead of naming the source of trouble, they opt for a posi-tively idealistic advocacy of cultural development, and offer a vague solution to problems not made clear (2004, 100). *In from the Margins* questions openly neo-liberal globalisation in the form of European com-petition with US interests, while also acknowledges loss of conviction in traditional state intervention and the problematic unity of European culture. In fact, the ETCD report asserts that the key question is the choice between market forces and public intervention. The answer is that (public) cultural policy is more important now than ever, its prime objec-tive becoming the promotion of diversity. Previous solutions, such as increased welfare, should be abandoned, while surrender to the force of neo-liberal globalisation is neither an option. Instead, change should be 'managed' along the principles of identity, creativity, participation and diversity – buzzwords without referents, and various loose ends, says McGuigan critically (101). Not wishing to deny the good intentions of this new cultural policy, Anne Cronin is equally critical of both reports, and argues that they serve to naturalise inequalities by 'culturalising' difference. Despite the explicit aim of both the UNESCO and the Coun-cil of Europe's reports to enfranchise marginalised groups (especially women and ethnic minorities) through consumerist rights of access to culture and cultural legitimacy, they actually produce new forms of marginalisation (2002). Cronin considers how these policy documents define culture 'as a belonging' – a consumer right of ownership of citizenship status. However, the 'new politics of European belonging' mean that this new articulation of cultural rights may result in further exclusion and cultural dispossession.

Cultural policy-making in the EU

In Marshall's classic social-democratic agenda the aim was to reduce class inequality. Subsequently, the agenda was developed to include policies for removing gender and racial discrimination. Questions of further entitlement were raised including this time issues of cultural policy, such as access to the arts, multiculturalism and the recognition of difference. The growing concern with cultural citizenship and identity reflects, to some extent, how issues that were once considered 'social' came increasingly to be thought of as 'cultural'. Questions of identity and belonging have superseded questions of material entitlement in much social and cultural theory as well as in public policy and cultural politics (McGuigan 2004, 34). The love affair of development studies with political economy and neo-liberal economics has begun to wane in the nineties, and culture has taken centre stage in the development agenda (99). Following Raymond Williams's (1984) distinction between cultural policy 'proper' (public patronage of the arts, media regulation, and construction of cultural identity), and cultural policy as display (national aggrandisement and economic reductionism), cultural policy-making among the members of the European Union falls within the former category (McGuigan 2004, 65). In this sense, any member-state will have an administrative apparatus for the implementation of its own cultural policies on a national, regional, local scale, and concurrently will participate in inter-state enquiry according to a common Europeanness (a typical example being the mapping document, whereby the Council of Europe sends out international groups of experts to map and evaluate the cultural policies of member states). EU members have, residually at least, some form of welfare-state model of cultural policy, contrary to the US where cultural policy 'proper' is marginalised by the free-market imperative. Having said that, given the recent undermining of the welfare state by neo-liberalism and global capitalism, there is an uncertainty about the actual value of cultural policy 'proper' even within its bastions – as exemplified in the shift from a 'cultural industries' rhetoric to a 'creative industries' one in a reductively economic perspective undertaken by the New Labour in Britain (*Creative Industries-Mapping Document*, Department of Culture, Media and Sport 1998). Evidently, when the action in the cultural and creative industries is largely dictated by market forces, government action is marginalised whatever the rhetoric.

Citizenship

Until the 1980s, citizenship was largely ignored by social scientists, while the Left dismissed 'rights' as a bourgeois irrelevance. Since then citizenship has become increasingly politicised as parties on the Left and the Right, at both national and European level, have tried to appropriate its symbolic and semantic association with words like 'empowerment', 'participation', 'community' and 'rights' (Shore 2004). Attention should be drawn to the fact that the concept of citizenship is not only modern but Western as well, which means that contrary to modernisation assumptions, Western-style citizenship is not the inevitable outcome of industrialisation and the expansion of the public sphere as the case of Japan and the newly industrialised countries of South-East Asia have demonstrated. Similarly, despite the existence of cities and a strong urban tradition, Western-style citizenship did not evolve in the nations of Islam (Sassen 1996).

Most authors would agree that citizenship is a widely used yet highly contested concept (Shaw 1997; Lehning 2001, 241; Shore 2004), if not a 'slippery' one (Riley 1992, 180). A lot of the confusion stems from the fact that 'citizenship' is usually confounded with 'nationality', and sometimes the two, conceptually different, terms, are regarded as identical and used interchangeably (Meehan 1997). At the dawn of the modern constitutional state the two terms differed greatly. The contemporary view holds that 'nationality' is the legal concept that defines the legal membership of an individual of a state. It is a legal identity from which no rights need arise, though duties might. 'Citizenship', on the other hand, is a practice, a form of belonging resting on legal, social and participatory entitlements, which may be conferred or denied irrespective of nationality, as has been in the case of women, and religious and ethnic minorities. How exactly individuals become legal members of a state depends on the state's nationality legal regime, and the criteria for the acquisition and loss of nationality vary significantly (Meehan 2000, 1993; Preuss et al. 2003).

What citizenship actually means in any one place depends on particular local history and politics.[2] For example, sections of the British Left throughout the twentieth century denounced the discourse of citizenship as a 'bourgeois charade' disguising the invidious inequalities of class division, while others embraced its rhetoric, seeking to develop a version of 'active citizenship'. Similarly, the term 'citizen' carries a different history of ideological baggage in former state socialist societies. In Slovakia, it was associated with being a 'citizen of gypsy origin', a group negatively stereotyped among the rest of the population. It is only in recent years that the concept of citizenship is being rehabilitated and associated with freedom and democracy (Jamieson 2002, 519).

Discussions on modern citizenship take off from T. H. Marshall's classic essay *Citizenship and Social Class*, who argued that citizenship is about membership in a community, and identified three layers of citizenship rights: civic, political, and social. These constitute the traditional components of the welfare state where every individual is guaranteed full membership in these rights (1950). The Marshallian notion of citizenship

---

[2] Some writers opine that the citizenship debate is merely a case of being 'lost in translation', and claim that the English term 'citizenship' conflates two distinct meanings in French: citoyenneté, which refers to membership in a political community, and nationalité, which refers to the legal bond between the individual and the state (Neveu 2001 in Shore 2004, 31). French republicanism expects from immigrants the unreserved acceptance of the 'universal' principles embedded in French political culture, aiming at their eventual assimilation (Preuss et al. 2003). The civic understanding prevailed during the German re-unification in 1990, and the new nationality law enacted in 2001, facilitated the attainment of German nationality by foreign residents. Germans exercise 'social' citizenship in settings such as professional chambers, churches, social security corporations, and large enterprises. In fact, the German concept of citizenship posits that citizens shape political decisions both as part of the sovereign 'people' and as members of particular corporations. The British experience of citizenship is interplay between natural rights, customary common law, and legislative sovereignty. Individual Britons are not seen as members of the political community of the state, but are 'represented' within it by the Parliament. The divergence of citizenship and sovereignty facilitated the inclusion of immigrants and consolidated multiculturalism (Preuss et.al. 2003, 9-11). In Greece, different facets of pervasive clientelism from 1863 onwards, has resulted in a gargantuan state sector, a weak civil society and a political culture dominated by partocratic orientations and personalistic discourses which render issues of social reform peripheral. All of this means that Greece, compared to Western Europe, has a political system that provides fewer civil and political rights to its citizens – due to its weak civil society (Mouzelis 1995 ; Diamandouros 1994).

is challenged by the emergence of increasing social and cultural pluralism and the fact that despite the existence of common rights, some members may feel excluded. As a result, definitions of citizenship need to be revised so as to accommodate the pluralism of modern societies and supersede the lack of a shared heritage: the concept of 'liberal democratic citizenship' is a case in point through which a 'shared citizenship identity' can be developed (Lehning 2001, 245-6). Saskia Sassen has introduced the concept of 'economic citizenship' to explain the way in which traditional citizenship is challenged (1996). The emergence of 'postnational talk' demonstrates the shift from state to 'social citizenship' wherein identity is understood as a complex social formation with sufficient space for contradictory identities. An argument in this direction is Yasmin Soysal's model of 'post-national membership' (1994). Soysal draws inferences about how global factors transform the national order of citizenship based on emerging forms of incorporation and membership of migrants. Others have argued about the construct of 'cultural citizenship' (see above, McGuigan), 'ecological citizenship' (van Steenbergen 1994), or 'global citizenship (Falk 1994) while there is a wide range of feminist perspectives on citizenship, namely Ruth Lister's approach according to which human agency should be seen as the basis for a feminist theory of citizenship. Lister offers the concept of 'differentiated universalism' in order to reconcile the universalism embedded in citizenship with the demands of a politics of difference (1997, 28).

European citizenship: an empty promise or a truly 'post-national' demos?

The oldest criticism of EU citizenship starts from the limitations of the Treaty of Rome as a, restricted, basis for rights (i.e. freedom of movement for goods, capital, labour and services). These rights addressed the 'citizen-as-worker' instead of reflecting the normative principle that people are citizens because they are human beings. Concerns about the narrowness of rights began to be acknowledged in the mid-1970s, gained further momentum in the eighties and were reflected in the Maastricht Treaty. Critics note that the status and rights of EU citizens continue to rest upon member state nationality, in itself a prerogative still of national governments (Meehan 2000). Two issues arise from the Maastricht Treaty's definition of citizenship: first that there is no uniform pan-European meaning of citizenship, and second that it hardly eliminates the democratic deficit it was designed to address (Bhabha 1998).

There is ambivalence among critics regarding European citizenship. Is citizenship, in its conventional conception, still a useful concept in a world where globalization has challenged the sovereignty of the nation state? European citizenship is described by Percy Lehning as a 'condition' by which people from different nations should have similar rights towards the European public courts and public officials, a condition which has been largely fulfilled within the EU (2001). What is missing is a conception, and a construction, of European citizenship where people share a common identity, a common purpose. And why do we need a notion like European citizenship, one might ask? Because the citizens of member states enjoy rights and have responsibilities emanating from Union organs rather than their respective national parliaments. However, as these organs do not articulate the will of a European people, or *demos*, there is a legitimation gap within the Union caused by the growing EU power and the (lack of) consent of member states citizens. This absence of accountability at European level has the implication that European public policy can only deal with a limited range of issues. At this point, the role of civil society to generate trust among strangers at the national level, so argues Lehning, can be extended at Union level. The creation of a European-wide public sphere would involve a continuous civic conversation among a critical mass of 'citizens of the European Union' on a variety of issues (267-8).

Lehning's answer to the Union's legitimation gap is passing authority on certain matters to the organs of the supranational community in the form of 'transnational federalism' (258), the mirror image of federalism on national scale. European citizenship must entail accountability not to the 'separate peoples of Europe', but to the 'people of Europe as a whole' instead. Citizens may become members of a federation, under the provision the latter is based on an overlapping consensus. This consensus will, in its turn, generate a 'shared citizenship identity' to supersede all rival identities based on national belonging before it leads on constitutional patriotism on a federal level (262-3). It is accepted that within the 'shared citizenship identity', citizens do not have similar language, ethnic and cultural origins; they form multicultural societies instead. Consequently, the European demos is not founded on the premise of ethnic homogeneity, but encompasses heterogeneity and pluralism.

One of those vehemently opposed to European citizenship was Raymond Aron who already in 1974 argued that professional civil servants in Brussels have formed a bureaucracy that is detached from democratic processes. Not only that, but Aron sees citizenship rights as not being able of being guaranteed by anything other than the state, more particularly the nation state, and certainly not by a regime like the EU which is not a state at all (1974). There are other, much more critical, voices regarding European citizenship. Meehan (1997) agrees that the Union citizenship rhetoric is mainly symbolic and intends to camouflage the lack of real developments in the field of social rights. A similar, if not more cynical, view, is the realization that 'no one falls in love with a common market', which is why EU policy-makers have invested so much political capital in such a problematic and contested construct (Shore 2004, 28). The poverty of provisions associated with Union citizenship, as seen in the Citizenship Charter of the Maastricht Treaty where few 'new' rights were recognised for member state nationals and none duty, leads Shore to question the motives of this initiative, offering a number of plausible explanations: that the EU was frustrated at the lack of flexibility and mobility in the European labour market and wanted to create a Single Market in which citizens-workers would perceive the whole of Europe as their domestic labour market; that it was a public relations stunt; above all, that the key rationale was to strengthen the legitimation of the EU by fostering feelings of belonging, which would gradually lead into a new basis for allegiance to the Union. The side effect has been that under these circumstances, 'European citizenship' represents nothing more than a 'blank banner', 'a mobilizing metaphor' which is there to 'invent (...) a European public', thus granting EU institutions the cultural legitimacy they lack – nothing more, nothing less than a case study in 'cultural hegemony and the manufacture of consent' (: 31). Additional confusion originates from the fact that although the Treaty of Rome aimed to bring closer together the *peoples* of Europe, Union citizenship drives towards a singularly conceived European *people*, the absence of which undermines the legitimation of the entire EU project. It is not surprising, then, the fervour with which the EU cultural policy has promoted its 'Unity in diversity' concept in the attempt to mould a 'shared cultural heritage', for the only way to prevent the Union from breaking up is the construction of a European nation.

Joseph Weiler, one of the most prolific authors on European polity, argues (1999) that the EU promotes a consumer-style political style wherein the Union has become a 'product' within a context of 'brand development', and only the construction of a European 'demos' could amend this. The problem is how to create this demos without resorting to traditional nation-building activities. Weiler proposes a 'Third way', based on Habermasian 'constitutional patriotism' (Habermas 1996), whereby patriotism is separated from citizenship and EU's *supranational* identity is accentuated, and goes on to suggest the creation of co-existing 'demoi' which operate in 'concentric circles' and allow individuals to belong simultaneously to multiple demoi. The supranational EU can play a civilizing and modernizing role by decoupling political and civil rights from their nationalist framework. Shore (2004) is critical of Weiler's model of supranational citizenship, embedded on ethnocentric assumptions. Is it possible, demands Shore, to have a democracy without a demos? He thinks not because a European demos does not exist, hence to suggest that a European citizenship is established without having a European public, press, or pan-national political parties is an illusionary fabrication.

'Citizenship' as part of the EU rhetoric

A clear marker of belonging within Europe is EU citizenship, established as a direct political link between the Union and the people in an attempt to address the Union's democratic deficit. Union citizenship is not about full rights to democratic participation and representation since Article 8(1) of the Treaty of the European Union (where the European Community became the European Union, and is also known as the Maastricht Treaty) provides that 'every person holding the nationality of a member state shall be a citizen of the Union'. The rights defined in Article 8 of the Maastricht Treaty also include, among others: the right to move and reside freely within the member states; the right to vote and stand in municipal elections and in European Parliament elections (for citizens residing in member states of which they are not nationals). Such a list of citizenship rights is exceedingly limited and hardly compares with domestic understandings of citizenship. The most notable feature, nevertheless, seems to be the one founded on free movement, a right EU nationals already enjoyed – for years in many cases. In that respect, Article 8(1) seems to add nothing new (Shaw 1997). Not only that, but, as we shall see later on, Union citizenship, as stipulated in Article 8, has been heavily criticised about its failure to achieve a direct political link between the EU and its citizens, or to articulate a programme of social policies constitutive of citizenship.

In effect, only nationals of EU member states are Union citizens, and the determination of who is a national, and thus, who belongs, depends entirely on individual member states. This in itself raises several questions as to who has a legitimate right to belong to this Union. In this sense, the definition of European citizenship under the Maastricht Treaty establishes a unitary basis for *exclusion* rather than a coherent set of criteria for *inclusion*. (Bhabha 1998, 604). De Búrca corroborates this view and warns that citizenship is not necessarily an integrative force within the EU; instead, it may be exclusionary and divisive because at present it draws directly upon the notions of member-state nationality and citizenship to define the scope of membership, while excluding a priori all third-country nationals from that membership (1996; Shore 2004, 39). 'Citizenship' became part of the EC/EU discourse in the early seventies[3] and since then Union citizenship policymaking entailed the policy objectives of 'special rights' for Union citizens (right to vote and stand for elections) and a 'passport union'. Union citizenship represents a first challenge to the modern concept of Marshallian citizenship – due to its

---

[3] During the early 1970s, the policy objectives of 'special rights' for European citizens and a 'passport union' aimed at the creation of a feeling of belonging (Wiener 1997, 539). In the 1980s, citizenship practice introduced a different policy paradigm. At the time, market-making was on top of the Community agenda exemplified by Jacques Delors's 1992 policy 'Europe Without Frontiers'. This new mobility policy targeted non-worker groups as a strategy to make the best use of European human resources towards the creation of a European identity. 'Foreigners', that is Community citizens working in another member state, were awarded a series of social rights, something that served to accentuate the 'democratic deficit' of the European Community, for once citizens moved, they lost access to political participation. To overcome this, the Commission proposed the establishment of voting rights for 'foreigners' in municipal elections. During this third period of the developing practice of European citizenship, political rights were adopted and rights of free movement and residence for those employed, their families and also for other persons were stipulated. Following the fall of the Berlin Wall, two types of resources were mobilised: rights of free movement, residence, establishment, voting and standing for municipal and European elections at the place of residence were to be granted, as was the uniform passport. These resources were to receive legal status in Article 8 of the EC Treaty in Maastricht. Post-Maastricht, another debate was articulated by the European Parliament, this time requesting citizenship for every citizen holding the nationality of a member state as well as for every person residing within the territory of the EU. A few years later, in 1997, the Treaty of Amsterdam contained a number of provisions relating to human rights and amended the general principles of the Union as laid down in the Maastricht Treaty (Meehan 2000).

decoupling of rights and identity, and adhering to civic and political norms rather than ethno-cultural ties (Shore 2004; Shaw 1997; Habermas 1992; Bhabha 1998; Weiler 1999). The other stems from processes of decolonization, migration and social movement mobilization. All these suggest that what David Held calls 'the language of citizenship' has become eroded, and that democratic citizenship should be dissociated from the notion of citizenship as state membership altogether (Wiener 1999, 530). By introducing Union citizenship, the EU has borrowed an established concept with a political and legal heritage, which it has then struggled to incorporate into its own conceptual system. The problem is, however, that the 'currency' of citizenship carries a huge intellectual baggage regarding content, meaning and symbolism that cannot be side-stepped.

Let me now turn to the discussion of certain policy initiatives implemented by the EU. Why these initiatives have been selected? One reason is because they represent examples of the symbolic initiatives taken by the EU in its search for instruments of legitimization and of moulding a sense of common belonging, frequently referenced in existing literature (Sassatelli 2002; Morley and Robins 1995; Cronin 2002). Another reason, particularly as far as Culture 2000 and Priority 7 is concerned, comes from personal involvement with these policy instruments. Preparing and submitting project proposals for Culture 2000 and Priority 7 brought my attention to the almost iconic use of 'culture', 'identity' and 'citizenship' in EU cultural policy and triggered my interest in exploring them further.

'Culture 2000' describes itself as the cornerstone of EU's cultural activity, in itself the culmination of previous policy initiatives on heritage protection, translation and artistic cooperation – such as the Kaléidoscope programme, aimed at encouraging 'artistic and cultural creation and co-operation of a European dimension' and the Raphaël programme, aimed at 'supplementing member state policies in the field of cultural heritage of European importance'. All of them put an emphasis on popular culture and the media in the creation of a European cultural identity and citizenship (Cronin 2002). 'Culture 2000', initially conceived as a four-year policy initiative, but later awarded two more years of life till 2006, was adopted by the European Parliament and the Council in 2000 and aims to create a cultural area common to the European peoples by promoting cultural dialogue. In fact, the Europa-Culture homepage explicitly states that 'since its inclusion on the Treaty on the European

Union, cultural cooperation has become a new community competency'
(http://europa.eu.int/ comm/culture). Other objectives include: highlighting cultural diversity and developing new forms of cultural expression; sharing the common cultural heritage of European significance;
fostering intercultural dialogue and mutual exchange between European
and non-European cultures; improving participation in culture for as
many citizens as possible. Dance, theatre, the visual and plastic arts,
cinema, literature, music – all forms of creative activity are encouraged,
as is the conservation of cultural heritage across the Union (Culture
2000). The EU has provided for additional instruments to ensure heritage conservation, the European Regional Development Fund being a
case in point. The above Euro-lingua explicitly recognizes culture both
as an economic factor and a factor in social integration and citizenship,
and requests that all future projects under the Culture 2000 banner must
address the citizen and provide a link between tradition and innovation.

Priority 7, 'Citizens and Governance in a knowledge-based society',
of the sixth Framework Programme and the Specific Programme *Integrating and Strengthening the European Research Area*, intends to mobilise,
strengthen and integrate European research in order to understand new
forms of relationships between the citizens of Europe within an emerging knowledge-based society. This priority is broken down into seven
distinct research areas, however, direct attention on the study of 'citizenship' within the EU is channeled through the following two research
sub-divisions: (a). 'Implications of European integration and enlargement
for governance and the citizen', with the objective of clarifying European
integration and enlargement, as well as issues of democracy, and citizen
well-being. It comprises the following topics: democracy in a supranational context; new EU borders, new visions of neighbourhood; and
governance for sustainable development. (b). 'New forms of citizenship
and cultural identities', aiming at promoting citizen involvement and
participation in European policy making and studying the coexistence of
multiple identities. This sub-theme consists of the following: towards a
European public sphere; gender and citizenship in a multicultural context; and values and religion in Europe.[4]

---

[4] The other sub-divisions are: 'improving the generation, distribution and use of
knowledge and its impact on economic and social development' with the objective of
understanding the ways in which policy-making organizations learn and of assessing
the role of knowledge in the formulation and implementation of policies; 'options and

Other policy initiatives have included the 'European City of Culture', whereby selected cities receive funds to organise a wide range of cultural events and exhibitions; the EU Town-Twinning Scheme, where towns, cities and villages across Europe forge long-lasting ties; various 'Heritage days'; projects like the Netd@ys Europe and Netd@ys week, where the public at large is invited to use new technologies for education and culture and their active participation in cultural life is encouraged; the Debora project, involving digital access to books of Renaissance, and wishing to offer more access to culture and heritage to the peoples of Europe. Similarly, the EU is interested in maintaining linguistic diversity, thus actively helping to preserve regional and minority languages; encouraging language learning; and developing programmes such as eContent to produce language-engineering resources and promote European digital content; the educational and vocational training programmes of Socrates and Leonardo da Vinci, feature cultural and artistic training and tuition; audiovisual policy is served by the MEDIA programme, which intends, among other, to provide support for various workshops and film festivals, and encourage media professionals to improve their techniques. In order to 'make citizenship work', particular attention is paid to the direct involvement of European citizens in the integration process, and especially the young people. The YOUTH programme, established in 2000 to end in 2006 and with a view to adopting its successor for the period 2007-2013, intends to mobilise the participation of young people in democratic life; contribute to their active citizenship and feeling of belonging in Europe; develop their sense of solidarity and mutual understanding, and consequently contribute to European social cohesion (COM 2004b).

The Commission is taking the enlargement of the Union and the increased mobility and migratory flows resulting from the single marker seriously, and has not given up its efforts to construct a 'European citizen-

choices for the development of a knowledge-based society' with the objective of showing how a knowledge-based society can promote the EU societal objectives of the Lisbon summit; 'the variety of paths towards a knowledge society', with the objective to provide comparative perspectives across the EU; 'articulation of areas of responsibility and new forms of governance', aiming at the development of forms of multi-level governance; 'issues connected with the resolution of conflicts and restoration of peace and justice', aiming at supporting conflict resolution (FP6, Priority 7: Citizens and Governance in a knowledge-based society , Work Programme 2004-2006).

ship', as demonstrated by its proposal to declare 2008 'European Year of intercultural dialogue' (COM 2005). In more detail, intercultural dialogue is seen as a raising-awareness tool towards the promotion of active European citizenship and the implementation of the renewed Lisbon strategy for 'growth and employment in a knowledge-based society'. It is hoped that the dialogue among European citizens, 'and all those living in the Union temporarily or permanently' as the revised, all-inclusive meaning of 'active European citizenship' goes, and the initiatives planned in the fields of culture, lifelong learning, youth, and citizenship will help combat social exclusion, racism and xenophobia and contribute to European integration and cohesion. This alteration in the articulation of Union policy making marks a significant improvement from the Treaty of Maastricht.

At first look, Culture 2000 and Priority 7 yield some interesting points which highlight the need for deeper and more rigorous investigation:

233 European cultural projects have been offered grants in 2004, and another 217 pan-European projects were supported in 2005-2006, sharing 32 million and 33 million euros respectively, reads the Culture 2000 website. Cultural operators and organizations from the 25 Member States, the EEA countries (Iceland, Liechtenstein, Norway), and two acceding countries (Bulgaria and Romania) took part, leading the Commissioner for Education, Training, Culture and Multilingualism, Ján Figel to say: 'Once again, the projects selected .... are an illustration of the extreme diversity of European cultures .... [and] will actively participate in the constant development of pan-European cooperation in the field of culture' (http://europa.eu.int/rapid/pressreleases). Appearances may be deceptive, nevertheless. The fact that a large number of countries are being represented in the projects funded by Culture 2000, does not necessarily guarantee that all member states and candidate countries are *equal* participants in the culturally diverse European universe, as the following example from 2000-2002 will illustrate: cultural operators and organizations from as many as twenty-six countries were funded through Culture 2000 showing disparities in participation. There were 29 operators from Austria, 30 from Belgium, 2 from Bulgaria, 8 from the Czech Republic, 49 from Germany, 17 from Denmark, 1 from Estonia, 44 from Spain, 19 from Finland, 88 from France, 50 from Greece, 7 from Hungary, 6 from Ireland, 8 from Iceland, 114 from Italy, 6 from Lithuania, 6

from Luxembourg, 3 from Latvia, 28 from the Netherlands, 28 from Norway, 5 from Poland, 6 from Portugal, 5 from Romania, 33 from Sweden, 1 from Slovakia, and 27 from the United Kingdom. Even if these numbers were population-weighted, the inequalities in representation prevail, hence the 'purity' of the diversity argument is compromised.

As far as Priority 7 is concerned[5], in Citizens-1 (the first part of this call, open only to large-scale, big-budget network projects, Networks of Excellence and Integrated Projects) only five projects were eventually funded out of 70 proposals submitted. Two of these approved projects covered the research sub-topic 'Multilevel governance, democracy and new policy instruments', and one the sub-topic 'Migration, immigration and multiculturalism as challenges for the knowledge-based societies'. 74% of the researchers involved in the projects submitted were male, leaving women researchers in the minority, and further exacerbating Doreen Massey's argument about 'high-tech fantasies' (1991) regarding the (under)representation of women, not in science parks this time, but in a Commission-funded programme on citizenship. Citizens-2 comprised the second part of this call in 2003 and involved the much smaller in scale and budget projects, STREPs and Coordination Actions. There were 17 distinct research sub-categories available, of which the following five are more significant, in my view, for the study of European citizenship: 'Citizens' attitudes and civic values', 'Transformations in the candidate countries', 'Human rights', 'Active civic participation', and 'The European public sphere'. Of 194 proposals submitted, 39 were selected for funding. The gender ratio slightly improved in comparison to the previous part of the call, with 66% of those involved being male. Citizens-3 was again open to NoEs and Ips only, and of 169 submitted proposals, 15 were finally selected for funding. Of the 12 research topics available, I believe that five stand out as more directly relevant to the study of European citizenship: 'Social cohesion in the knowledge-based society', 'Deepening and widening of the European Union: lessons from the past and visions of the future', 'Global governance, regulatory frameworks and the role of the European Union', 'European citizenship and multiple identities', and 'Cultural dialogue and the European society'.

---

[5] I am focusing on the first call, in 2003, since there were no detailed data available for subsequent calls at the time of writing. All data and charts originate from Henry Scott at the National Documentation Centre in Athens, Greece (2005).

Another point worth pressing here, and investigating further, is the degree of diversity in Priority 7 in terms of representation in proposals either with regard to countries or to the number of participants per country. Bearing in mind the paucity of available data, it appears that a trend emerges: in terms of country participation in proposals, charts 1 and 2 indicate an uneven distribution amongst countries (either member-states, associate members or accession countries), both as regards to projects submitted (hence evaluated), and to those which passed the evaluation threshold.

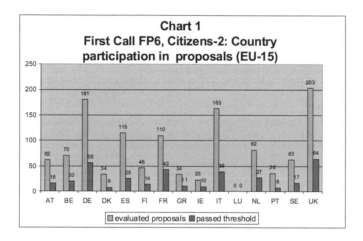

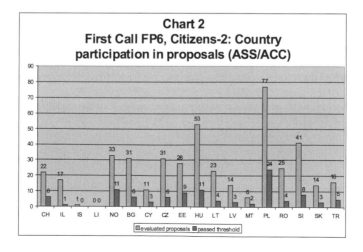

The 'big five', Germany (181 submitted proposals), Spain (115 submitted proposals), France (110), Italy (163) and the UK (203) are well above an intermediate group which comprises Austria (62 submitted proposals), Sweden (63), Belgium (70), the Netherlands (82) from EU-15, and Poland (77) and Hungary (53) from accession and associate states. A third group consists of countries such as Denmark (34), Greece (34), Portugal (30), candidate Bulgaria (31), Estonia (28), Ireland (23), and Lithuania (23). Countries such as Latvia (14), Slovakia (14), Cyprus (11), candidate Turkey (10), Malta (6), and Iceland (1) present a much lower participation rates in terms of projects submitted.

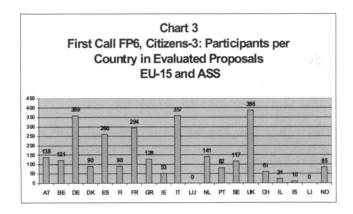

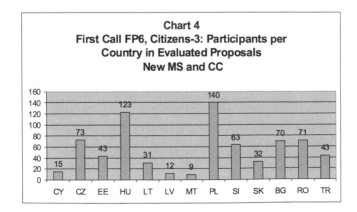

Charts 3 and 4 highlight the unevenness in the number of researchers in evaluated projects across the EU.

In this case too, there is a 'big five' group: Germany (353 partici-pants), Italy (357 participants), the UK (386), France (294), and Spain (260). An intermediate group includes countries such as the Netherlands (141), Austria (138 participants), Greece (128), Sweden (117), Hungary (123) and Poland (140); countries like Norway (80), the Czech Republic (73), candidates Bulgaria (70) and Romania (71), and Ireland (53) can be seen to form a third group, while Cyprus (15 participants), Latvia (12), Malta (9) are among those countries which demonstrate the disparity in representation across the Union.

Conclusions

In this article, I have shown that forging a European identity and citizen-ship has become an explicit target of EU policy. The extent to which policy initiatives taken by the Union have successfully managed to bring the 'common cultural heritage to the fore', as required by the Maastricht Treaty, is a different ball game, nevertheless. It may be that the EU has acknowledged 'culture' a special status, using it both as art and as enter-tainment, in order to form a common European consciousness and sense of citizenship. However, the extent to which the Union competently constructs its long-sought 'imagined European community' is still open for discussion. Also to be determined is the extent to which the Union manages to forge a notion of citizenship for its peoples. Are we witness-ing the emergence of a consumer's right to citizenship, as Anne Cronin (2002) argues, within the EU? This article has explored the ways in which the EU tries to forge and promote a sense of cultural belonging and citizenship for itself by way of a couple of cultural policy initiatives, hereby used as examples. Based on existing data at the time of writing, there is enough evidence to suggest that while a lot of ground has been covered by the EU insofar as the construction of a European demos (or demoi) is concerned, there is still much room for improvement. In fact, further research is much needed, from the part of the EU as well, if the concept of European citizenship and culture is to be fully understood and materialised.

In terms of gender representation, it appears that the EU, regardless of its wishful rhetoric, maintains existing gender disparities even within a policy initiative specifically geared towards the study of citizenship. In this respect, Framework Programme 6 merely reiterates the gender imbalance, or worse, the gender invisibility of previous European research policy agendas during the nineties, such as the 'Quality of Life' and 'Citizens First', and it seems that in the beginning of the twenty-first century we have to ask the same questions all over again: 'Why So Few (women)?' (Rose 1999, 37). 'Gender mainstreaming' (Woodford-Berger 2004), that is the social engineering of gender equality, should hence become part and parcel of Union policy, discourse and administration and not remain a wishful rhetoric. There is no available data regarding gender representation for Culture 2000. This is a blind spot which the EU should take in and monitor closely.

The fact that so many diverse research cultures appear to be represented in Priority 7 is encouraging indeed, but more in depth analysis is needed before any concrete conclusions can be drawn. It could be that this apparent diversity may be overestimated. Playing devil's advocate, I can only offer a number of possible contingent factors that may lead towards such a trend: the degree of information provision available regarding funding initiatives from the Commission, and Priority 7 more particularly; the comparative advantage of those researchers, principally from the more advanced and older member states, who have already succeeded in the past, and whose success rate, hence representation eventually, will be higher in relation to some unknown newcomers from an associate state; the degree in which researchers in any one country are driven towards Commission funding because of lack of resources in their own country. All in all, Priority 7, having the ambition to integrate European research in economic, political, social sciences and humanities, risks becoming all-inclusive, a 'one-term-covers-everything' blanket. As a result, direct attention on the study of 'citizenship' within a research priority committed to 'citizens and governance' is restricted to too few, in my view, sub-topics, which do not receive the research attention they deserve. An EU rationale on 'making European citizenship' should tackle research issues in a more coherent and targeted manner if it truly wishes for European citizenship to be appropriately studied, understood and realised, and the trust gap between civil society and the Union itself to be bridged. As far as Culture 2000 is concerned, the apparent diversity of participant countries in Culture 2000 may also run the risk of being hyped up, as mentioned above. There is significant funding disparity among countries involved – even after making allowances for a proportional representation according to population. My reading of the data is that some countries are better at the game of informal networking in Brussels than others – once again, proving the need for robust investigation.

The enlargement which took place in May 2004 has accentuated divergence within the EU and its repercussions are yet to be determined since the increased diversity can deepen the problem of legitimacy and lack of a European public sphere or a European demos. Not only that, but, in the aftermath of the enlargement process, the Union has been trying to strike the right balance between unity and diversity. Recognizing the increased diversity of the Union, the Commission has called for a holistic integration policy in order to give a concrete meaning to the notion of European citizenship (COM 2003). Union policy demands that due attention be given to encouraging citizen dialogue with institutions, citizen exchanges, and participation in cross-border projects. The Commission believes that 'by fostering the mobility of citizens, artists, cultural and audiovisual works, European citizens can take advantage (...) of the opportunities offered by their rich and diverse cultural heritage' and accepts that there is a 'developing European identity, an identity which complements those (national, regional, ethnic, religious) that citizens already have' (COM 2004a). The assertion of a common cultural identity is not without its problems, nevertheless. The 'unity in diversity' claim of European culture may work to create anxieties and a sense of cultural disorientation. Internal tensions have led to the flourishing of cultural regionalism and small nationalisms (Basques, Scots, and so on), while more and more migrant and diasporic populations living across Europe feel excluded from the European cultural psyche (Morley and Robins 1995). It may be that for some difference is a value. However, this notion of 'multiple identity' remains ambiguous, a formal solution with no substance, a superficial if successful motto that may easily fall into Eurocentric triumphalism (Sassatelli 2002, 440). Not only that but this simultaneous widening and deepening of the EU may constitute a serious challenge to the European integration process, and serves to highlight existing problems of identity, legitimacy, borders, democracy and citizenship. The point I want to press here is that the extent to which the Union is a true 'unity in diversity', deriving its legitimacy from its plurality, or whether it has a limited proclaimed diversity is still open to deliberation.

The debate around the accession of Turkey as a 'significant other' highlights this further.[6]

Despite the apparent limitations of the particular cultural policies that aim to construct the European citizen that I examined in this article, I would not like to come out as a total non-believer in the ability, or need, of the EU to invent a notion of citizenship for itself. The Commission, in its long quest for a new common European identity, an identity that allows for a high degree of diversity at the same time, has rightfully decided the implementation of a variety of cultural policies. The initiatives mentioned above and those examined more closely, are, in my view, steps in the right direction and do indeed articulate 'a new politics of cultural belonging' for the EU. What is now needed is an introspective look and an evaluation of the work done so far so as to identify weaknesses and monitor gaps. In this way, the next round of cultural policy initiatives introduced by the Commission will work better towards the construction of a European citizenship and culture. And the much sweated for diversity may not suffer as a result.

References

Aron, Raymond. 1974. Is Multinational Citizenship Possible?. *Social Research* 41 (4): 638-656.

Baykal, Sanem. 2005. Unity in Diversity? The Challenge of Diversity for the European Political Identity, Legitimacy and Democratic Governance: Turkey's EU Membership as the Ultimate Test Case. *Jean Monnet Working Paper 09/05*. New York University School of Law.

Bhabha, Jaqueline. 1998. Get Back to Where You Once Belonged': Identity, Citizenship, and Exclusion in Europe. *Human Rights Quarterly* 20(3): 592-627.

---

[6] Baykal makes a very interesting case, tying inextricably the future of the EU as a 'European' collective political identity to its decision on Turkish membership, and argues that the challenge of diversity is multiplied both by the size of Turkey as a prospective member, and by the perception of the country as non-European. Turkey's accession, if realised at all, will alter the perception of the Union as a rich, western, Judeo-Christian entity (2005: 8-9). The basic rationale of enlargement was the democratisation and liberalization of the former Eastern Bloc countries, mainly because it was seen as a moral obligation, a kinship-based duty of inclusion of the 'kidnapped West'. The inclusion of Malta and the Greek Cyprus can be explained on the basis that these countries constituted the 'us', were 'European' that is, for the EU. Inclusion of Turkey has never been seen in a similar frame (26).

Bondebjerg, Ib and Peter Golding, eds. 2004. *European Culture and the Media*. Volume 1. *Changing Media-Changing Europe Series*. Bristol: intellect.

Búrca de, Gráinne. 1996. The Quest for Legitimacy in the European Union. *Modern Law Review* 59: 356-361.

COM. 2003. 336 final of 3.6.2003 on *Immigration, Integration and Employment*.

COM. 2004a. 154 final of 9.3.2004 on *Making Citizenship Work: Fostering European Culture and Diversity Through Programmes for Youth, Culture, Audiovisual and Civic Participation*.

COM. 2004b. 471 final of 14.7.2004 on *Creating the YOUTH IN ACTION Programme for the Period 2007-2013*.

COM. 2005. 467 final of 5.10.2005 on *Concerning the European Year of Intercultural Dialogue (2008)*.

Cronin, Anne M. 2002. Consumer Rights/Cultural Rights. A New Politics of European Belonging. *European Journal of Cultural Studies* 5(3): 307-323.

Department of Culture, Media and Sport. 1998. *Creative Industries-Mapping Document*. London: DCMS.

Diamandouros, Nikiforos. 1994. Cultural Dualism and Political Change in Postauthoritarian Greece. Estudio/Working Paper 1994/50, Centro de Estudios Avanzados en Ciencias Sociales, Instituto Juan March.

European Commission. 2000. *Culture 2000 Framework Programme: Specifications for 2006*. DG for Education and Culture/ Decision No 508/2000/EC.

European Commission. 2002. *e-Europe: An Information Society for All*. Luxembourg: European Communities.

European Task Force on Culture and Development (ETCD). 1997. *In from the Margins: A Contribution to the Debate on Culture and Development in Europe*. Strasbourg: Council of Europe.

Falk, Richard. (1994), 'The Making of Global Citizenship', in van Steenbergen, B. (ed), *The Conditions of Citizenship*, London: Sage.

Habermas, Jurgen. 1996. The European Nation State, its Achievements and its Limitations: on the Past and Future of Sovereignty and Citizenship. *Ratio Juris* 9(2): 125-137.

Habermas, Jürgen. 1992. Citizenship and National Identity: Some Reflections on the Future of Europe. *Praxis International* 12(1): 1-19.

Jamieson, Lynn. 2002. Theorising Identity, Nationality and Citizenship: Implications for European Citizenship Identity. *Sociológia* 34(6): 507-532.

Kleberg, Carl-Johan. 2000. The Concept of Culture in the Stockholm Action Plan and its Consequences for Policy Making. *International Journal of Cultural Policy* 7(1): 49-69.

Lehning, Percy B. 2001. European Citizenship: Towards a European Identity?. *Law and Philosophy* 20: 239-282.

Lister, Ruth. 1997. Citizenship: Towards a Feminist Synthesis. *Feminist Review* 57: 28-48.

Marshall, T. H. (1992)1950. *Citizesnhip and Social Class*. London: Pluto.

Mcguigan, Jim. 2004. *Rethinking Cultural Policy*. Maidenhead: Open University Press.

Meehan, Elizabeth. 1997. Political Pluralism and European Citizenship. In *Citizenship, Democracy and Justice in the New Europe*, eds. Percy B. Lehning and Albert Weale, 69-85. London: Routledge.

Meehan, Elizabeth. 2000. *Citizenship and the European Union*. Center for European Integration Studies, Bonn. Discussion paper C63, http://www/zei.de. Accessed January 2006.

Morley, David and Kevin Robins, 1995. *Spaces of Identity: Global Media, Electronic Landscapes and Cultural Boundaries*. London: Routledge.

Mouzelis, Nikos. 1995. Greece in the Twenty-first Century: Institutions and Political Culture. In *Greece Prepares for the Twenty-first Century*, eds. Dimitris Constas and Theodore Stavrou. Baltimore: John Hopkins University Press.

Neveu, Catherine. 2001. European Citizenship, Citizens of Europe and European Citizen. In *An Anthropology of the European Union*, eds. I. Bellier and T. Wilson. Oxford: Berg.

Preuss, Ulrich. K., Michelle Everson, Mathias Koenig-Archibugi, and Edwige Lefebvre. 2003. Traditions of Citizenship in the European Union. *Citizenship Studies* 7(1): 3-12.

Riley, Denise. 1992. Citizenship and the Welfare State. In *Political and Economic Forms of Modernity*, eds. John Allen, Peter Braham and Paul Lewis. Cambridge: Polity Press.

Rose, Hilary. 1999. A Fair Share of the Research Pie or Re-Engendering Scientific and Technological Europe? *The European Journal of Women's Studies* 6: 31-47.

Sassatelli, Monica. 2002. Imagined Europe: The Shaping of a European Cultural Identity through EU Cultural Policy. *European Journal of Social Theory* 5(4): 435-451.

Sassen, Saskia. 1996. *Losing Control? Sovereignty in an Age of Globalization*. New York: Columbia University Press.

Shaw, Jo. 1997. European Citizenship: The IGC and Beyond. *European Integration online Papers*. http://eiop.or.at/eiop/texte/1997-003a.htm. Accessed January 2006.

Shore, Cris. 2004. Whither European Citizenship? Eros and Civilization Revisited. *European Journal of Social Theory* 7(1): 27-44.

Soysal, Yasmin. N. 1994. *Limits of Citizenship: Migrant and Postnational Membership in Europe*. Chicago: University of Chicago Press.

Van Steenbergen, Bart.1994. Towards a Global Ecological Citizen. In *The Condition of Citizenship*, ed. Bart van Steenbergen. London: Sage.

Weiler, Joseph. H. H .1999. *The Constitution of Europe: 'Do the New Clothes Have An Emperor?' and Other Essays on European Integration*. Cambridge: Cambridge University Press.

Weiler, Joseph. H. H. 1997. To be a European Citizen: Eros and Civilization. *Journal of European Public Policy* 4(4): 495-519.

Weiler, Joseph. H. H. 1995. Does Europe Need a Constitution? Reflections on Demos, Telos and the German Maastricht Decision. *European Law Journal* 1: 219-253.

Wiener, Antje. 1997. Making Sense of the New Geography of Citizenship: Fragmented Citizenship in the European Union. *Theory and Society* 26: 529-560.

Williams, Raymond.1984. State Culture and Beyond. In *Culture and the State*, ed. L Apignanesi, 3-5. London: Institute of Contemporary Arts.

Woodford-Berger, Prudence. 2004. Gender Mainstreaming: What is it (About) and Should We Continue Doing it? IDS Bulletin 35(4): 65-72.

World Commission on Culture and Development (WCCD). 1996. *Our Creative Diversity*. Paris: UNESCO.

EUROPEAN STUDIES 24 (2007): 183-202

THE EU AND THE PRESS:
POLICY OR NON-POLICY?

David Hutchison

Abstract

Several aspects of the current situation of the newspaper press in the EU are discussed, and attention is drawn to significant economic and social trends. The reluctance of the Commission to deal with the issues of pluralism and concentration of ownership is noted, and the impact of other EU interventions and non-EU interventions on the operations of the press in the countries of the Union is considered. It is suggested that the EU will increasingly have to engage in debate on the limits on free speech and, in that context, an analysis of the reactions to the publication of cartoons depicting the prophet Muhammad by a Danish newspaper in 2005 is offered. Finally, it is suggested that non-intervention may not be a sustainable policy.

Introduction

There is much about the media to be found on the Europa website of the EU: one page on 'Media in the Information Society' tells the reader:

> The European Commission deals with media. Its policy objective is to contribute towards creating a genuine 'European media area' that guarantees and reinforces citizens' choices, particularly as regards television or radio channels and programmes and the press, by ensuring freedom of establishment for companies in the media sector and the free movement of the services they offer (Europa 2005).

This statement is not accompanied, as one might expect, by an image derived from television or the cinema, areas in which the EU has taken initiatives in the shape of the Television Without Frontiers Directive and the MEDIA programme, but by a picture of a middle aged man reading

what looks like an upmarket newspaper. The irony here is that the EU
has apparently opted out of major interventions in the press policy arena,
most obviously in its abandonment of action in the matter of concentration of ownership in relation to pluralism of expression. The question
might then be 'does the EU have any press policy at all?' This chapter
aims to seek answers to that question, and in doing so it will consider the
overall position of the press in the EU and highlight critical issues currently facing it. The emphasis will be on newspapers rather than magazines, not only because of space constraints but also because it is in
newspapers - and journals of comment and reporting - that issues of
public policy are most discussed in the print media.

The Press in the EU

Newspaper circulations vary remarkably in the countries of the Union,
ranging from 450 copies per thousand inhabitants per day in Sweden,
through 310 in the Netherlands to 90 in Greece and 38 in Portugal; high
consumption is much more a northern than a southern European habit.
(Bens 2004, 18). Circulations generally are falling throughout the Western world. A Staff Working Paper produced by the Commission, which
makes the point that within the publishing sector in the 25 member
states newspapers account for 36.8% of that sector and Periodicals
31.9% (European Union 2005, 10), goes on to comment:

> The decline in newspaper circulation in Europe has been ongoing for two
> decades, with little sign of recovery. Evidence from research suggests that
> the decline is general across all age groups. Taking into account that circula-
> tion has also been falling in the US and Japan, it seems reasonable to as-
> sume that this decline is of a structural nature (Ibid, 22).

It should be noted however that the World Association of Newspapers is
rather more upbeat on the matter, and claims 2004 as a positive year,
since circulation worldwide went up two per cent, and in the five-year
period ending then, by almost five per cent (World Association of Newspapers 2005, 3). But most of the circulation gains have been in Asia,
South America and Africa, although the drop in the EU overall is as little
as 0.7% in one year and 0.4% in five. However circulation increases in
several countries in the five year period – Austria (3%), Ireland (29%)
and Poland, (44%), for example – were counterbalanced by declines in
rather more countries, with significant drops in for example Germany
(8%), France (6%) and the United Kingdom (11%).

The current situation then may not be one of significant decline across the EU taken as a whole, but in major countries that is the reality. It is not difficult to enumerate the factors which have contributed to this decline: increased competition from other media, the growth of the Internet, the inelasticity of time devoted to media activity (people do have other pursuits with which to occupy themselves) are among the more obvious causes which can be adduced. In addition, there is the matter of the orientation towards public affairs of many young people: as Williams has commented, ' (they) … have exerted their spending power on a range of other media and leisure activities, such as popular music, drinking, clubbing and eating out, which are seen as more preferable pastimes than newspaper reading' (Williams 2005, 32). What must be starting to concern newspaper executives is whether there is a plateau on which circulations will bottom out or whether the decline will continue indefinitely. Companies have tried a range of strategies in order to counteract the decline, the most striking of which is the introduction by the Swedish company Kinnevik, of its free *Metro* daily papers which now have a circulation of five million copies per day across Europe (*Guardian* 28.11.05). These are financed entirely by advertising and the operation is claimed to be profitable but, certainly from the perspective of a reader of *Le Monde* or *Die Welt,* it is hard to regard *Metro* as anything other than a condensed version of a newspaper proper, and indeed it is is difficult not to see it as a dangerous innovation, for if the consumer can have a newspaper with a brief but adequate summary of what is going on in the world free of charge, why should he/she pay money for an expanded version? On-line versions of titles seem a rather better way of seeking to compensate for circulation declines, provided adequate revenue can be raised through advertising and subscriber charges.

The British observer always has to remember that the structure of the newspaper market in the UK is not typical. London based titles dominate throughout England and Wales, and even in Scotland, which has historically had a strong press of its own, they have a very significant share of the market. The reasons for this pattern are rooted in history. Strong regional titles existed in the earlier part of the nineteenth century but as the railways expanded and printing technology became more efficient, it was possible for the capital's newspapers to exploit their closeness to the centre of government, and print in London from the early evening on, then employ the British railway network, which radiates to and from the capital in a way that is much less true of continental countries, to ensure that copies were available in the most populous parts of the land by early the next morning. That was not possible in France or in Germany, which in any case was only in the process of becoming the nation state it now is in the latter part of the nineteenth century. Overnight distribution of titles produced in capital cities in Scandinavian countries like Norway and Sweden was obviously a geographic impossibility in landscapes of mountains and fjords. So it is not surprising that to this day the best selling newspaper in France is not the Paris based *Le Figaro* but *France Ouest*, and while Germany does have the national mass circulation *Bild*, many of its leading newspapers are regionally based; in Sweden, although metropolitan newspapers have become much more important than once they were, there are still a large number of provincial daily titles. Clearly political factors are at work alongside the geographical ones. In the case of Germany, for example, there are strong provincial governments in the Länder with accompanying strong regional identities. There is perhaps a parallel here with the situation in the USA, where, although modern satellite technology has enabled a paper like the *New York Times* to become in effect a national title, and *USA Today* to be established as the country's first coast to coast newspaper, it is striking how regional loyalties have been only slightly eroded, so that *USA Today*, despite its efforts to woo readers since its inception in 1987, has struggled to reach a circulation of two million, which is very low in relation to the potential market.

What does not vary so much across Europe is the growth of concentration of ownership. This is a reflection of the situation worldwide. As in the United States a company like Gannett is one of three dominant players, so in Germany the Axel Springer company has over 20% of the daily market (Kleinstuber 2004, 80), and in Britain the Murdoch dominated Newscorp has over 30% of that market by circulation (Tunstall 2004, 263). A similar process has taken place in France, Italy and elsewhere in Western Europe (Kelly et alii 2004, passim). The situation in the former Eastern Bloc countries is similar: indeed the growth of concentration in the newspaper markets there is startling. Gulyas has calculated that between 1992 and 2003 the two largest groups in the Czech Republic and Hungary increased their shares of the national dailies market from around 30% to over 70% (Gulyas 2006, 18). Gulyas also notes the tendency in these countries for control of media companies in gen-

eral to pass into foreign hands, with the market share in the daily newspaper markets of non-indigenous companies having reached 70% in the
case of Hungary and 80% in the case of the Czech Republic by 2003
(ibid, 14). The German companies, Springer and Bertelsmann, and the
Norwegian conglomerate Orkla have been particularly active. Expansion
abroad is not only a feature of the Eastern European scene. Newscorp,
which, depending on how one configures it, is either Australian or American, has acquired publications in many other parts of the globe, while
the Gannett company through its British subsidiary, Newsquest, has
been building up a strong position in British weeklies and regional dailies, but the speed with which the Eastern European press has been
acquired by foreign investors is remarkable.

Another common feature of the ownership pattern throughout Europe, as elsewhere, is cross media involvement. Companies with interests
in one medium often have interests in others and indeed in non-media
businesses. So, for example, Bertelsmann, which began life as a publisher
of bibles in the nineteenth century, has interests in its home country of
Germany in both press and broadcasting, while also owning publishing
companies in the United States. The French company Vivendi, until a
rapid decline in fortunes in recent years, amassed a range of interests
including water companies in France – its base operation – and Universal Studios in the USA.

Such organisations are not at liberty to buy and sell just as they
please. They face domestic and foreign restrictions on their operations.
Many European countries have provisions in place to limit concentration
within specific sectors and across sectors. In the United Kingdom, for
example, powerful newspaper companies when they go on the acquisition trail can find their proposals subject to public interest tests by government agencies and by the media regulator Ofcom. In Germany early
in 2006 KEK (Kommission zur Ermittlung der Konzentration in
Medienbereich), the German regulatory body, blocked a proposed take-
over by the Springer group of ProSiebenSat.1, the country's largest commercial broadcaster, on the grounds that the new entity would have too
great a potential sway over public opinion. The decision produced a
sharp response from Springer's chief executive: 'What ... (the regulators)
... have overlooked is a global shift in media competition into digital
distribution markets – as though that were some kind of delusion of new

economic yuppies gone wild. This opinion is not only false, it's negligent (*Guardian* 11.1. 2006).

This line, much favoured by such individuals, emphasises both the growth of digital media and the international context in which companies now operate, and as such it does mirror some of the thinking at Commission level in the EU.

Newspapers are financed by sales and advertising. The balance varies from country to country and also by type of newspaper, with, for example, the British mass circulation titles traditionally drawing around half of their income from advertising, while upmarket titles tend to rely for 60-70% of their revenue on this source. 50-60% is the current norm across Europe (European Union 2005, 20). The major difference between the United Kingdom and the European mainland is the existence of subsidies in many countries, subsidies which are designed to bolster publications which might otherwise be put out of business by stronger competitors. Norway and Sweden have the most developed systems of subsidy and offer the same justification, namely that in the interests of pluralism of news sources and opinion, it is civically desirable that public money be provided to sustain titles which the market left to itself would not support. Sweden, with a population of nine million, currently spends €56m annually on its programme (Swedish Press Subsidies Council 2005). Subsidy schemes are also to be found in countries as different as Austria and France. In addition, many countries offer other aid such as grants and loans for capital equipment, subsidised telcommunications, cheap postal rates and lower rates of VAT than are generally levelled. The Anglo American reaction to subsidy is often hostile, but it can also be sympathetic, if careful to note the potential pitfalls:

> … he who pays the piper can often call the tune. State support for the press, it has been pointed out, can result in an unwelcome dependency on state beneficence. Newspapers which feed from the hand of the state might not always be disposed optimally to perform their watchdog function. They may not hold the political executive to the same degree of account that genuine financial independence might allow for (Humphreys 1996,107).

And even a continental observer such as Murschetz, having examined subsidy regimes in four European countries, expresses doubts about the effectiveness of such policies and their sensitivity to changing market conditions (Murschetz 1998). It should be noted however that when commentators from the other side of the Atlantic berate such schemes they often forget that in the United States the Newspaper Intervention Act has allowed competing titles to merge their commercial operations in defiance of free market principles (Hutchison 1999, 171). And the continuing process of concentration in the US and the UK ought to give Anglo-American observers some pause for thought about the limitations of the free-market model when it comes to the sustaining of pluralism of ownership.

It has been argued that there is a marked difference between European and Anglo-American styles of journalism, with the latter much more fact oriented and the former more willing to mix opinion and fact, and indeed to see journalism as a branch of political activism (Williams 2005). It is certainly true that papers like the *New York Times* and the *Daily Telegraph* pride themselves on reporting what is going on in the world with reasonable accuracy and on containing rather more hard news than *Le Monde*, for example, does. On the other hand, the British mass market press does not pretend to offer its readers a diet of political and social facts, but presents a mixture of slanted news, opinion, gossip and celebrity chat, while more upmarket titles in the UK have in recent years expanded the ranks of their columnists/commentators at the expense of their news coverage. The UK press could therefore be said to contain both the 'objective' and 'committed' styles, and although the distinction has traditionally paralleled the upmarket/mass market one, the recent move of the *Independent* towards being a 'viewspaper' has blurred that distinction. In a recent challenging study Hallin and Mancini have argued that to understand Western journalism as a whole we need to forsake the libertarian and social responsibility models as articulated half a century ago in Siebert, Peterson and Schramm's *Four Theories of the Press*, in favour of three new models. These they call, rather inelegantly, Mediterranean/Polarised Pluralist, Northern European/Democratic Corporatist and North Atlantic/Liberal; furthermore, they argue that when one subjects the media–state–citizen relationship to detailed scrutiny country by country, many hybrid cases emerge (Hallin and Mancini 2004). A proper judgement on the continuing prevalence of distinctive and varying approaches to news and comment throughout the European press calls for rather more linguistic expertise and textual analysis than the present writer - with only a working knowledge of French, very poor German and Italian glimpsed fitfully through its progenitor, Latin, to draw on - has at his disposal, or is able to engage in.

One matter, which can be discussed with some confidence however is the issue of professional regulation, which varies from country to country. Sometimes this is done on a voluntary basis, sometimes on a statutory or quasi-statutory one. In Sweden the Press Council and Press Ombudsman ensure that a Code of Ethics is adhered to, the Council having the power to issue adjudications, which must be published by the newspaper concerned, and to levy small fines. A Press Complaints Commission exists in the United Kingdom and its Code of Practice is supposed to be adhered to by all British journalists but the Commission is operated and financed by the press on a voluntary basis, in marked contrast to the way in which complaints about broadcasting are dealt with in Britain, for Ofcom has the power, rather like the Swedish Press Council, to issue adjudications and to levy fines; the UK Press Complaints Commission does require its adjudications to be published but it has no power to impose financial penalties. There are a number of codes of practice in different sectors of the French press but no national one, while in Hungary the Association of Hungarian Journalists has promulgated a Code of Journalistic Ethics and can impose sanctions, including temporary suspension of membership of the Association, on those who break it. In Germany there is also a Press Council and, in addition, a statutory right of reply. The Television Without Frontiers Directive has required such a right since its first promulgation, and there has recently been discussion about that provision being extended into the electronic sphere. The reaction of the European Newspaper Publishers Association, which claims to represent 5000 titles in 24 countries, is less than enthusiastic at such a prospect; the Association is clearly worried that the German system might at some point be applied much more widely:

> ENPA is not aware of any problems which have risen as a result of the lack of a European enforced right-of-reply. The situation has evolved that a different system regulating right-of-reply applies between Member States, but this does not affect competitiveness in ENPA's opinion because of the predominately national identity of newspapers in Europe. The right-of-reply practice according to each Member State rather than at European level is effective because it suits the legal environment of that Member State (ENPA 2005a, 5).

While the argument here is couched in economic terms, specifically in relation to on-line versions of titles, it is obvious that ENPA would be very resistant to any EU wide initiative in the traditional print sphere too. In its opposition to an extension of the scope of the TWF Directive to on-line material, the proprietors have the active sympathy of the UK government, whose Broadcasting Minister announced early in 2006 that he was seeking the support of other member states in order to block regulation of new media services; the Commission's proposals, he stated would mean 'the creation of a basic tier of pan-European content regulation of the Internet' (*Guardian* 26.1.06). This was said despite the relevant Commissioner's declaration a few months earlier that she had no wish to move in such a direction, although it was clear that she did want to take action against some on-line operators such as purveyors of child pornography and racial hatred (Reding 2005a).

The EU approach to date

It is not only right of reply provision, which concerns the newspaper companies. In responding in 2005 to a Commission Issues Paper on Media Pluralism published as part of the on-going debate about the revision of the TWF Directive, ENPA was forceful in its rejection of any suggestion that an EU wide initiative was needed – 'Regulation of media pluralism is a matter for the Member States... which is subject to the subsidiarity principle' (ENPA 20005b 1). In the same paper the proprietors go on to argue that there are many benefits arising from media consolidation, and while there has been an increase in concentration of press ownership in national markets, 'the impact of this concentration must be taken in its relative context.' (Ibid 5). The views of MEPs are cited in support of this position, which is intriguing, given that, as Sarikakis points out in her study of the European Parliament's involvement in media policy, that body has constantly pressurised a reluctant Commission to take an anti-concentration initiative (Sarikakis 2001, passim). It is certainly true that the Commission did indeed publish a Green Paper on the matter in 1992 and engaged in fairly lengthy consultation prior to publishing a draft Directive in 1996, but ultimately, in the face of sustained opposition from media businesses, it decided no action would be taken at EU level. As Doyle has pointed out, 'at the collective European as well as at the national level, the perceived economic opportunity costs of restricting indigenous media firms have completely overshadowed concerns about safeguarding pluralism' (Doyle 2002, 166). Early in 2006 the Parliament rather plaintively reminded the Commission that it had 'long demanded' that a Green Paper on concentration of ownership be produced, without much hope, one suspects, of a positive response from Brussels (European Parliament 2006).

Yet there are signs that the Commission does continue to be concerned about the problem. There have been specific interventions under Competition Legislation, (ibid 167ff), and the Staff Working Paper referred to earlier on the EU Publishing Sector has much to say about how the position of the press might be strengthened through improving productivity and efficiency, and sustained by cheap and effective postal services, particularly for periodicals, but the Paper is also concerned with 'the potential of publishing ... (in promoting) ... the diversity of opinion and culture that the peoples of Europe need in order to derive the richest benefits from the information society' (European Commission 2005, 5). The convolutions of the Commission on the matter are discussed in far more detail elsewhere in this volume, but it does seem likely that for the foreseeable future it will be left to a body outside the EU, the Council of Europe, to agitate at the pan-national level, and to argue that 'Competition regulation does not give a satisfactory protection against media concentrations which are contrary to freedom of expression and information, and to the level of media pluralism which is desirable in a democratic society' (Council of Europe 2002, 11).

The issue is a complex one, and it does not necessarily follow that pluralism of ownership will automatically lead to a diversity of views being expressed, for it is perfectly possible to envisage a situation where, despite diversified ownership, there might be remarkable unanimity of social and political perspectives. That would normally favour the right, since newspapers are businesses and business tends to be politically conservative. In practice reality is a little less tidy than that. What is clear however is that while pluralism of ownership does not necessarily guarantee diversity of perspectives, concentration of ownership, whether at national or pan-national levels, almost inevitably means a restriction of perspectives.

Relegating action on the concentration of ownership front to member States does make it easier for the EU to avoid discussing the awkward fact that subsidies and other financial measures in various countries have produced widely differing environments in which newspapers operate. To say there is a lack of uniformity is to put it mildly and there can be little doubt that such variations in the commercial television arena would produce an immediate response from the Commission. But of course there is a crucial difference between the two areas: in one there is significant cross-border traffic, whereas in the other there is considerably less. Newspapers are very much of their own time and place, which is one reason why, to take an example from the other side of the Atlantic, Canadian cinema and television may have been swamped by American material, but the newspaper market has been only marginally affected; on the other hand, the Canadian magazine market has been significantly penetrated by American publications, despite several government initiatives designed to counter the cross border flow (Hutchison 2002). Where there is a common language, as in the case of Austria and Germany or southern Belgium and France, there is bound to be some cross border traffic. And, to take the first case, there are clearly barriers to open competition, since Austria subsidises the press in a variety of ways but Germany does not. One can only assume that this is a sleeping dog the Commission would rather let alone, and the failure to act on the concentration issue makes it easier to do so.

Despite the reluctance to take initiatives on that front, the fact remains that because of the sheer quantity of EU legislation, there is a significant impact on press policy in the member states. A few examples can be cited. The UK Office of Fair Trading decreed in 2004 that in order for British competition law to be aligned with the relevant EU law, then the existing monopolies granted to individual wholesale distributors of newspapers and magazines in specific geographical areas would be ended. Under the terms of the current provision, in return for this regional monopoly, a wholesaler guarantees that all outlets, from supermarkets to corner shops, will be supplied with whatever newspapers and magazines they request, the clear understanding being that there is significant cross subsidy within each distribution network. The OFT proposal to remove magazines from this arrangement - at one point it seemed intent on removing newspapers also - has led many in the trade to predict that it would inevitably mean that wholesalers, now under pressure from competitors, would ignore small outlets in favour of supermarkets; this could ultimately mean the closure of many corner shops and the disappearance of more specialist magazine titles (*UK Press Gazette* 18.3.2005). In the face of a skilful campaign organised by the periodicals industry, which has succeeded in making an effective case, the OFT has delayed its final decision, which at the time of writing is still awaited. What is already clear is that if the OFT were to persist with its original proposal, the EU, not a popular institution in the UK at the best of times, would be perceived to be the villain of the piece, and one which is actively contriving to diminish pluralism in the British magazine sector, however unjust such a conclusion might be.

The Commission called in September 2005 for a media code of conduct designed to ensure that broadcasting and the press do not offer help, deliberately or accidentally, to terrorists. While it is clearly the Internet which is most open to criticism in this regard – and perhaps the terrorism issue is one of the factors which has persuaded the Commission to begin talking about regulating the Internet, as it did in 2005 – the press will be affected by whatever initiative is developed. One can see how in countries with large Islamic populations, enforcing any code will be, to say the least, complicated.

The Market Abuse Directive, which appeared in 2002, requires that financial journalists who recommend specific share purchases to readers are obliged to make certain that nothing they publish could be open to the accusation that it is misinformation. The sanctions against those found to have breached this law include jail terms, although the EU did agree to an amendment to the Directive, which means that account must be taken in any specific case of the role of self-regulatory mechanisms – such as Codes of Conduct and Press Councils – in the relevant states.

The European Court of Human Rights is also having an increasing impact on the press in EU and non-EU countries alike. After several German publications printed pictures of her cycling, shopping and sunbathing, Princess Caroline of Monaco won a ruling in 2004, which drew on Article Eight of the Convention on Human Rights on Privacy, as against Article Ten on Free Speech, to the effect that private photographs taken without the consent of the individual concerned, and in which there was no legitimate public interest, should not be published. It would appear that this ruling was in the mind of a court in Munich in 2005 when it awarded damages to a gay man who was photographed in an intimate embrace at a festival in Würzburg; two years after the festival the picture appeared in a Munich tabloid purporting to illustrate the gay scene in that city, and as a consequence the man's sexual orientation became known to his family, which up until that point had been unaware of it (*UK Press Gazette* 7.10.05).

The Court also works to protect journalists – and may even do so to protect them from the EU! The case of the Belgian Hans-Martin Tillack illustrates this. In 2002 Tillack published an article in the German magazine *Stern* which drew on a leaked EU memorandum on fraud. The relevant EU department, the Anti-Fraud Office, sought aid from both the Belgian and German police. The latter declined to act, but the former decided to consider whether there had been a breach of professional secrecy and raided the journalist's home and office, seizing various records and papers. After the EU Court of Justice supported the Anti-Fraud Office, Tillack indicated that he would take his case to the ECHR, and, in what looked like a move born of embarrassment, the Belgian government proposed a law guaranteeing the protection of journalistic sources, a legal provision which had not existed prior to 2004; and one which British journalists, for example, who do not enjoy the same protection, can only envy (*Daily Telegraph 18.10.04, UK Press Gazette* 22.4.05).

Courts in one EU country may seek to have an impact on journalistic practice in another. In 2003, for example, the then German chancellor, Gerhard Schröder, obtained an injunction from a court in his own country in an endeavour to stop the British *Mail on Sunday* from repeating allegations it had made about the politician's supposed affair with a a television presenter. The paper gleefully denounced the Chancellor under the headline 'Sorry, Herr Schröder, but you don't rule Britain…at least not yet', and went on to claim that there was a proposal, driven by the Germans and the French, to introduce an EU wide privacy law (*Mail on Sunday* 19.1.03). Even more extraordinary was the attempt in 2005 by the Barclay Brothers, owners of the *Daily Telegraph* to sue the rival *Times* newspaper in the French courts over allegations about how the Barclays were conducting their business in France. Their motive for doing so appears to have been the prospect of a rather faster procedure than would normally be available in the English courts. (*Guardian* 25.4.05).

The Commission could legitimately regard all of these cases as incidental, even when they involve EU legislation, as the British magazine case does, in that they do not arise because of the existence of any specific press policies promulgated by the Union. However there is one rather difficult area where, even in the absence of specific policy, it is hard to see how interventions can be avoided. The European Union is an association of democratic liberal states, in which it is to be expected that freedom of the press is a given; Chapter 2 of the Union's Charter of

Fundamental Rights refers specifically to 'freedom of expression and information'. Yet in recent years, there have been a number of disturbing events. At the beginning of 2006 Andrzej Marek, editor of a Polish weekly magazine, was jailed, having been convicted of libelling a public official whom his publication had accused of obtaining his post through blackmail, and of using it to advance the interests of his advertising agency (International Press Institute 2006); he served two days before Poland's highest constitutional court suspended his sentence. Early in 2005 in the same country the eminent journalist Jerzy Urban was found guilty of insulting the head of a foreign state in his satirical magazine after he berated the then Pope for staying in office as his health declined, and employed lavatorial references to make his point; Urban was spared jail but was fined (*UK Press Gazette* 4. 3.05). It is not only in the newer member states that such cases arise. The Italian journalist, Oriana Fallaci, in mid-2005 found herself in court accused by the president of the Muslim Union of Italy of insulting the Muslim faith in a book she had just published (*UK Press Gazette* 3.6.05). This particular case echoes the Urban one in Poland, for it turns on two different approaches to the place of religion in society: are religious beliefs an entirely private matter, or are some of them so important that the state is required to offer them protection? And if that is the case, how is the state supposed to deal with radically different views of the relationship between politics and religion within one country? And how should a pan-national body like the European Union respond to the dilemma?

That question raised itself dramatically in the early part of 2006. In September 2005 the Danish newspaper *Jyllands-Posten* published a series of cartoons depicting the prophet Muhammad. The paper had commissioned the cartoons, on learning that a Danish writer who was working on a book about the prophet aimed at children, apparently found that he could not persuade artists to produce illustrations, as they feared criticism and possible physical violence, since for large sections of Muslim opinion such depictions are inherently blasphemous. The paper decided to test the limits of free speech in Denmark by commissioning the cartoons. To non-Muslims some seem straightforward enough, one for example has the prophet leading a donkey, but others are clearly designed to cause controversy: one shows the prophet with a turban in the shape of a bomb, while another has him telling suicide bombers at the entrance to heaven 'Stop, stop, we have run out of virgins', a clear reference to the promise apparently made to some young men who set out on suicide bombing missions that they will be rewarded with forty virgins in the after life. Many Muslims in Denmark were offended, and then, after being visited by a delegation of Danish imams, several Islamic countries demanded apologies from the Danish government, and a boycott of Danish goods began. Denmark's Prime Minister initially robustly defended the freedom of the paper to publish; when, at the end of January 2006 *Jyllands-Posten* apologised for offence caused, though still insisted that it had the right to publish, the Prime Minister welcomed the apology but did again make the point that he had no power to censor the press. By this juncture other papers had reproduced the cartoons, apparently as an act of solidarity with *Jyllands-Posten*. So readers of several Norwegian titles, and of *France Soir*, *Die Welt*, and *Magyar Hírlap* could form their own judgement, something British readers were initially unable to do other than through the Internet – the *Guardian* and *Times* helpfully provided the relevant link while declining to print the cartoons – although several broadcasters showed them briefly in television news bulletins. Protest escalated to a remarkable degree and armed militants in Gaza made violent threats against citizens of Norway, Denmark and Germany and forced the EU's office to close. There are ironies here: the EU is a major financial supporter of the Palestinian Authority; the militants appeared to be bearing out the points made by at least two of the cartoonists; and, as anyone with a knowledge of European history knows, medieval Islamic Spain was far more tolerant of Jews and Christians than the Catholic Castilian regime which succeeded it was of Muslims. As the temperature rose, Danish government property in the Middle East was incinerated and in Afghanistan several people died when police opened fire on demonstrators.

The response of a number of national leaders in Europe, particularly in France and Germany, was supportive of the right to publish, and the proposition that free speech inevitably means the right to cause offence; the British Foreign Secretary however criticised the re-publication of the cartoons as 'disrespectful' (BBC News 2.3.06). The reactions of EU Commissioners were rather similar to Mr Straw's. The Trade Commissioner, Peter Mandelson, declared that newspapers which republished the drawings had been 'deliberately provocative' and Franco Frattini, the Justice Commissioner, said that *Jyllands-Posten* had been wrong to publish in the first place (*Guardian* 3.2.06). A more robust response, while acknowledging unambiguously the offence caused, could have drawn attention to the fact that both residents of and visitors to a Muslim country such as Saudi Arabia have no option but to accept aspects of that society – public floggings, amputations and executions, for example - which may not be to their taste, and therefore Muslims in the EU have likewise to accept the liberal tradition of free speech which may not be to their taste. Furthermore, it could have been pointed out that non-Muslims seeking to worship, let alone proselytize, in a number of Arab countries, face considerable impediments, whereas Muslims in the EU are at liberty to worship and evangelise at will; the price of a desirable freedom may be the toleration of one which seems rather less desirable.

As the EU has expanded, it has taken in countries which do not have strong democratic traditions; indeed several have emerged from Communist rule with relatively weak civil societies, and have been obliged to satisfy the Union that their democratic credentials are now completely in order. The current application from Turkey is bound to lead to a difficult negotiating process for several reasons, not least the fact that it is an Islamic country, although a secular state. But it is also a country, which in some matters takes a rather limited view of the importance of freedom of expression. In October 2005 Hrant Dink, the editor of a bilingual Turkish/Armenian weekly paper, was given a suspended jail sentence for 'insulting and weakening Turkish identity' by calling on the Armenian diaspora to abandon the anger they felt towards Turkey on account of the massacres committed in 1915 (*Observer* 9.10.05). Just to mention that such massacres took place is to invite serious trouble in Turkey, which seems to be in denial in the matter.

All of the cases mentioned above and others like them have attracted attention outside the countries involved, and there have been protests from various bodies concerned with human rights and freedom of expression, but it is important that the public voice of the European Union is heard too. Sometimes private diplomacy is more effective than public but there is a danger for the EU if it uses this route too often, or is reluctant to take a stance at all, that it appears to be less concerned with upholding the freedom of the press than it ought to be. It did take a public approach when the Turkish writer Orhan Pamuk, who was awarded the Nobel Prize for literature in 2006, found himself in court accused in similar terms to those under which Hrant Dink was charged, namely 'insulting Turkishness' in remarks he made about the Armenian massacres and treatment of the Kurdish minority in the country. The EU made it clear that the outcome of the case was highly relevant to Turkey's application for membership. Early in 2006 proceedings were dropped and the Enlargement Commissioner was quoted as saying that the decision was 'good news for freedom of expression in Turkey', but that the Turkish government needed to do more to deal with aspects of the law which could restrict freedom of speech (*BBC News* 24.1.06). It is to be hoped that equally vigorous statements will be made to the governments of existing members if they fail to ensure that chapter 2 of the Charter is fully adhered to, and that it is not left to other bodies, such as the Organisation for Security and Cooperation in Europe, which commented forcibly on the Polish cases, to take the lead initiative.

Conclusion

In 2005 the EU established a Directorate-General Information Society and Media headed by Viviane Reding; it is now responsible for audiovisual policy, which was previously handled by the Education and Culture Directorate, and publishing, formerly the responsibility of the Enterprise Directorate. This seems an eminently sensible change, given the likely pace of convergence. However it may also have the effect of highlighting the difference between the Commission's approach to broadcasting and film on the one hand, and the press on the other.

It should be obvious from what has been written above that newspapers in Europe have a range of problems to cope with. In the first place, the huge variations in consumption among the member states do raise issues about the extent to which citizens are fully informed about what is going on in their own countries and in the EU as a whole. Radio, television and on-line services are no doubt very valuable in providing basic information, and public service broadcasting systems are much more likely to be trusted as news purveyors than the press. But it remains the case that the presence in a society of a vibrant newspaper sector is vitally important in raising and sustaining the level of public debate. Even although the British mass market press, for example, often fails miserably to do any such thing, the UK's upmarket sector usually fulfils that role admirably, as do many newspapers across Europe. Low or declining readership of newspapers is not a symptom of rude democratic health. Likewise, the financial pressure which the press is suffering, as other media seek a greater slice of available advertising revenue, can lead to cutbacks in expenditure on journalism, particularly the time consuming journalism which raises awkward political and social questions. And increasing concentration of ownership can mean significant diminution of pluralism of expression.

The response of Commissioner Reding thus far has been to indicate in a speech to a European Publishers Forum at the end of 2005 that she is concerned to ensure that there is in place 'an early warning system in order to signal whether new policy initiatives would damage the editorial or commercial freedom of the media' (Reding 2005b). To this end a Media Affairs Coordination Group has been established. It remains to be seen whether it will move beyond the perfectly sensible objective which the Commissioner has set it, and consider whether the EU needs to be much more proactive in its support of the press.

On the other hand, a sceptical observer might wish to argue that while there is currently no EU press policy of any substance, nor is there likely to be, that is not a bad thing. After all, it could be said, the results of the efforts in other media areas are not very impressive: Television without Frontiers has not had a great impact in expanding European television production, not least because of the weak enforcement mechanisms in place; the MEDIA programme has never had the resources necessary for major investment such as are available in the United States. Both enterprises might have been bureaucratic success stories but the evidence on the small and large screens is rather scanty. France has made a much better job of protecting its cinema industry than the EU has; the British system of public service broadcasting survives - despite the more commercial orientation initiated by the 1990 Broadcasting Act and enthusiastically promoted by Ofcom, since its establishment in 2003 - because successive British governments have felt obliged to ensure that the BBC is properly funded. In other words the subsidiarity which ENPA wishes to continue as far as the press is concerned, has been much more effective in areas where the EU has sought to take initiatives, initiatives which pale into insignificance when set alongside what individual states have done for themselves.

This is an attractive argument to a citizen of the UK or Sweden or Germany. However it might not be nearly so appealing to citizens of a number of other EU countries, not least some of those which have recently joined. Can a fair minded British, German or Swedish observer really be happy, for example, at the pace of concentration and the extent of foreign ownership in some of these states? In such countries might the price of the EU commitment to subsidiarity be far too high for the general civic good? The policy statement quoted at the beginning of this essay talks about guaranteeing citizens' choices in the media, and ensuring freedom for companies to establish themselves and to be able to trade without impediment. Citizens' choices, as far as the press is concerned, may need rather more attention than they have been given to date, and freedom for companies rather less.

References

Bens, Els de. 2004. Belgium. In *The Media in Europe*, eds. Mary Kelly, Giianpietro Mazzoleni, and Denis McQuail, 16-30. London: Sage.

Commission of the European Communities. 2005. *Strengthening the Competitiveness of the EU Publishing Sector*. Brussels: Commission of the European Communities.

Council of Europe 2002. *Media Diversity in Europe*. Strasbourg: Council of Europe.

Doyle, Gillian. 2002. *Media Ownership*. London: Sage.

Europa. *Media in the information society*. http://europa.eu.int/comm/internal_market/media/index_en.htm

European Commission. 2005. *Strengthening the Competitiveness of the EU Publishing Sector*. Brussels: Commission of the European Communities.

European Newspaper Publishers Association. 2005a. *Response to the Commission Issues Paper on Regulation of Audiovisual Content*. Brussels: ENPA.

European Newspaper Publishers Association. 2005b. *Response to the Commission Issues Paper on Media Pluralism*. Brussels: ENPA.

European Parliament. 2006. *Press Briefing: A Knowledge Based Society Open to All*. Strasbourg :European Parliament.

Gulyas, Agnes. 2006. European Integration and East Central European Media. In *European Culture and Media*, ed.Ib Bondebjerg. Bristol: Intellect.

Hallin, Daniel C. and Mancini, Paolo. 2004. *Comparing Media Systems*. Cambridge: Cambridge University Press.

Humphreys, Peter J. 1996. *Mass Media and Media Policy in Western Europe*. Manchester: Manchester University Press.

Hutchison, David. 1999. *Media Policy*. Oxford: Blackwell.

Hutchison, David. 2002. Canadian Cultural Policy, Maclean's Magazine and the Coverage of the Death of Pierre Trudeau. *London Journal of Canadian Studies* 18: 15-39.

Kelly, Mary, Mazzoleni, Gianpietro, and McQuail, Denis. 2004. *The Media in Europe*. London: Sage.

Kleinstuber, Hans J. Germany. In eds. Mary Kelly, Giianpietro Mazzoleni, and Denis McQuail, op cit.

Murschetz, Paul. 1998. State Support for the Daily Press in Europe: a Critical Appraisal. *European Journal of Communication* 13, 3: 291-313.

Organisation for Security and Co-operation in Europe. OSCE media freedom representative asks Poland to remove prison sentences from libel law. www.osce.org/item/8874.html.

Reding, Viviane 2005a. *Better regulation for Europe's media industry: the Commission's approach*. Brussels: European Commission.

Reding, Viviane 2005b. *Reinforcing the competitiveness of Europe's publishing industry*. Brussels: European Commission.

Sarikakis, Katharine 2001 *The Role of the European Parliament in the Formation of Media Policies*. Glasgow: Glasgow Caledonian University (PhD thesis).

Swedish Press Subsidies Council 2005. Press Subsidies Council. www.presstodsnamnden.se/english.htm.

Tunstall, Jeremy. 2004. The United Kingdom. In eds. Mary Kelly, Giianpietro Mazzoleni, and Denis McQuail, op cit 262-74. London: Sage.

Williams, Kevin. 2005. *European Media Studies*. London: Hodder Arnold.

World Association of Newspapers 2005. World Press Trends. www.wan-press.org/article7321.html?var_recherche=circulation+figures.

EUROPEAN STUDIES 24 (2007): 203-226

DIVERSE JOURNALISTS IN A DIVERSE EUROPE? IMPULSES FOR A DISCUSSION ON MEDIA AND INTEGRATION[1]

Sonja Kretzschmar

Abstract

This article examines policies in the US and in the EU that aim to integrate women and ethnic minorities in the media. According to democratic theory, media are essential for the creation of a European public sphere, which integrates all members of the increasingly diverse European society. The article compares and analyses US policies to achieve newsroom diversity within the media with policies to increase the diversity in EU media. The development for media diversity in the EU is twofold: on the one hand, problems of dis-integration of ethnic minorities in the EU are getting increasingly obvious, and the pressure to find political solutions for the situation is rising. On the other hand, the situation on the EU media markets is favouring 'mainstream' content, reflecting diversity only insufficiently. Suggestions to change this situation are discussed in this article, addressing the question of the possibility of a diverse public sphere, which has an active part in the realisation of an EU democracy.

[1] For critical comments and creative ideas, co-operation in turbulent times, patience and courage I thank Dr. Katharine Sarikakis, my friend and colleague. I thank Prof. Christoph Neuberger for literature tips and cross-reading, as well as Sarah Zielmann. Karina Brink's help with linguistic matters was priceless.

Burning cars in Paris in autumn 2005, burning mosques in the Netherlands after the murder of Theo van Gogh[2] and the 'murders of honour'
of Muslim women in Germany – every now and then, the discussion
about 'failed integration' in the states of the European Union (EU)
makes headlines in the media. Questions of integration and integration
policies become the focus of attention in the EU. The media, offering a
platform of dialogue for people belonging to diverse ethnic composition
groups in the European society, play a crucial role in this debate. In
democracies, this role is twofold: to communicate the needs and demands of social groups to politicians and vice versa, and to communicate
policies back to the citizens (Schäfers 1986). A functioning public sphere
which integrates all underprivileged groups of the society, ethnic minorities as well as women, is essential for the formation of public opinion
and decision-making, particularly in the case of the EU, where criticism
on the basis of a 'democratic deficit' renders the role of the media in
alleviating part of this problem significant.

This paper focuses on the analysis of anti-discrimination and diversity
policies in the EU related to the media, which form the basis of the
public sphere within the European society. Because the question of
gender and ethnic diversity policy is relatively recent within the EU, the
legal framework and diversity journalism in the United States of America
(USA) offers an interesting case of existing efforts to address issues of
diversity in the media, from which to draw tentative conclusions. It
discusses the main EU policies against discrimination and addresses
media diversity policies with the aim to determine the level of success in
building a platform for a multi-ethnic public sphere. The paper will try to
answer the following questions: have policies fulfilled the aims for which
they were initiated? What kind of developments can be expected and
which measures should be taken for the functioning of a democratic
public sphere in the EU?

The word 'diversity' in the context of media often leads to the expres-
sion 'media diversity', which refers to the heterogeneity of media (Van
Cuilenburg 2005, 301) in media markets (Van der Wurff 2005, 293-324).
The idea is, that various, *diverse* media, which reflect diverse points of

---

[2] Theo van Gogh made a film about the suppression of Muslim women, 'Submission I', which was broadcast in the Netherlands in 2004. In connection with this film
he was murdered in November 2004. Discussion in: Ali, Ayaan Hirsi 2005; De Leeuw,
Marc and Sonja van Wichelen, 2005; Mak, Geert 2005.

view, in their sum reflect society as a whole. But as different groups of society often do not have the same economic possibilities to make their voices heard, and mainstream media tend to reflect only mainstream opinions, media policy often tries to balance out the equation between these media, sometimes by supporting minority media, which carry on minority opinions. The concept of diversity generally is seen twofold: on the one hand in the market, with diverse single media, on the other hand in the product of media; e.g. public service broadcasters have the duty to reflect diverse opinions in their programme. Therefore, the analysis of media economics (D'Haenens 2005, 293) and an extensive discussion about diverse media markets and media content exists (Van Cuilenburg 2005, Van der Wurff 2005, Vergeer 2005, Vettehen 2005).

Within this discussion, one question remains open: can a variety of perspectives be reflected sufficiently in the media, while journalists are recruited predominantly from a particular demographic mainstream group? Is this reflection complete, when ethnic minorities and women are not equally represented within this group?

Surely it is part of the journalistic apprenticeship to be able to reflect reasonably diverse groups in society. However, in the USA, insufficient coverage of topics connected with gender and ethnic minorities[3] led to a debate of diversity among journalists and has lately become of interest in the European media.[4] Newsroom diversity means therefore a heterogeneity of media journalists, ideally in the same demographic proportion with the audience or readership of their media.

---

[3] The term 'ethnic minorities' cannot be defined easily; here, the EU definition based on the Council of Europe Recommendation 1201 (Council of Europe 1993) is used: 'The expression 'national minority' refers to a group of persons in a state who: reside on the territory of that state and are citizens thereof; maintain longstanding, firm and lasting ties with that state; display distinctive ethnic, cultural, religious or linguistic characteristics; are sufficiently representative, although smaller in number than the rest of the population of that state or of a region of that state; are motivated by a concern to preserve together that which constitutes their common identity, including their culture, their traditions, their religion or their language'.

[4] The crucial role of the European media in the process of integration of ethnic minorities was addressed at a conference in Essen, Germany, in November 2006. The conference was organised by the public broadcasters from Germany (WDR, Westdeutscher Rundfunk and ZDF, Zweites Deutsches Fernsehen) and France (France-Télévision) by order of the European Broadcasting Union (EBU). Another conference is planned in Paris in 2007 (WDR 2006a).

The Roots of the Diversity Debate

This paper takes as its point of departure the experience of the US in its role as the 'archetypal' immigration country. Claims of social justice and anti-discrimination policies in the USA derived from the powerful history of the civil rights movement and the women's rights movement. For the purposes of my paper, the development of integration policies is mostly related to initiatives taken in relation to the media and the journalistic profession. In the US, the question of ethnic diversity entered the public sphere most dynamically during the American Civil Rights Movement in the 1960s. One of the movement's early aims was to redress racial discrimination in employment. Kennedy's Executive Order 10925 of 1961 required federal contractors to take 'affirmative action' (AA) as a measure to end racial discrimination (Kelly and Dobbin 1998). A non-technical definition of affirmative action is 'the expenditure of energy and resources by an organisation in the quest for equality among individuals from different, discernible groups' (Crosby 2004, 5). AA, a policy initiative aiming to overcome the lingering effects of racism and sexism, has been highly controversial in the USA ever since (Crosby 2004, Skrentny 1998, Miller 1997, Miller, Reyes and Shaffer 1997, Miller and Clark 1997), as well as in other countries around the world that adopted the policy e.g. in India, Malaysia, Sri Lanka and Nigeria (Sowell 2004). Although a thorough discussion about the problems associated with the means of implementation within companies is beyond the scope of this paper, it is important to draw attention to the Equal Employment Opportunity (EEO) Act, which grew out of the Equal Rights Movement of the 1960s. In contrast to AA, federal laws based on EEO prohibit employment discrimination based on race, colour, religion, sex or national origin. These approaches differ in the ways of implementing their aims: AA implies a pro-active stance against discrimination, EEO implies a more passive or reactive one (Crosby 2004, 5), but they both hold the same goal: 'to decrease, or eliminate if they can, discrimination against individuals' (Crosby 2004, 5).

Newsroom Diversity: the answer to content diversity?

The development of a legal framework had two important consequences. First, AA and EEO are the basis for longitudinal data gathering on newsroom diversity in the USA. Second, the tradition of data gathering has been institutionalised. Several institutions monitor newsroom diversity regularly, such as the American Society of Newspaper Editors (ASNE) and the Knight Foundation. In addition, special surveys are carried out in the academic field, e.g. by the University of Maryland (Callahan 2004). The data form the basis for discussion on diversity in the media (Poynter Institute 2005). It allows an open, mostly controversial, but in any case lively, discussion within the American society about the integration of minorities in the media and the newsroom (Benson 2005; Robertson 2004; Henry 2003; Monroe 2003; McGowan 2003; Hoyt 1999), which includes original and creative approaches to the topic, such as the interactive Newsroom Diversity Game (Robert C. Maynard Institute for Journalism Education 2005). Moreover courses on diversity reporting became part of US based journalism education (Ross and Patton 2000); a development, which is only in its infancy in Europe (Röben 2004)[5].

What does US generated data tell us about newsroom diversity? The most profound data is gathered by ASNE, which started its initial survey in 1978 and repeats a Newsroom Employment Census annually. The goal of the survey is to monitor the degree of diversity in the media and to push for the acceptance of a minimum proportion of minorities in newsrooms nationwide equal to the percentage of minorities in the nation's population by 2025. The data shows constantly rising figures; in ASNES's initial survey in 1978, minority journalists comprised 3.96 percent of the total newsroom workforce (with an estimated number of 43,000 journalists in total). In 2004, the number of minority journalists was at 13.42 percent, from an estimated number of 54.000 journalists in total (ASNE 2005). At a first glance, it appears that diversity in the US newsroom has increased since 1978. But a closer look at the data reveals a stagnation during the late 1990s onward, after an increase during the 1970s and 1980s.

In the six largest US newspapers non-white employment has been even sliding, and in the smaller newspapers figures do not look very different. To determine the relation between the percentage of minority staff and the total percentage of minorities in the US population, ASNE uses figures from the 2000 US census, which do not take into account the rapid growth of the non-white population. This means that if a newspaper is only maintaining the same non-white staff percentage, it is los-

---

[5] A research project, with the aim to develop a curriculum for intercultural education of journalists could not be realised due to lack of funding.

ing ground and putting ASNE's goal of parity further out of reach each year (Dedman and Doig 2005). One of the major reasons why the figures do not look even worse is based on a fact that is not connected with diversity progress: due to buyouts, layoffs and attrition in the newspapers, the total number of journalists has been sliding down generally in recent years. These cuts tend to affect older journalists, mostly members of the majority staff group. As a result, the non-white percentage is increasing without additional non-white journalists being hired (Dedman and Doing 2005).

Similar results, lack of change and stagnation in the struggle for equity employment can also be found for women in journalism and mass communication education in the US (Rush et al. 2004, 97-128). Although women are not a minority, they are still an underprivileged group when it comes to jobs and positions within the mass media workforce (Rush, Oukrop and Creedon 2004, 97-128; Rush 2004, 263-272). This fact has not changed in the last twenty-five years since gender inequality became formally recognised and despite the fact that many measures have been taken to redress gender imbalances. The ideal development of a straight-line increase of women in mass communications did not take place: only a third of the workforce is female and this figure seems to be stagnating worldwide (Rush 2004, 266). Neither gender equality nor newsroom diversity is progressing effectively since the Civil Rights Movement of the 1960s.

Despite the long standing provision of AA and EEO laws and guidelines from the 1960s, depending for their implementation on the particular president, and having changed names and means during the 1990s to the more 'modern' Diversity Management (DM) (Kelly and Dobbin 1998), the outcome is not satisfying. Data collection on diversity policies exists, but a clear formula for success cannot be given, neither for ethnic minorities, nor for gender balancing (Bulkeley 2004, Endres, Creedon and Henry 2004; Kern-Foxworth 2004).

When one turns to the situation in Europe, two questions arise: first, why have policies such as AA and EEO not taken off in the EU, and second, what is the EU's approach to ethnic diversity and gender balance in European media?

Diversity Policies in the EU: an Overview

The EU is founded on the principles of liberty, democracy, respect for human rights and fundamental freedoms as they are written down in Article 6(1) in the Treaty on EU.

But as the lack of pan-European information and data on the situation of ethnic minorities was a main obstacle for the construction of effective EU policies, the European Centre on Racism and Xenophobia (EUMC) in Vienna was established by Council Regulation in 1997 and commenced its activities in 1998. Its primary task is to provide the Member States with reliable and comparable information and data on racism, xenophobia, islamophobia and anti-Semitism at the European level.

With the Amsterdam Treaty, which entered into force in 1999 (European Union 1997) new powers were given to the EU to combat discrimination on the grounds of racial or ethnic origin, religion or belief, disability, age and sexual orientation. In 2000, the Council adopted two directives: the Racial Equality Directive 2000/43/EC (RED) (EC 2000a), and the Employment Equality Directive 2000/78/EC (EED) (EC 2000b). The RED aims to implement principles of equal treatment between persons irrespective of racial or ethnic origin, whereas the EED establishes a general framework for equal treatment in employment and occupation. The directives define basic guidelines regarding discrimination and integration in the countries of the EU; in addition to that, every country is allowed to implement additional guidelines to facilitate the integration of racial and ethnic minorities into the employment market. These guidelines had to be incorporated into national law by 2003, which was achieved by the majority of the EU member states. Four member states – Germany, Luxembourg, Austria and Finland – failed to satisfy the requirements of both directives and were therefore referred to the EJC (EUMC 2005b). As the practical implementation of these directives is not yet complete, the EU will not move forward to any new challenges in that field (EP 2005c).

With the enlargement of the EU, the policy faces new challenges of integration of ethnic minorities, such as the Roma[6]. This led to the Green

---

[6] The Roma are the biggest ethnic minority group in Europe. Romas live in several states, 80 per cent in the states of Bulgaria, Czech Republic, Romania, Hungary and Slovakia. The European Union and the World Bank started the 'Decade of Roma Inclusion' from 2005-2015, eight Central- and Southeast-European countries (Bulgaria, Croatia, Czech Republic, Hungary, Macedonia, Serbia and Montenegro, Romania and

Paper entitled 'Equality and Non-Discrimination in an Enlarged European Union' (European Commission 2005), which fed into the EU Social Policy Agenda (Commission of the European Communities 2005).

The European Parliament expressed its concern about the degree of success of current policies:

> The Commission notes that the EU has some of the most advanced anti-discrimination legislation in the world, but that evidence from legal experts, NGOs and other sources indicates that this legislation is not yet operating to its full effect. The Commission therefore, considers that further efforts should be made in order to ensure the effective implementation and enforcement of the current legal framework. These efforts should include: completing the transposition into national law; the establishment of effective specialised equality bodies in all member States, additional training and awareness-raising measures (EP 2005c).

As part of awareness-raising the Social Policy Agenda has determined that 2007 will be the European year of equal opportunities (EP 2005b). The aim is to make Europe's diversity visible as a 'source of socioeconomic vitality which should be harnessed, valued and enjoyed' (EP 2005b). Moreover he EU faces the 'European year of intercultural dialogue 2008' with the aim to raise respect for as well as promote 'cultural diversity in Europe and develop an active European citizenship'; in this year, various initiatives are being financed to promote intercultural dialogue focused on communication and awareness-raising (EP 2006a). In the meantime, the European Commission is running a Community Action Programme, a five-year pan-European information campaign (2001-2006) on combating discrimination on the grounds of racial or ethnic origin, religion or belief, age, disability and sexual orientation. With the slogan 'For Diversity. Against Discrimination', the campaign includes various initiatives with a more symbolic character, such as the European Truck Tour 'For Diversity. Against Discrimination' or 'Runs for Diversity'. Although the mass media are a crucial part of European societies in respect of the integration of European citizens (Klaus and Lünenborg 2004), they do not play a central role in the campaign. Only one initiative is connected directly to the media as part of the 'Community Action Programme to Combat Discrimination': The Journalist Award, honour-

Slovakia) are participating. George Soros, from Hungarian descend, and his Open Society Institute took an active part in initiating this decade. Main emphasis lies on education, habitation, work and health of the Roma. Whether the decade will be a success is still an open question (Soros 2005, Jungle World 2005, Café Babel 2005).

ing journalists who contribute with their work to the benefits of diversity and to the fight against discrimination in employment.[7]

Equality policies in the EU and US: a retrospect

Europe and America have distinct immigration histories. Until the 1960s, the expectation of traditional immigration countries, such as Australia, Canada, and the USA, was the 'anglo-conformity model' (Kymlicka 1999, 70), meaning that immigrants had to shake off their cultural heritage and to adapt to existing norms of the 'hosting' country. With the Civil Rights Movement at the end of the 1960s, all three countries rejected the conformity-model and confessed to a more tolerant and pluralistic policy concerning immigrants. Especially in the US with its history of slavery and the segregation of the black population, 'collective guilt' (Teles 1998) became a strong factor in implementing a legal framework such as AA and EO. Its lack in the EU may be also explained by demographics: more than one quarter of the population in the US identify themselves as members of ethnic minorities, whereas European countries are still overwhelmingly homogenous. In Britain e.g. more than 93 percent identified themselves as white (Teles 1998).

With growing experience in a culturally diverse society in the US, the anglo-conformity model was more or less abandoned, as well as in other 'classic' immigration countries, such as Canada. But limits of the new model, multiculturalism, the acceptance of cultural differences, were also seen by politicians in immigration countries. Today, the limits of multicultural policy in a liberal state are clearly visible: not only equality between ethnic groups but also freedom for members of several groups have to be respected (Kymlicka 1999). That means that an ethnic group may neither suppress another group nor may a group suppress its own members by shortening their civil or political rights (Kymlicka 1999, 62-63). In the EU, a substantial debate about limits of the multicultural policy has started only recently, e.g. connected with Hirsi Ali (Ali 2005;

---

[7] The winner of The Journalist Award 2005, announced in April 2006, was the Irish Fiona Ness, features editor at the *Sunday Business Post* with her article 'Disabled and Dismissed' which reported on the lack of employment and education opportunities for the disabled and the attempts through legislation to address this issue. The Journalist Photo Award, bestowed for the first time, was won by Robert Matwiejczyk, a student from Leeds, with a photo of black and white hands playing the piano.

Hitchens 2006). The discussion of where the rights of cultural groups interfere with individual rights are still in their infancy in the EU.

Diversity Policies in the EU: Gender

As well as ethnic minorities and disabled people, the support of women as another historically discriminated against group is given some attention through plans for a European gender institute (EP 2005a, 2006b) which will be a clearing-house for information and exchanges of good practices, approximating the European Monitoring Centre on Racism and Xenophobia (EUMC). But although policies for gender equality exist, their success is also viewed critically: the European 'Parliament was deeply disappointed to note that, after a quarter of a century of equal treatment policies, the gender gap has hardly closed at all' (EP 2005c). This echoes the results Rush (Rush 2004) sees for the situation of women in journalism and mass communication education: stagnation without much progress.

Any attempt to bring about a policy similar to AA, for example, would be probably blocked in the European countries by national and EU law. A regulation comparable to AA put in place in Germany to correct discrimination against women in sectors where they are under-represented, by giving them priority when applying for a job in competition with equally qualified men, was ruled as sex discrimination by the European Court of Justice[8]. As the European Court of Justice (ECJ) does not favour 'preferential treatment' of women, it would be unlikely to accept a policy targeting ethnic minorities (Teles 1998, 1020-1021).

The EUMC Study on Racism and Cultural Diversity in the Mass Media

Parallel to these EU policies a number of small initiatives, run mostly by NGOs and funded or supported partly by the EU or media organisations, came into being in several European Countries. Ter Wal collected examples of good and negative practice within the EU Member States in the years 1995-2000 for the European Monitoring Centre on Racism and Xenophobia (EUMC). Based on these findings, recommendations were made on how cultural or ethnic diversity can be effectively promoted in the media. According to EUMC media professionals, media organisa-

---

[8] The case Kalanke vs. Freie Hansestadt Bremen (Teles 1998, 1020-1021).

tions, advisory bodies, political organisations and ethnic minorities groups should work together to achieve:

– more visibility, voice and better access for migrant and ethnic minority groups, especially in mainstream media and routine news making, and in all news genres;
– more possibilities for background and investigative reporting and introduce more positive news frames or formats, instead of the predominant 'problem' format;
– increased awareness of the necessity to check information from official sources and of the impact of the language of political and official actors; and recognition of the need to comment upon or balance these when appropriate (not following the official perspective only);
– support initiatives in training and programming areas to increase access, participation and improve representation of ethnic, cultural, religious minorities in the media;
– support cooperation and information exchange among media and minority organisations to promote ethnic, cultural, religious diversity in the media (Ter Wal 2002, 75-76).

In various EU Member States, some of the recommendations have already been acknowledged and even implemented, in other states this is still not the case.[9] All in all, the EUMC study classifies the European states into two groups: first, in countries with a long colonial history, such as the UK and the Netherlands. In these countries, models of participation of ethnic, cultural or religious minorities are easier accepted and adopted. The second group comprises countries where a lack of labourers existed after the Second World War, and an official recruitment of workers from foreign countries took place. That these countries became de facto immigration countries themselves has often been denied in politics, so that only some integration policies were established there. In these countries marginalisation of migrant discourses is stronger.

---

[9] Detailed Member State reports for Belgium, Denmark, Germany, Greece, Spain, France, Ireland, Italy, Luxembourg, the Netherlands, Austria, Portugal, Finland, Sweden, United Kingdom to be found in: Ter Wal 2002, 90-418.

Diversity Policies for EU-media, a EUMC Proposal

As a means to ameliorate the situation in all EU Member States, pro-active policies for equal treatment and representations of ethnic, cultural and religious minorities were proposed by the EUMC in 2002. Policy propositions can be grouped into three areas: training, programming and information exchange at the level of media organisations (Ter Wal 2002, 84-86). Above all, active participation of minorities in the production of programmes and content is indispensable.

The last field for recommended European diversity policies contains:

– information exchange,
– co-operation and self-regulation at the level of media organisations;
– a network for the exchange of information on good practice among concerned parties (media, public authorities, NGOs etc.) covering also self-regulatory initiatives in traditional and new media, to combat racism and intolerance;
– a central European institution for the monitoring of programmes to assess sufficient coverage of concerns and interest of minorities;
– exchange and collaboration among Europe's public broadcasters at the level of programming to promote cultural diversity in the media.

Two general strands of recommendations are given by the EUMC for future policies: Continuous monitoring by media organisations to check not only the compliance of guidelines that deal with the treatment of minorities in the media, but also to check how a combined enforcement of recommendation sets are realised within the media. For instance, cultural diversity in the entertainment programming should be counter-balanced by current affairs and background news reporting.

Ultimately, mobility between personnel of mainstream and ethnic minority programmes should be made possible, and a network of major-ity and minority media and journalists could enable the media to offer a diversity of perspectives, and to allow a variety of voices to gain expres-sion.

The collection of examples of both, unsuccessful and good practice, and the recommendations of the EUMC provide a good basis from where to address the current situation in the EU. Without the claim of completeness, the following important good practice initiatives collected in different EU countries may offer an overview of the status quo in Europe.

Further Examples of Diversity Policies in the EU-Media

A variety of initiatives exists in the UK, a country with a long post-colonial history. Channel 4, using a special financing model, is the only public service broadcasting channel where multicultural programming is already part of the programme guidelines. The aim of content is here not to put the minority aspect in the focus of the programmes but to see it as a normal fact of everyday-life:

> The biggest challenge for us in Britain is not to get more blacks into television, we are doing it gradually, but to get them into programmes and stories which aren't about racism or race. So you have a person in a drama who has a love interest, and the fact that he's black isn't the story. The story is: he's falling for her, she is falling for him' (Patrick Younge, Multicultural Programming, Channel 4, in: Kretzschmar 2002, 325).

Not only Channel 4, but also the BBC, and especially BBC3, aim at integrating multicultural content into their programming. Both broadcasters try actively to integrate ethnic minorities into the staff (Kretzschmar 2002, 323-326). There are two European initiatives with an international focus that are worth mentioning: the UK-based Media Diversity Institute (MDI) and 'Online/More Colour in the Media' (OL/MCM), headquartered in the Netherlands.

MDI, an International Institute working worldwide, but with a European focus is funded by several international organisations, among others the Council of Europe. Its goal is to promote fair media coverage of diversity-related issues as an essential step toward strengthening human and minority rights. It aspires to reach its aims with a broad variety of approaches in a 'Reporting Diversity Network' such as cross-ethnic reporting projects, media training for minority NGO groups, and 'reporting diversity curricula' for journalism schools. These curricula are used by institutes and universities worldwide, with a focus on south-eastern European countries, such as Bosnia, Serbia, Albania, Bulgaria and Romania as well as overseas, e.g. Canada and Southern Africa. Especially in Southeastern European countries the MDI's journalistic guidelines for cautious everyday work (Pesic 2004, 121-158) can be seen as a reasonable tool in the peace-keeping process.

'Online/More Colour in the Media' (OL/MCM), established in 1997, is a network of NGOs, broadcasters, training institutes and researchers, it aims to improve the representation of ethnic minorities in broadcasting. OL/MCM operates a website (OL/MCM 2006) that serves as a tool collecting information about European initiatives, such as the 'European Week of Media and Minorities' that took place in March 2005. The website informs about public debates about Ethnic Media and Mainstream Media, European Media meetings of Ethnic Media in Europe. The OL/MCM initiative created a network of national platforms of ethnic and multicultural local radio and TV stations, and established the 'European Day of Monitoring'. Its initiatives are co-ordinated by several national OL/MCM partners. In addition, OL/MCM facilitates and coordinates transnational projects which are funded, among others, by the European Commission, like Equamedia, CREAM and LOG THE MEDIA. All these projects aim to integrate members of ethnic minorities into the media system, above all young people.

Taking into account developments until 2000, the EUMC study concludes that diversity policies in countries with a short history of immigration are not very widespread, while countries with a colonial history have more policies in place (Ter Wal 2002, 76). The situation does not seem to have changed since then. A closer look at two countries from both groups, Germany and the Netherlands, shows these differences.

In Germany only very few initiatives exist with the aim to integrate ethnic minorities into the media system, like a regional training programme for young ethnic minorities (WDR 2006b), the Civis Media Price, conferred for diversity coverage, and special radio and TV programmes for ethnic minorities (Zambonini 2004, Geißler and Pöttker 2005, Segadlo 2005). With the rise of the integration debate, there seems to be an increased interest recently, when a nation-wide initiative was founded in 2005: 'Integration and TV' (Bundesinitiative Integration und Fernsehen 2006), financed by the European Social Fund. In addition, a study about the working situation of migrants in German media has been carried out, ordered by the city of Berlin (Berufliches Qualifizierungsnetzwerk für Migrantinnen und Migranten, BQN) which states that migrants are clearly underrepresented in German media, and that media are not interested in changing this situation; a new programme for integrating members of ethnic minorities into media in Berlin is envisaged (Institut für Medien- und Kompetenzforschung 2005).

Apart from these initiatives, Germany is not taking part in most of the transnational OL/MCM initiatives, and even the majority of Public Service Broadcasters do not have internal policies to increase the number of ethnic minority members among their staff. Media diversity remains here a niche topic for daily media work.

In contrast to Germany, a variety of policies exist in the Netherlands (Esselink 2004) to integrate ethnic minorities with the help of the media (Peeters and D'Haenens 2005). The 'Stichting Omroep Allochtonen' (STOA now Mira Media), the organisation of ethnic minorities in the Netherlands, succeeded in securing the commitment of national broadcasters for a multicultural employment and programme policy since the 1980s. Public Service Broadcasters had to take into account multicultural aims and to report to STOA on their results and progress annually. Although Dutch initiatives were manifold, the success of integration is seen more critically by Dutch politics. As a consequence, two new projects, 'perslink' and 'multiple choice', were initiated by Mira Media. 'Perslink' is a media training programme for speakers of ethnic minority languages, making their voices heard in the Dutch public sphere. 'Multiple Choice' is an equal opportunities programme with the aim to encourage members of ethnic minorities to seek work in the media.

Even though such policies exist, recommended as good practice examples by the EUMC, complete integration did not take place neither; the murder of the Dutch film-maker Theo von Gogh and the following controversial discussion about integration in the Netherlands (Mak 2005, De Leeuw and van Wichelen, 2005) shows that deficits in integration politics cannot be compensated easily with policies in the media field.

Diversity Policies: successful solutions?

Obviously, integration of ethnic minorities with the help of the media into the society is a field where satisfying solutions have not been found yet, although a variety of attempts have been made, both in the US and in the EU. The perspectives given by media researchers are not too optimistic: an ideal development is outlined by Husband (Husband 2000; 199-214). He suggests that a heterogeneous citizenry may in the end produce a multi-ethnic public sphere, which is not free of conflicts, but opens up an arena to carry out existing tensions and conflicts in a democratic way.

Although this is a desirable development for a democratic society, where a lively public sphere should connect various groups of the society, one has to doubt its success. It becomes even more unlikely the more commercialised a media system is, as ethnic minorities often belong to low income groups, which are not commercially attractive audience groups for the media.

Looking back at the USA, where AA and EEO have been active for many years, what experiences have been made with these policies? Did ethnic minorities and female journalists, who came into the newsrooms, change the content of the media they were working for into multi-ethnic media, communicating in a multi-ethnic public sphere?

The socialization of young journalists in the newsrooms takes place within a set of promotions and sanctions, so that the mainstream variety of topics, which is typical for the particular media, is learned and repeated perfectly. Other factors strengthen this development: the tight daily pressure of news deadlines forces journalists to 'routinize the unexpected' (Cottle 2000, 20), which is done easier by relying on key institutional sources of news. The search for non-institutional voices and viewpoints is time-consuming and is left beside under time pressure, so 'the bureaucratic nature of news production is geared to privilege the voices and viewpoints of (white) social power holders, and not those excluded from powerful institutions' (Cottle 2000, 20).

Apart from the fact that with the multiplication of media outlets of newsrooms (online editions, news for mobile phones etc.) the pressure rises to produce more content with effectively fewer people, and new staff is rarely hired parallel to work multiplication, the nature of journalistic work is changing as well. New technologies in the newsrooms demand multi-skilled journalists, able to work with the same content for various media. As this takes up working time, the use of community members as journalistic sources is often undermined. In addition, community work has to be done increasingly on a high technical and professional level to be recognised by the media. This high level is often difficult to be met by citizen groups, and in the end, it undermines community source involvement (Cottle 2000, 21).

In addition, news values which favour stories connected with conflict, drama, controversy and deviance, enforce images of ethnic minorities connected to these topics. This may be a reason for the negative images of ethnic minorities detected by media research in various countries over the years. Public journalism, with its advocacy of democratic participation, may correct some views of mainstream media (Cottle 2000, 21).

Newsroom Diversity

What happens to the young ethnic minority journalists upon entering the newsrooms through a special training programme? They are confronted with several factors, which make it very difficult for them to bring possible media issues with their own personal perspective as minority members into the daily discussion.

Wilson (2000) looked at their development by taking black journalists in the US as an example: 'Their survival on the job depends upon how well they conform to newsroom policy expectations and how they 'fit in' with fellow workers. One black male reporter at the *Washington Post* said that the newspaper 'frequently seems to interpret equal opportunity as meaning that if minorities and women work hard and follow directions, they too can become white men" (Coleman et al. 1986, 4, in Wilson 2000, 97).

This seems to be a common development. Underprivileged groups, such as women and ethnic minorities, have two options: either to adapt, and let go of the idea of proposing women or ethnic minority topics, which are not part of the mainstream media ones. Or, to abandon the profession because of frustration: having analysed available data for black American journalists, Wilson argues that compared to the data of the 1980s more than 20 percent of black journalists planned to leave the profession in the 1990s (Wilson 2000, 97)[10]. The reason is that 'white editors still want them to think and report from the white perspective some 30 years after the Kerner Commission' (Wilson 2000, 99).[11]

To an even greater extent such facts as an unsatisfactory job situation and the pressure only to reproduce mainstream perspectives can be found among coloured women working in journalism and mass media (Kern-Foxworth 2004, 205-222). Being coloured and a woman at the same time seems to enforce the unsatisfactory job situation, and more

---

[10] For more detailed information on the situation of American journalists see Weaver and Wilhoit 1996.

[11] The Kerner Commission Report was released after street riots in 1968 in the US, named after the chairman of the commission. It stated the discriminating situation of blacks and suggested various means for the advancement of the situation. As one result, AA and EEO were established.

than half of all coloured female journalists believe that they 'still face barriers to career advancement that are not faced by their white and male colleagues.' (Kern-Foxworth 2004, 214).

This phenomenon, affecting both coloured women and men, may have been reinforced by the rising commercialisation of the US media. It is only marginally counter-balanced by public service broadcasters, which are the only media obliged to cover minority interests. As they are on the retreat worldwide, together with the export of a commercial media system all over the world (Herman and Mc Chesney 1997), future perspectives are not too bright.

What kind of future development can be expected? The commercialisation of the media system worldwide enhances a highly competitive media market. In neoliberal theory, not just diversity concerning underprivileged groups, but diversity in general, flourishes best in a free marketplace of ideas. However this thinking is based upon the classical economic market theory that assumes the existence of equally powerful individuals. Full competition in the marketplace will, in theory, most efficiently produce the best quality products at the lowest price possible (Van Cuilenburg, 1999). In practice, controversial developments should be taken into account: 'In markets with fierce competition, it is dangerous for producers to be different from their rivals, be it in terms of price or quality composition of their products, or both.' (Van Cuilenburg 1999, 195). As a result, producers are driven towards conservativism and risk-avoiding behaviour. In the end, in a highly competitive media market, 'media reflecting society inevitably ill perform regarding openness to a great variety of different social positions, and conditions' (Van Cuilenburg 1999, 191).

Conclusion

We witness a twofold development: on the one hand, competitive media markets enhance mainstream content, which mostly reflects ethnic majority opinions. Although some policies exist to pave the way for a multi-ethnic and gender balanced public sphere, as well in the US as, to a lesser degree, in the EU, and some progress can be seen in a few examples, a fundamental change is not in sight. The aim to integrate different voices of the society into the media system is reached neither in the US nor in the EU.

On the other hand, problems of disintegration of ethnic minorities are rising within western countries, especially in the EU states: in France, the banlieue riots of the autumn 2005 made disintegration problems open and visible. In Germany, the murders of Turkish women, justified by relatives on cultural grounds with 'stained honour', make headlines more and more regularly, and in the Netherlands the discussion about integration of the Muslim minority is very vivid since the murder of van Gogh.

The gap between the necessity to build a multi-ethnic public sphere, where media newsrooms are also multi-ethnic and gender balanced, and the reality, where different groups live beside but not with each other, is not closing. To change the situation, supporting policies will not be enough: movements of concerned citizens are needed, coalitions between underprivileged groups, like women and ethnic minorities, have to be established. Only then, a working democracy, offering equal rights for all members of the society, will be in sight. (Rush, Oukrop and Sarikakis 2005).

It is the challenge of responsible media researchers to analyse the current unsatisfying situation and to deliver reliable data to confront politicians with the results. New guidelines for media policies have to be developed which will make democracy work within a multi-ethnic public sphere, integrating diverse opinions and cultures. A first step would be the gathering of data about diversity policies in the EU media in a central institution, with a regular evaluation system of the implementation of these policies. Second, even when women and members of ethnic minorities are integrated successfully into newsrooms, the culture around them should be targeted to become friendlier to their perspectives and voices, so that they can actively participate in the programme and news making.

Especially for Public Service Broadcasters, who have the duty to reflect society as a whole with all its minority groups, regular programme supervision should take place, where the goal to produce programmes for all society members is achieved through real programming. Obstacles which prevent new, different programme ideas from realisation should be identified, so that a form of diversity quality control for media can be implemented on a regular basis. A diverse public sphere could lift a heavy part of the European democratic deficit and make EU democracy work.

References

Ali, Ayaan Hirsi. 2005. *Ich klage an. Plädoyer für die Befreiung der muslimischen Frauen.* München: Piper. English translation in print, 2006. The Caged Virgin. *An Emancipation Proclamation for Women and Islam.* New York: Free Press.

American Society of Newspaper Editors (ASNE). 2005. News Staffs Shrinking while Minority Presence Grows. www.asne.org/index.cfm?id=5648

Benson, Rodney. 2005. American Journalism and the Politics of Diversity. *Media, Culture & Society* 1: 5-20.

Bulkeley, Christy. 2004. Whose News? Progress and Status of Women in Newspapers (Mostly) and Television News. In Seeking Equity for Women. In *Journalism and Mass Communication. A 30-Year Update*, eds. Ramona R. Rush, Carol E. Oukrop and Pamela J. Creedon, 183-204. Mahwah, New Jersey, London: Lawrence Erlbaum Associates.

Bundesinitiative Integration und Fernsehen. 2006. www.bundesinitiative.org.

Café Babel. 2005. 'Auch heutzutage erleben wir immer noch eine Apartheid gegenüber den Roma'. www.cafebabel.com/de/article.asp?T=T&Id=3592

Callahan, Christopher. 2004. Lagging Behind. www.ajr.org/Article.asp?id=3738

Commission of the European Communities. 2005. Communication from the Commission on the Social Agenda. http://europa.eu.int/comm/employment_social/social_policy_agenda/spa_en.pdf.

Cottle, Simon. 2000. Introduction. Media Research and Ethnic Minorities: Mapping the Field. In *Ethnic Minorities and the Media*, ed. Simon Cottle, 1-30. Buckingham/Philadelphia: Open University Press.

Council of Europe. 1993. http://www.us.es/mhrd/Mat.Ferrero.4.pdf.

Crosby, Faye J. 2004. *Affirmative Action is dead: Long Live Affirmative Action.* New Haven/London: Yale University Press.

Dedman, Bill, and Stephen K. Doig. 2005. Newsroom Diversity Has Passed its Peak at Most Newspapers, 1990-2005 Study Shows. http://powerreporting. com/knight/.

D'Haenens, Leen. 2005. Commentary and Debate Special Section Introduction: Defining Media Diversity. *Communications, the European Journal of Communication Research*, 3, 293.

De Leeuw, Marc and Sonja van Wichelen. 2005. 'Please, Go Wake Up!' Submission, Hirsi Ali, and the 'War on Terror' in the Netherlands. *Feminist Media Studies*, 3: 325-340.

Endres, Kathleen, Creedon, Pamela J. and Susan Henry, eds. 2004. Timeline and Vignettes. Exploring the History and Status of Women in Journalism and Mass Communication Education. In *Seeking Equity for Women in Journalism and Mass Communication. A 30-Year Update*, eds. Ramona R. Rush, Carol E. Oukrop and Pamela J. Creedon, 33-50. Mahwah, New Jersey, London: Lawrence Erlbaum Associates.

Esselink, Hana. 2004. Mira Media. In *Interkulturelle Kompetenz und Medienpraxis*, ed. Jörgen Klußmann, 159-197. Frankfurt am Main: Brandes & Apsel.

European Commission. 2005. *Green Paper on Equality and Non-discrimination in an Enlarged European Union* http://ec.europa.eu/employment _social/publications/2004/ke6004078_en.html.

European Council (EC). 2000a. Council Directive 2000/43/EC. http://europa.eu.int/comm/employment_social/fundamental_rights/pdf /legisln/2000_43_en.pdf.

European Council (EC). 2000b. Council Directive 2000/78/EC. http://ec.europa.eu/employment_social/fundamental_rights/pdf/legisln/ 2000_78_en.pdf

European Monitoring Centre on Racism and Xenophobia (EUMC). 2005a. Activities of the European Monitoring Centre on Racism and Xenophobia, EUMC Annual Report 2004/2005, Part 1. http://eumc.eu.int/eumc/ material/pub/ar05/AR05_Sum_EN.pdf.

European Monitoring Centre on Racism and Xenophobia (EUMC). 2005b. Racism and Xenophobia in the EU Member States. Trends, developments and good practices. Annual Report 2005 – Summary. http://eumc.eu.int/ eumc/material/pub/ar05/AR05_p2_EN.pdf.

European Parliament (EP). 2006a. *European year of Intercultural Dialogue 2008: Respect and Promote Cultural Diversity in Europe and Develop an Active European citizenship* http://www.europarl.eu.int/oeil/file.jsp?id=5279532.

European Parliament (EP). 2006b. *Gender Equality: Establishment of a European Institute for Gender Equality.* http://www.europarl.eu.int/oeil/file.jsp?id =5238252.

European Parliament (EP). 2005a. *Development Co-operation: Promoting Gender Equality.* http://www.europarl.eu.int/oeil/file.jsp?id=235342.

European Parliament (EP). 2005b. *Non Discrimination and Gender Equality: European Year of Equal Opportunities for all .* http://www.europarl.eu.int/oeil/ file.jsp?id=5253822.

European Parliament (EP). 2005c. *Protection of Minorities and Anti-discrimination Policies in an Enlarged Europe.* http://www.europarl.eu.int/oeil/file.jsp? id=5223932.

European Union (EU). 1997. The Treaty of Amsterdam. www.eurotreaties.com/ amsterdamtreaty.pdf.

European Union (EU). 2005. www.stop-discrimination.info/24.0.html.

Geißler, Rainer and Horst Pöttker, eds. 2005. *Massenmedien und die Integration ethnischer Minderheiten.* Bielefeld: transcript Verlag.

Henry, Neil. 2003. *Racial Reverberations in Newsrooms* After Jayson Blair. Nieman Reports, 3: 25-27.

Herman, Edward S. and Robert W. McChesney. 1997. *The Global Media. The New Missionaries of Corporate Capitalism.* London/Washington: Cassell.

Hitchens, Christopher. 2006. *The Caged Virgin.* www.slate.com/id/2141276/.

Hoyt, Mike. 1999. *Reporting Race: Diversity Fatigue? Here's a Tonic. Columbia Journalism* Review, 9/10, http://archives.cjr.org/year/99/5/race.asp

Husband, Charles. 2000. Media and the Public Sphere in Multi-ethnic Societies. In *Ethnic Minorities and the Media*, ed. Simon Cottle, 199-214. Buckingham/ Philadelphia: Open University Press.

Institut für Medien und Kompetenzforschung. 2005. *Multikulti zwischen Wunsch und Wirklichkeit. Berufseinstieg und Beschäftigung von Migranten im deutschen Journalismus.* MMB-Trendmonitor III/2005. www.mmb-michel.de/2004/ pages/trendmonitor/Trendmonitor-Downloads/Trendmonitor_III_ 2005.pdf.

Ireland, Patrick R. 1994. *The Policy Challenge of Ethnic Diversity.* Cambridge, London: Harvard University Press.

Jungle World. 2005. *Roma à la carte.* www.jungle-world.com/seiten/2005/ 05/4797.php.

Kelly, Erin and Frank Dobbin. 1998. How Affirmative Action Became Diversity Management. *American behavioral scientist*, 7: 960-984.

Kern-Foxworth, Marilyn. 2004. Women of Color on the Frontline in the Mass Communication Professions. In *Seeking Equity for Women in Journalism and Mass Communication. A 30-Year Update,* eds. Ramona R. Rush, Carol E. Oukrop and Pamela J. Creedon, 205-222. Mahwah, New Jersey, London: Lawrence Erlbaum Associates.

Klaus, Elisabeth and Margret Lünenborg. 2004. Cultural Citizenship. *Medien und Kommunikationswissenschaft,* 2: 193-213.

Koch, Ralf. 1996. *„Medien mögen's weiß'. Rassismus im Nachrichtengeschäft. Erfahrungen von Journalisten in Deutschland und den USA.* München: Deutscher Taschenbuch Verlag.

Kretzschmar, Sonja. 2002. *Fremde Kulturen im europäischen Fernsehen.* Wiesbaden: Westdeutscher Verlag.

Kymlicka, Will. 1999. *Multikulturalismus und Demokratie. Über Minderheiten in Staaten und Nationen.* Hamburg: Rotbuch Verlag.

Mak, Geert. 2005. *Der Mord an Theo van Gogh. Geschichte einer moralischen Panik.* Frankfurt am Main: Suhrkamp Verlag.

Miller, Fayneese. 1997. The Political Rhetoric of Affirmative Action. Infusing the Debate With Discussions About Equity and Opportunity. *American behavioral scientist*, 2: 197-204.

Miller, Fayneese and Mary Ann Clark. 1997. Looking toward the Future. Young People's Attitude bout Affirmative Action and the American Dream. *American behavioral scientist*, 2: 262-271.

Miller, Fayneese, Xaè Reyes and Elizabeth Shaffer. 1997. The Contextualization of Affirmative Action. *American behavioral scientist*, 2: 223-231.

McGowan, William. 2003. *Coloring the News: Collides With Journalists.* Nieman Reports, 3: 31-33.

Monroe, Bryan. 2003. *Newsroom Diversity: Truth vs. Fiction.* Nieman Reports, 3: 29-31.

Online/More Colour in the Media (OL/MC). 2006. http://www.olmcm.org/.

Peeters, Allerd L. and Leen D'Haenens. 2005. Bridging or Bonding? Relationships Between Integration and Media Use Among Ethnic Minorities in the Netherlands. *Communications*, 2: 201-231.

Pesic, Milica. 2004. Ein Journalismus der Vielfalt: Medien als ein Mittel der Integration. In *Interkulturelle Kompetenz und Medienpraxis*, ed. Jörgen Klußmann, 121-158. Frankfurt am Main: Brandes & Apsel.

Poynter Institute (PI). 2002. *Counting Diversity: Who measures up?* www.poynter.org/content/content_view.asp?id=9761&sid=5.

Quandt, Siegfried. 1998. Der Umgang mit kulturellen Unterschieden. Herausforderungen, Chancen, Grenzen. In *Deutschland im Dialog der Kulturen*, eds. Siegfried Quandt and Wolfgang Gast, 25-34. Konstanz: UVK.

Röben, Bärbel. 2004. Umgang mit Differenzen als Schlüsselqualifikation. Projekte zur Einführung einer interkulturellen Perspektive in die JournalistInnenausbildung. In *Die Zukunft der Kommunikationsberufe. Ausbildung, Berufsfelder, Arbeitsweisen*, eds. Kurt Neubert and Helmut Scherer, 265-275. Konstanz: UVK.

Robert C. Maynard Institute for Journalism Education. 2005. *The Newsroom Diversity Game*. www.maynardije.org/resources/game.

Roberston, Lori: What Works? 2004. *American Journalism Review*, August/September www.ajr.org/Article.asp?id=3734.

Ross, Felicia Jones and Jamila P. Patton. 2000. The Nature of Journalism Courses Devoted to Diversity. *Journalism & Mass Communication Educator*, 1: 23-39.

Rush, Ramona R., Carol E. Oukrop and Katharine Sarikakis. 2005. A Global Hypothesis For Women In Journalism And Mass Communications. *Gazette, The International Journal For Communication Studies*, 3: 239-253.

Rush, Ramona R. 2004. Three Decades of Women and Mass Communication Research. *In Seeking Equity for Women in Journalism and Mass Communication. A 30-Year Update*, eds. Ramona R. Rush, Carol E. Oukrop and Pamela J. Creedon, 263-272. Mahwah, New Jersey, London: Lawrence Erlbaum Associates.

Rush, R.R., C.E. Oukrop, L. Bergen, J.L. Andsager. 2004. Where Are the Old Broads? Been there, Done that ... 30 Years Ago. An Update of the Original Study of Women. In Journalism and Mass Communication 1972 and 2002, eds. Ramona R. Rush, Carol E. Oukrop and Pamela J. Creedon, 97-128. Mahwah, New Jersey, London: Lawrence Erlbaum Associates.

Schäfers, Bernhard, ed. 1986. *Grundbegriffe der Soziologie*. Opladen: Leske und Budrich.

Segadlo, Stefan. 2005. *Fremde Kulturen im öffentlich-rechtlichen Fernsehen am Beispiel von 'Cosmo TV'*. Münster: unpublished master thesis.

Skrentny, John David. 1998. Introduction: Affirmative Action: Some Advice for the Pundits. *American behavioral scientist*, 7: 877-885.

Soros. 2005. www.soros.org/initiatives/roma/focus_areas/decade.

Sowell, Thomas. 2004. *Affirmative Action Around the World.* New Haven/London: Yale University Press.

Taylor, Charles. 1997. *Multikulturalismus und die Politik der Anerkennung.* Frankfurt am Main: Fischer Taschenbuch Verlag.

Teles, Steven M. 1998. Why Is There No Affirmative Action in Britain? *American Behavioral Scientist,* 7: 1004-1026.

Ter Wal, Jessika, ed. 2002. *Racism and Cultural Diversity in the Mass Media. An Overview of Research and Examples of Good Practice in the EU Member States, 1995-2000.* Vienna: European Monitoring Centre on Racism and Xenophobia.

Treibel, Annette. 1990. *Migration in modernen Gesellschaften. Soziale Folgen von Einwanderung und Gastarbeit.* Weinheim: Juventa Verlag.

Van Cuilenburg, Jan. 2005. On Monitoring Media Diversity, Media Profusion, and Media Performance. Some Regulator's Notes. *Communications, the European Journal of Communication Research,* 3: 301-308.

Van Cuilenburg, Jan. 1999. On Competition, Access and Diversity in Media, Old and New. *New Media Society,* 2: 183-207.

Van der Wurff, Richard. 2005. Media Markets and Media Diversity. *Communications, the European Journal of Communication Research,* 3: 293-301.

Vergeer, Maurice. 2005. Measuring Diversity and Level of Aggregation. *Communications, the European Journal of Communication Research,* 3: 312-319.

Vettehen, Paul Hendriks. 2005. 'Open Diversity' Statistics: An Illusion of 'Scientific Thoroughness'? *Communications, the European Journal of Communication Research,* 3: 308-312.

Weaver, David Hugh and Grover Cleveland Wilhoit. 1996. *The American Journalist in the 1990s.* Mahwah, New Jersey: Lawrence Erlbaum Associates.

Westdeutscher Rundfunk (WDR). 2006a. *Integration auf allen Kanälen.* www.wdr.de/themen/kultur/rundfunk/wdr/europaeische_medienkonferenz /index.jhtml?rubrikenstyle=kultur.

Westdeutscher Rundfunk (WDR). 2006b. *Journalistische Talentwerkstatt 'WDR grenzenlos'.* www.wdr.de/unternehmen/jobs/stellenangebot/stellenangebot_f.jhtml?druck=1.

Wilson, Clint C. 2000. The Paradox of African American Journalists. In *Ethnic Minorities and the Media,* ed. Simon Cottle, 85-99. Buckingham/Philadelphia: Open University Press.

Wilson, Clint C. and Félix Gutiérrez. 1995. *Race, Multiculturalism, and the Media.* Thousand Oaks, London, New Delhi: Sage Publications.

Zambonini, Gualtiero. 2004. Funkhaus Europa, das kosmopolitische Mehrsprachenprogramm des WDR. In *Interkulturelle Kompetenz und Medienpraxis,* ed. Jörgen Klußmann, 93-100. Frankfurt am Main: Brandes & Apsel.

EUROPEAN STUDIES 24 (2007): 227-249

WHITHER CULTURAL DIVERSITY:
THE EUROPEAN UNION'S MARKET VISION
FOR THE REVIEW OF TELEVISION
WITHOUT FRONTIERS DIRECTIVE

Mark Wheeler

Abstract

Technological convergence and the globalisation of communications services have brought new entrants into the European television sector. The European Union's regulation of television services was established in the 1989 Television without Frontiers Directive (TWF) which provided liberalising rules to stimulate production so a harmonised single European audiovisual market could compete with US imports. In 2000, the Education and Culture Commissioner Viviane Reding announced the Commission would review TWF to consider whether its focus on television remained appropriate, and this process culminated in the publication of the draft Audiovisual Media Services Directive in December 2005. Throughout this review, the EU opened up the European audiovisual sector to market opportunities, while placing matters of cultural diversity and democratic opportunity to one side. Moreover, this supranational policymaking has conformed to the changes accompanying a transformation from 'government to governance' which has emerged in modern statecraft.

Introduction

Technological convergence, economic opportunity, and the globalisation of communications services have brought new entrants and consumer services into the European television sector. With the expansion of audiovisual services, there has been a diversification of revenue streams available to media, new media, telecommunications, mobile telephone and Internet companies. Consequently, the European Union (EU) has developed policies to facilitate a sustainable audiovisual market in the global marketplace.

The EU's regulation of television services was established in the 1989 Television without Frontiers Directive (TWF) (89/552/EEC). TWF provided liberalising rules to stimulate production by stemming inefficiencies resulting from unnecessary national regulations so a harmonised single European audiovisual market could compete with US imports. TWF was amended in 1997 to provide Member States with national measures to protect public access to free-to-air coverage of major societal events.

In 2000, the Education and Culture (now Information, Society and Media) Commissioner Viviane Reding announced the EC would review TWF to consider whether its focus on television services remained appropriate in an era of reforming technologies and economic expectations. Subsequently, in 2002, the European Commission (EC) set out three major reviews to discuss whether TWF's measures, including quotas and controls over advertising to promote the production and distribution of European television programmes, were adequate. After a two-year period of consultation with commercial stakeholders, this policy process culminated with the EC draft revision of TWF entitled the Audiovisual Media Services Directive (COM (2005) 646final)) in December 2005. This broadened the scope of EU regulations as the Commission believed an expansion in its jurisdiction would sustain the competitive advantage of European television and television-like services. (Ward 2002, 71)

The first section of this analysis considers the context for reforming TWF with regard to changes within the role of governance of communications services. It assesses the Information, Society and Media Directorate's approach to the regulation of audiovisual services by placing them within the framework of the 'hollowing out the state.' (Rhodes, 1994) Therefore, there has been a greater devolution of power to the interests of stakeholders, while simultaneously an expansion of forms of supranationalism as the EU operates as a 'network state' to define governance for the interests of global capital. (Castells 2000) This marketisation of the 'regulatory state' has led to the EC placing the principles of enterprise above those of cultural diversity and citizen representation.

Consequently, the second section of this analysis reviews the ideological values which have underpinned the EU's audiovisual policy process concerning the relaxation of EU regulations and the issues associated with culture, citizenship and the democratic flow of information. Finally, the study outlines the draft Audiovisual Media Services Directive's recommendations for extending the scope of regulation; the relaxation of advertising rulings; protections for minors and human dignity; matters of cultural diversity and media pluralism.

From 'government to governance' in the converging communications environment

The EC's approach to audiovisual policy reflects the changes resulting from a process of 'government to governance' which has occurred in accordance with the decline of the nation state. This has been accompanied by the privatisation of public monopolies, the deregulation of market economies and the use of private solutions for welfare provision. These developments have been exacerbated by technological reforms to modern information and communication systems, in which the previous determinants of time, space and geography have imploded, thereby allowing for the international flow of finance. In effect, there has been a collapse of national sovereignty in which governments' roles have been transformed from policy initiation to the facilitation of the global exchange of capital.

This process has been associated with changes to national policy-making since the end of the Keynesian consensus and rise of the 'regulatory state'. It has been described as 'the hollowing out of the state' (Rhodes 1994) in which power has devolved from central government to subsidiary regulators and quangos so the 'state [has become] ... fragmented and diversified.' (Gamble 2000, 290) There has been a collapse in state unity, wherein the lines of accountability have become muddied, and governments' ability to formulate policy substantially reduced.

Paul Smith has shown how this 'hollowing out of the state' detrimentally affected the UK Government's Digital Television policy in the 1990s, resulting in its failure to launch digital terrestrial services (DTT) for public consumption, thereby enabling Rupert Murdoch's BSkyB to enhance its monopolistic power in the subscription based satellite digital television (DST) market. (Smith, Summer 1999; Smith 2004) This failure to affect control over the digital television systems occurred due to the marketisation of broadcasting, the collapse of national regulation and the growing power of supranational governance:

> Overall, since the 1980s, there has been a shift from a mode of governance based on direct state intervention, supported by power to tax and spend, to one characterised by rule making and the extensive delegation of powers to institutions operating at arms length from government. ... In effect, government by regulation, as the introduction of digital television in the UK illustrates, is government by proxy (Smith, Summer 1999, 12).

Smith was concerned that UK governments understood their role to be the facilitators of market opportunities for digital providers, rather than conceiving that such services should operate as a *public good*. In turn, with the privatisation and deregulation of communications markets, commercial interests have lobbied for their competitive rights above the social or cultural dissemination of information and knowledge. (Smith, Summer 1999)

Conversely, this process has evidenced 'hollowing-up' in which power flows from the nation state to supranational tiers of authority. Such de-nationalisation has resulted from the cessation of national sovereignty to European integration. This transformation of sovereign power conforms to Manuel Castells' conception of the EU as a 'network state' in which the Euro-polity is characterised by a complex network of European, national and sub-national institutions. These bodies have been involved in a convoluted combination of federal, supranational and intergovernmental arrangements which are 'organised around global networks of capital, management and information.' (Castells 2000, 502)

In the area of modern communications, these developments have been most profoundly felt with the globalisation of audiovisual services, as technological convergence, economic opportunity and public-choice ideologies have undermined normative national regulations governing broadcasting and telecommunications. With regard to the European television economy, the EU responded to market changes in the 1989 TWF Directive by abolishing national sovereignty over television services by allowing for the free movement of broadcasting services across frontiers to stimulate audiovisual production. The EU employed the Maastricht Treaty's concept of mutual recognition which meant, as long as minimal regulations were met by the provisions of the originating Member State, the justifications for another Member State to impede the reception or retransmission of broadcasts were removed (Collins 1994, 59-60).

While the 'country of origin' objective remains secure, the EC feels TWF's scope is too limited to facilitate such a growth of new services. (Reding, 7 April 2005) And it is upon the basis of the supranational marketisation of communication services that the Information, Society and Media Directorate has sought to affect a strong, integrative European audiovisual industry. It argues *harmonised*, pan-European regulations based on country of origin principles are required to provide legal certainties for all European broadcasters, irrespective of their platforms or methods of delivery. In turn, the Commission's approach has been dictated by its concern to devolve power to corporate stakeholders in the global economy through the *liberalisation* of audiovisual services. In such a manner, the EU contends its will respond to the competing demands of new information services, while enhancing consumer choice and citizenry in the global communications market place.

Liberalisation and Intervention in the converging European audiovisual sector

The EC has favoured a liberalised approach to audiovisual regulation to enhance technological change and business opportunities, while conforming to the principles of proportionality and subsidiarity. Consequently, it has defined minimal amounts of regulation to ensure consumer protections, to achieve net benefits for citizens by encouraging innovation, to hold guarantees of legal certainty and to maintain technological neutrality. These rules should be enforced as locally as possible and where appropriate by self-regulation (BSAC, 12 September 2005, 2).

For the Commission, the convergence of discrete communications systems (telecommunications, broadcasting and computers) has led to new opportunities for investment and innovation within digital forms of broadcast television, high-speed broadband Internet Service Providers (ISPs) and third generation mobile telephone networks. These information society services offer consumers with goods 'normally provided for remuneration, at a distance, by electronic means and at the individual request of a recipient of the services' (European Union, 8 June 2000).

Within the converging European audiovisual market place, the digitisation of broadcasting may transform the deliverance of traditional forms of programming, while providing consumers with greater access to downloadable services. According to EU Commissioner Reding, there are over 50 million broadband connections across Europe and the information and communications sector accounts for 5.3 per cent of the EU's GDP, 3.4 per cent of its employment and 25 per cent of its productive growth. (Gow, 24 January 2006) Thus, as service providers and consumers exchange information services; the value of information as a commodity has been enhanced.

These imperatives provide many challenges for the supranational regulation of information and communication services. And the EC has responded by seeking to enlarge its scope by providing rules to cover new media services and differentiating between linear and non-linear television services. Linear services refer to traditional forms of scheduled programming operating on broadcast, internet or mobile telephone services which have been pushed by suppliers to audiences that are subject to normative regulations. Non-linear services are forms of content such as on-demand films or news which viewers pull from a media service provider on the basis of choice. Consequently, consumers may control the programming they want to watch through video-on-demand, mobile telephony or internet downloads. Moreover, as the new services have liberalised consumer choices, the EC believes European citizens can access the widest array of content.

This position accorded to the principles of the 2005 EU Lisbon agenda which referred to the Commission's adoption of the 'i2010: European Information Society.' This was a comprehensive strategy to encourage the digital economy by modernising and deploying EU policy instruments, regulations, research and industrial partnerships. Consequently, in reviewing the Directive, the EC had two purposes; the amendment of the existing regulations for television services, including the relaxation of advertising rules, and the creation of a regulatory framework for emerging broadband services to put in place:

> ... The conditions to respond to the expectations of both business and consumers while, at the same time, stimulating the European content industry and the European Information and Communications Technologies (ICT) industries. This necessitates the establishment of conditions for healthy competition, of clear rules and greater legal certainty (Reding, 30 May 2005).

However, the Directorate is also responsible for providing social, cultural and democratic levels of oversight in the expanding audiovisual sector. Thus, within an era of single market integration and commercial opportunity, the Commission is required to protect what it perceived to be the core values and strengths of the European broadcasting economies. These include:

- Pluralism, the most fundamental public objective in the media sector;
- Cultural diversity, especially regarding the preservation of national identities; and
- The enhancement of citizen's choice, in which consumers will be able to enjoy a wide degree of access to the new opportunities provided by market innovation (Ungerer, 13 February 2002, 4).

The Treaty on the European Union, which came into force on 1 November 1993, requires Community to take all cultural aspects into account in its actions concerning audiovisual services. (European Union, 7 February 1992) In 1999, the Prodi Commission defined its position concerning the regulation of content in a Communication entitled 'Principles and Guidelines for the Community's audiovisual policy in the digital age' which was endorsed by the Council and the European Parliament. (European Union, 14 December 1999)

The Communication reaffirmed regulation within the audiovisual sector must safeguard such public interest objectives as: pluralism; cultural and linguistic diversity; copyright protection; the right of reply, and the protection of minors. Thus, the Commission commented the extent of any subsequent regulation should be determined by the failure of the market to realise these objectives. Therefore, any revision of TWF would be required to maintain regulations concerning circumscribed forms of information; fundamental human rights; freedom of expression; freedom of establishment; the protection of minors; matters of public order; watersheds and viewers' rights to reply.

Concurrently, the Directorate is committed to continuing TWF's protections for heritage and cross-cultural exchanges which exist through quotas and subsidies such as the MEDIA Plus programmes. These measures raise questions referring to the definition of 'European content' and through the promotion of cross-frontier provision extend to concerns about media pluralism, news production and independent production rights. And consumer protections are required for on-demand services such as the defence of minors and controls stemming incitement to hatred.

The EU argues TWF has proved effective in maintaining cultural and democratic rights across the European television market, and will remain appropriate in the converging communications market. In Article 4 of TWF, the Commission established quotas requiring broadcasters to reserve a majority proportion of their transmission time for European works (excluding news, advertising and sports events) 'where practicable' and through appropriate means. Within Article 6, the Directive provided a definition for 'European works' suggesting these were productions originating from Member states and third party states (non-EU European countries) as defined by the Council of Europe's European Convention on Transfrontier television.

Yet, both these rulings provided limited cultural protections as they defined 'European' as referring to 'any legal or natural person domiciled in any of the member states of the Council of Europe.' (Collins 1994, 70) This was a permissive definition suggesting American media companies based in Europe may be understood as being 'European'. Additionally, the articles contained get-out clauses concerning practicability and stated their aim for European production 'should be achieved progressively' (Humphreys 1996, 277).

Thus, from 1989 until 1997 the quotas were 'valued increasingly in terms of the symbolic rather than real' (Levy, 1999, 48). Only a few EU dirigistes, who called for the quotas to become obligatory rather than being observed through choice, believed these measures could offset the growing reliance by European broadcasters on imports. In the event, the 1997 revision of the TWF Directive signalled an end to this debate when the European Parliament decided to vote against the toughening up of the quotas (Levy 1999, 48).

Therefore, TWF's clauses concerning cultural diversity and the democratic dissemination of information have been ineffectual in preserving European content and providing a wide range of services for citizens. And the EC's underlying approach to the amended Audiovisual Media Services Directive, by framing the consultation squarely within the limits of economic opportunity, has by-passed key concerns about the *public* worth of Europe's television services in a more complex communication environment with severe implications for citizens' rights. In effect, rather than audiences being able to extend their choices across a plurality of communication services, this commercial vision may be seen to have limited opportunities for cultural diversity by extending corporate interests and leaving media concentration under the auspices of the Competition Directorate. Consequently, in developing its regulatory approach to audiovisual services, the EU's response has signaled a conflict between the economic priorities of industrial competitiveness on the one hand and a highly qualified desire to maintain the principles of European cultural identity on the other (Iosifidis, Steemers and Wheeler 2005, 97):

> Broadcasting and the audiovisual has therefore been a notable site where one of the 'grand narratives' of the Community has been played out, the battle between the interventionists and free marketers, between *'dirigistes'* and 'ultra liberals' (Collins 1994, 23).

The review and adoption of the draft 2005 Audiovisual Media Services Directive

To establish a regulatory framework for audiovisual content, the EC commissioned three investigations in 2002 concerning the TWF's measures over quotas, advertising and the production and distribution of European television programmes. (Iosifidis, Steemers and Wheeler 2005, 99) These reviews concluded Article 4 and 6 of TWF, referring to the definition of 'European' works, quotas and subsidies, had sustained a satisfactory framework for the promotion of European production and cultural diversity. However, this decision to continue with TWF's rulings regarding cultural diversity and media pluralism into the amended Directive ignored key concerns about the social, cultural and democratic dimensions of European television and new media services.

Similarly, in accordance with their market-led philosophies, the reviews urged the relaxation of advertising regulations (Articles 10-20) which had exacerbated differences over commercial breaks between Member States characterised by highly regulated and deregulated regimes. They placed emphasis on the need for clear rules covering product placements and brand integration which were vital for securing new revenues. In response, the EC decided its goal for product placement should be increased consumer information, while acknowledging it as a legitimate form of advertising.

To assist these reviews, the Commission published the Fourth Report to the Council of Europe and the European Parliament on the application of the TWF Directive in 2003 which recommended the Directive's scope should be widened to cover all audiovisual media services irrespective of their delivery. Subsequently, the Commission launched a first consultation round in 2003 which included public hearings and written submissions from interested parties. In turn, the Directorate drew up its conclusions in the Communication on the Future of European Regulation. Following this, focus groups were created to analyse the issues in greater detail and they summarised their positions at a seminar in Luxembourg held on 30 and 31 May 2005.

On 11 July 2005, the EC published six issue papers concerning the scope of the proposed directive, the impact of the relaxation of advertising controls and consumer protections. In response, over 200 interested parties were invited to submit further submissions in anticipation of the Liverpool Audiovisual Conference held from 20-22 September 2005. This meeting concluded TWF needed substantial revision as the current rules aggravated unjustifiable differences in regulation over services which were distributing identical or similar forms of media content. Therefore, the EC argued restrictive rules must be liberalised or abolished to affect a decisive step towards Audiovisual Media without Frontiers in Europe's single market.

On 13 December 2005 the Commission adopted the legislative proposal for the Audiovisual Media Services Directive. It aimed to reduce the regulatory burden on Europe's providers of TV and TV-like services by establishing a flexible framework for single market integration and greater freedoms in advertising revenues. Moreover, as the revised Directive reaffirmed TWF's country of origin principle, it removed many of the complexities service providers faced concerning different Member States rulings.

The Directive established a level playing field for companies offering TV-like services, irrespective of the technology used to deliver them (e.g. broadcast, high-speed broadband, third generation mobiles) and harmonised disparate national rulings on the protection of minors, incitements to racial hatred and the surreptitious use of advertising through EU-wide standards of protection. Subsequently, the Directorate contended a strong, creative European communications economy could expand multimedia opportunities, boost competition and consumer choice, while protecting minors, cultural diversity and the plurality of provision.

Expanding the Regulatory Scope of Audiovisual Media Services
Under the Commission's principle of technological neutrality, the Directive defined audiovisual services to comprise from all scheduled (linear) and on-demand (non-linear) forms of television or television-like

programmes. Moreover, it extended the scope of audiovisual to include advertisements, teleshopping, and moving images with or without sound which accompany television services promoting goods across terrestrial, cable and satellite networks, the internet, telecommunication networks or any electronic network.

However, this scope is limited by the basic European Treaty which differentiates between audiovisual media services aimed at consumers for commercial exploitation and non-commercial forms of private communication such as websites. The Directive similarly excludes the regulation of radio channels, electronic newspapers, magazines and audio transmissions. Thus, it defines an audiovisual service as a form of mass communication which provides scheduled programming to inform, educate and entertain.

In turn, audiovisual service operators must comply with the rules laid down by the Directive, whereas ISPs have not been placed under any new licensing requirements or liability regimes. Moreover, an ISP is considered to be exempt from the EU's regulatory scope if it only pipes information to its customers from the web, provides private on-line forms of information such as e-mail or communications which are not primarily intended to distribute audiovisual content to consumers such as a website that carries ancillary TV-like services. Yet, if it offers a video-on-demand service, the ISP has to comply with the Directive's regulations.

The main aim of the Directive was to extend the scope of its regulations in a platform-neutral manner so the same rules apply to the same set of services, but to be differentiated by the nature of that service. Presently, the TWF Directive covers broadcast television, whereas the ICT sector is subject to the e-Commerce Directive. Although, this Directive is based on the country of origin principle, it allows for a wide-range of Member State derogations. As a result, EU Member States have no common rules governing on-demand audiovisual services in the key areas addressed by the TWF Directive.

Consequently, by establishing a European tier of content regulations for all audiovisual-services the Directive defined rules for both linear and non-linear forms of programming. With regard to traditional television broadcasts, the Directive provides flexible content regulations concerning citizen safeguards such as the explicit identification of television suppliers and universal access to events which have a public worth.

These include the provision of news bulletins and short excerpts of key events even if the rights are held exclusively by a specific broadcaster.

Conversely, the Directive establishes only minimum principles for non-linear services concerning the liability of service providers and content owners. As a consequence, a basic set of pan-European content provisions exist including the protection of minors, the prevention of incitements to racial hatred, the identification of a media service provider, the identification of a commercial communication, the promotion 'where practicable' of the production of and access to European work, the prohibition of the transmission of films outside the licence period and the outlawing of surreptitious advertising (e.g. for alcohol or targeted at minors).

Although non-linear services are subject to lower levels of regulation than traditional broadcast channels these controls extend beyond general laws. With regard to identification, each site will be required to provide contact details covering the name of the service provider, its geographical address and information concerning the ISPs' national regulator. Moreover, a television channel transmitted over the internet will remain subject to the same rules by which it would be governed if it were broadcast across terrestrial airwaves. (Purnell, 26 January 2006) This means, for the first time, the EC has affected pan-European content regulations governing the internet.

The EU has faced fierce resistance to its harmonisation of consumer protections covering the new media. Through this form of regulatory intervention, the EC has been accused of attempting to regulate the Internet and compromising individual rights to free expression. Concurrently, while industrial actors, Member State regulators and governments favoured the Commission's liberalisation of linear services, they remained unconvinced about the economic desirability of its regulation of non-linear programming. From this business perspective, the EC's critics argue the Directorate has placed intolerable burdens on on-demand services.

Several regulators and industry lobbyists suggest the EC's definition between linear and non-linear will prove highly confusing. For instance, if a radio programme is transmitted over the internet does the buffering which is required by the switching of protocols make the broadcast linear or non-linear? When does the buffering equate with downloading of content and make the service non-linear? Moreover, with so many technologies becoming available to users, if individuals put up their own video material on a website should they be considered as providing linear services and be liable to licensing? Further, if consumers receive new services through on-demand, linear, time-shifted, live and non-commercial mechanisms will the distinction between linear and non-linear services remain workable? And is it justifiable to provide different regulations for the same programme due to the nature of its transmission? :

> It would make sense increasingly to have a level playing field but this is an arbitrary decision as to where old roots stop and new roots begin. Thus the linear and non-linear approach was by no means a perfect way of dealing with this ... if consumers are not differentiating between the services, neither should regulators (Pitts, 12 October 2005).

In sum, these critiques contend the EC's differentiation between linear and non-linear frontiers will disappear with further convergence and may undermine user rights for private communications. They suggest the Information, Society and Media Directorate has placed unfair restrictions on the future development of ICTs which need time to evolve without premature intervention. In this respect, the Commission has contravened its better regulation principles by using the Directive to impose a traditional licensing system on new media platforms and ignoring the e-Commerce Directive rules already in place:

> The internet is not the Wild West. The internet is already regulated by the general law, just like the print media and the theatre. The music industry in the UK is now actively pursuing people found illegally pirating copyrighted music material on peer to peer file-sharing networks (Hooper, 29 August 2005).

Most especially, industrial actors argue the amended Directive's regulatory burdens will undermine the competitiveness of EU-based new media services in the global communications market. They contend these rules will raise entry costs, stem new services and create jurisdictional anomalies. For instance, if a telecommunications operator provides on-demand services featuring an Electronic Programme Guide (EPG) it may be deemed to provide scheduled services and be subject to traditional forms of broadcast licensing. In turn, if a service 'streams' live content over mobile broadcasts it will be considered to be linear, but if the content is downloaded once it has been recorded it could be regarded as being as non-linear. Critics point out the Directive cannot stop new media companies from moving outside the EU's boundaries and such interventionist regulations will force Europe's knowledge entrepreneurs to move overseas, thereby losing the opportunity for innovation and growth.

Finally, as no other trading bloc will be subject to these regulations, the EC's opponents argue the Directive will place European new media companies at a considerable disadvantage against their international competitors. This criticism was articulated by the United Kingdom (UK) government's Secretary of State for Culture, Media and Sport Tessa Jowell and the former Minister for Film and Broadcasting James Purnell who spoke against the extension of the EU's regulatory scope. And Purnell lobbied several EU Member States including the Netherlands, Spain, Finland and Estonia to propose the Commission should adopt a self-regulatory approach to the new media (Deans, 26 January 2006).

Advertising and the protection of human dignity
In accordance with its 'light-touch' approach to regulation, the Directive recommended restrictions over advertising revenues should be reduced. However, the EC recognised a dichotomy existed between the need to provide the broadcasters with greater flexibility to finance, while maintaining fair levels of protection and choice for consumers, viewers and rightholders. Thus advertising rulings must provide safeguards for the public interest but remain proportionate to their objectives. The EC also hopes industrial responsibility will be enhanced through voluntary codes resulting in the greater deregulation of the advertising market.

Instead of providing detailed prescriptions on how often and under which conditions programmes may be interrupted by advertising, the Directive simplified the rules to encourage greater flexibility and to enhance self-regulatory conventions. The revision contends broadcasters rather than regulators will determine when to insert an advert during a programme rather than being subject to the regulations requiring a 20 minute gap between commercial breaks. It abolished the daily cap of three hours of advertising and dropped quantitative controls regarding teleshopping.

However, the Directive maintained the existing 12 minutes of advertising per hour ceiling and limited slots between news, films made for television, cinematographic works and children's programmes to once every 35 minutes. Further, it determined that all electronic audiovisual commercial communications (both linear and non-linear) must comply with specific requirements and basic qualitative rules governing adverts (e.g. human dignity, protection of minors, advertising for alcohol, tobacco and pharmaceuticals).

Furthermore, the Directive supported the expansion of new forms of brand integration such as split-screen, virtual and interactive advertising. The Commission accorded with the arguments of advertisers, commercial broadcasters and independent producers that traditional 30-second ads are declining as viewers' record programmes and fast-forward through breaks. To this end, the Directive facilitated greater opportunities for product placement by providing a legal framework to extend the range of advertising on linear and non-linear audiovisual services. Therefore for all television and television-like channels (with the exception of news and current affairs and those catering to children on whom advertising is proscribed) consumers will receive clear statements concerning product placement at the beginning of a programme. In such a manner, the Directive contended audiences would receive appropriate protections while broadcasters could access alternative forms of finance.

The amended Directive reaffirmed the rules governing protection of minors and human dignity on the linear services. In the light of submissions received from Member States, public service broadcasters, religious authorities and consumer organisations, it confirmed they should apply to non-linear services by establishing basic pan-European rules concerning content and identification of service providers.

In line with the principles of subsidiarity, these supranational regulations do not stop Member States from adopting self and co-regulation mechanisms when implementing these provisions. For instance, with regard to advertising aimed at minors, the Commission contended media literacy or education programmes delivered by public authorities, industry and consumer groups could prepare children for adverts. Moreover, the Directive complies with the principles recognised by the Charter of Fundamental Rights of the European Union and does not prevent Member States from applying their constitutional rights concerning press freedom and free expression.

Consumer groups believe the Directive's relaxation of advertising rules, most especially those reducing controls over product placement, were retrogressive. They have developed several arguments against the domination of broadcasting by advertising. First, they suggest clearly packaged commercial messages already intrude into social arenas ranging from the sponsorship of educational programmes at schools to the sale of public space on street corners. Second, new techniques are being employed by advertisers including pop-up ads on websites. Third, alternative forms of product placement and branding within films, television series, videos, DVDs, video games, books and 'adversongs' are leading to more covert forms of public influence. In turn, consumer groups have called for the disclosure of such commercial practices and refer to the scandal surrounding the placement of branded products in the ARD's (the German public channel) news programming. This practice undermines the democratic dissemination of information and the German National Association of Consumer Protection Centres argued it was 'a breach in the dyke around the freedom of information and of the press.' (EurActiv, 1 March 2006)

Thus, these advocates argue the EC has placed commercial considerations over the consumer protections. Previous safeguards will dissolve as self and co-regulatory codes will prove ineffectual in stemming advertisers from exploiting new techniques such as spot ads and split-screens. In particular, they contend the Commission's arguments about consumer power and media literacy are tenuous in the light of surreptitious branding aimed at children. They refer to surveys which demonstrate such advertising has a subliminal effect on children by shaping preferences for different toys, characters, life styles and subcultures.

Consequently, they believe such a usage of advertising undermines consumer protections and damages the rights of vulnerable groups. In turn, they have opposed Reding's declarations for greater self-regulation and have called for the extension of TWF rules concerning advertising. There should be a clear separation between a programme's editorial and advertising content, and the robust monitoring of rules stemming surreptitious messages aimed at children or easily influenced members of the public. These views have been endorsed by the EU Directorate General for Health and Consumer Affairs which responded to the Interservice consultation by demanding for greater advertising restrictions (Linx Public Affairs, 1 March 2006).

Such concerns have filtered into a more general debate about consumer rights in a converging communications environment. The Bureau Européen des Unions de Consommateurs (BEUC) has argued while new technologies offer greater choice, they undermine consumer confidence due to their complicated and confusing nature. Therefore, the BEUC has called for more effective forms of co-regulation in which statutory codes of conduct should be developed in consultation with representative bodies and national regulators. The Bureau also urged the Commission to extend its regulatory scope to ensure rapid market developments leading to media concentration do not undermine European citizens' rights to a plural and diverse range of content (BEUC, 15 July 2003, 3-4).

Promoting Cultural Diversity and Media Pluralism

The Sixth Communication from the Commission to the Council and European Parliament on the application of Articles 4 and 5 of Directive 89/552/EEC concluded there should be no changes to the quotas governing European based television programming as they reflected the interests of the content supply industry, the broadcast sector and the viewing public. They have promoted European production by offering diverse and high quality levels of scheduled programmes across Member States but within acceptable levels of derogation. Therefore, the amended Directive allows Member States to impose flexible content quotas in linear European television productions 'where practicable' while providing them with a wide margin of discretion.

Moreover, the EU argues these reforms correspond with the support measures it has developed through its MEDIA programme. These subsidies have strengthened the production capacity of European media systems, enhanced the circulation of European works to compete with international rivals, and preserved the Community's cultural diversity. Additionally, the Directive's modernisation of the rules governing advertising will safeguard the integrity of cinematographic works which can only be interrupted once in every 35 minutes and will stimulate new sources of funds for European audiovisual production such as product placement and brand integration.

The debate surrounding the appropriate EU regulatory instruments for the promotion of cultural diversity in the non-linear environment proved more problematic. As on-demand services represent differing degrees of user control, the EC felt transmission time and content quotas were inappropriate and might prove counter-productive. Conversely, it recognised the amended Directive would have to facilitate the free circulation of European non-linear services in the internal market. Thus, to square this circle, the Information, Society and Media Directorate reached a market solution in which Member States promoted consumer access to non-linear services where practicable and set out lower thresholds for new entrants so a vibrant European content industry might emerge.

From the consumer perspective, the essential role of media pluralism is to ensure the largest degree of choice from the widest array of channels to reflect different points of view and cultures. Therefore, the revised TWF Directive reaffirms the free exchange of media content across frontiers in linear services to stimulate the citizens' knowledge rights. The country of origin principle has a democratic dimension by facilitating the flow of services across borders to expand the range of available European channels. For example, within the 25 EU Member States, more than 160 broadcast services exist which originate from another Member State or non-EU country. The Directive extends the country of origin principle to the non-linear environment through the provision of a minimal set of harmonised rules. By establishing clear degrees of legal certainty, the EC contends on-demand services' commercial success; consumer choice and diversity will be enhanced.

While the availability of a wide number of television and television-like channels will aid consumer choice, further regulations are necessary to ensure a broad range of opinions. The amended Directive includes three measures to contribute to this more 'qualitative aspect' of citizens' information rights. First, it requires obligations from Member States to guarantee the independence of national regulators from state control. Thus, they should remain autonomous from governmental intervention; have their own apparatus and impartially award licences to comply with national and European rules covering the protection of minors, human dignity, non-discrimination and advertising. Second, media pluralism will be strengthened by the rights of free television services to receive short reports of newsworthy events and to have rights of access to events of societal importance. Finally, there will be the promotion of content from independent producers which accounts for 33 per cent of transmission time or 50 per cent of all European programming.

Consequently, the recommendations concerning any extension of cultural diversity and media pluralism remain marginal in the amended Directive. This accorded with the EC's market-led approach to new media services and demonstrated how matters of citizenship have been of secondary concern. Such an omission indicates the Directorate has responded to corporate lobbying over the needs of citizens. Therefore, while media entrepreneurs provide some limited degree of choice; this only exists within the context of *commercial viability* in which market competition provides the substructure and democratic preferences decline. (Keane 1991, 91) In effect, markets provide consumers with rival commodities which encourage individuals to seek private solutions to public problems, but exclude citizens from the income to enter the marketplace of ideas thereby undermining participation and empowerment. Thus, a conflict exists between the rights of possession and expression (Wheeler 1997, 138).

Conclusion

The convergence of communications systems has created new opportunities for innovation within linear and non-linear television and information markets. To facilitate these reforms, the EC engaged in a three-year policy process to revise the TWF Directive and published the draft Audiovisual Media Services Directive which proposes harmonised minimal rules to cover all audiovisual media services to accord with the rapid technological and commercial changes affecting the sector. It sought to reduce the regulatory burden on Europe's providers of TV and TV-like services by establishing a flexible framework allowing for single market integration and greater freedoms in advertising revenue.

This article has placed the review of TWF within the framework of the 'hollowed-out' state. The EU's approach to audiovisual services reflects both the dynamics of 'hollowing down' and 'hollowing up.' With regard to the former, the Directorate has devolved power to the interests of the commercial stakeholders whose arguments for greater deregulation readily caught the ear of Commissioner Reding. Simultaneously, in establishing a supranational approach to audiovisual policy, the Commission has indicated how it has operated as 'network state' in which the principles of global capitalism have shaped its marketisation of the European television industries.

Therefore, the EC favoured a *liberalised* approach to audiovisual regulation to enhance technological change and business opportunities. Through such measures the Commission believed it could advance a strong European communications economy by opening up multimedia opportunities, boosting competition and consumer choice, while protecting minors, cultural diversity and the plurality of provision. Consequently, the amended Directive was founded on the EU's principle of better regulation to affect reforms to EC's regulatory scope to cover linear services and non-linear services, the relaxation of advertising rulings, the extension of self and co-regulation to protect minors and human dignity, cultural diversity and media pluralism.

In the fall-out from the publication of the Directive, the EU has received criticisms from Member State governments, regulators and businesses concerning its attempt to harmonise minimum consumer protections covering the new media. These dissenting voices maintain it is unclear what should be defined as linear and non-linear, and that such a distinction will undermine the competitiveness of European based on-demand services. Industrial actors contend the Directive's rules will force Europe's knowledge entrepreneurs overseas, thereby losing the opportunity for growth. This position was advocated by the UK's Secretary of State Jowell and the former Minister for Film and Broadcasting Purnell who lobbied Member States to pressure the EC to drop its proposed regulation of new media services.

Elsewhere, consumer groups believe the EC's relaxation of advertising rules, most especially those regulations concerning product placement, will detrimentally affect viewers' rights. They claim the Commission has acceded to the interests of the advertising lobby and self regulatory codes cannot stop advertisers from exploiting new techniques such as spot ads, subliminal messages and product placement. These surreptitious forms of branding may unduly influence the purchasing habits of vulnerable groups and undermine the editorial autonomy of programme content.

The controversies surrounding consumer protections extend into a wider debate concerning the social, cultural and democratic worth of communication in the European television marketplace. Instead of proposing reforms to TWF measures concerning cultural diversity and media pluralism, the EC has retained inadequate quotas and definitions of European production. Similarly, there has been a limited degree of commentary from Member State governments and regulators concerning the democratic flow of information in the converging communications market.

Yet, the free and equitable distribution of linear and non-linear channels remains vital in the reform of any policy instrument designed to enhance the range of communications available throughout the European Union. In pursuing a market approach in the revision of TWF the EC may have accorded to its principles of integration and deregulation, but has missed a crucial opportunity to provide appropriate safeguards for European citizens. It is the intention of this small contribution to debate, by contending the EC's regulation of audiovisual services must extend beyond the limitations of business interest, will add to the growing calls for policy-makers to address the knowledge rights of Europe's citizens rather than to accede to the commercial interests of its information economy.

References

British Screen Advisory Council (BSAC). 12 September 2005. *The Television Without Frontiers Directive Submission to the European Commission prepared by the BSAC Working Group.* London: BSAC.

Bureau Européen des Unions de Consommateurs (BEUC). 15 July 2003. *BEUC's Response to the Commission's Consultation on Review of Television Without Frontiers Directive.* Brussels: BEUC.

Castells, Manuel. 2000. *End of Millennium: The Information Age: Economy, Society and Culture: Volume 3.* Oxford: Blackwell Publishers (Second Edition).

Collins, Richard. 1994. *Broadcasting and Audio-visual Policy in the European Single Market.* London: John Libbey.

Deans, Jason. 26 January 2006. Purnell Looks for EU Back-up on New Media Regulation. *The Guardian* http://media.guardian.co.uk/broadcast/story/ 0,,1695656,00.html.

EurActiv. 1 March 2006. Consumer Organisations: TV Without Frontiers Must Respect Limits. Brussels: Info Society www.euractiv.com/Article?tcmuri =tcm:29-142871-16&type=News.

Europe's Information Society Thematic Portal. 13 December 2005. *Modernising the TV without Frontiers Directive.* Brussels: Europa http://europa.eu.int/ information_society/newsroom/cf/itemlongdetail.cfm?item_id=2343.

European Union. 1989. *Council Directive 89/552/EEC of 3 October 1989 on the Coordination of Certain Provisions Laid Down by Law, Regulation or Administrative Action in Member States Concerning the Pursuit of Television Broadcasting Activities.* Brussels: European Council.

European Union. 7 February 1992. *Treaty on European Union,* (92/C 191/01), signed at Maastricht, 7 February 1992. Brussels: European Commission.

European Union. 30 July 1997. *Directive 97/36/EC amending the 1989 'Television without Frontiers' Directive,* OJ L 202. Brussels: European Commission.

European Union. 14 December 1999. *Principles and Guidelines for the Community's Audiovisual Policy in the Digital Age,* (Com 657 Final). Brussels: European Commission.

European Union. 8 June 2000. *Directive 2000/31/EC of the European Parliament and of the Council of 8 June 2000 on Certain Legal Aspects of Information Society Services, in Particular Electronic Commerce, in the Internal Market (E-commerce Directive); Directive 98/48/EC of the European Parliament and of the Council, 20 July 1998 Amending Directive 98/34/EC Laying Down a Procedure for the Provision of Information in the Field of Technical Standards and Regulations (Transparency Directive).* Brussels, European Commission.

European Union. 6 January 2003. *Fourth Report to the Council of Europe and the European Parliament on the Application of the TWF Directive.* Brussels: European Commission.

European Union. 13 December 2005. *Proposal for a Directive of the European Parliament and of the Council Amending Council Directive 89/552/EEC on the Coordination of Certain Provisions Laid Down by Law, Regulation Or Administrative Action in Member*

States Concerning the Pursuit of Television Broadcasting Activities Com (2005) 646 Final. Brussels: European Council.

Gamble, Andrew. 2000. Policy Agendas in a Multi-Level Polity. In Dunleavy, P. Gamble, A., Holliday, I. and Peele, G (eds.), *Developments in British Politics 6.* Basingstoke: Macmillan, 290-307.

Gow, David. 24 January 2006. Half of EU Set to be on 'Triple Play' of TV, Broadband and Phone by 2010. *The Guardian.* http://media.guardian.co.uk/broadbandbritain/story/0,,1693629,00.html.

Humphreys, Peter J. 1996. *Mass Media and Media Policy in Western Europe.* Manchester: Manchester University Press, 1996.

Hooper, Richard. 29 August 2005. *Regulation in a Convergent Environment Content Regulation in the Multiplatform Multichannel Digital Age (Selected Sections on New Electronic Media),* Seminar in Hong Kong hosted by the Hong Kong Broadcasting Authority and the Office of the Telecommunications Authority.

Iosifidis, Petros, Jeannette Steemers and Mark Wheeler. 2005. *European Television Industries.* London: British Film Institute.

Keane, John. 1991. *The Media and Democracy,* Oxford: Polity Press.

Levy, David A L .1999. Europe's Digital Revolution: Broadcasting Regulation, the EU and the Nation State. London: Routledge.

Linx Public Affairs: Legal and Political News affecting ISPs and Internet Users. December 2005. *The Audiovisual Services Directive.* http://publicaffairs.linx.net/news/?p=417.

Pitts, Simon. 12 October 2005. Discussion on the Television without Frontiers Directive Consultation and the Outcomes of the Audiovisual Conference in Liverpool. London: British Screen Advisory Council (BSAC).

Purnell, James. 26 January 2006. *Lessons for EU Regulation: How Does the Revised TVWF Directive Affect Competitiveness?* London: The Foreign Policy Centre.

Radaelli, Claudio M.. 1999. *Technocracy and the European Union,* London: Longman.

Reding, Viviane. 30 November 2000. Member of the European Commission Responsible for Education and Culture, Community Audiovisual Policy in the 21st Century Content Without Frontiers? London: British Screen Advisory Council (BSAC) http://www.europa.eu.int/comm/index_ en.htm10.

Reding, Viviane. 7 April 2005. Commissioner Information Society and Media, 'Address to British Screen Advisory Council (BSAC)'. London: BSAC.

Reding, Viviane. 30 May 2005. Seminar of the Luxemburg Presidency on the Revision of the Television Without Frontiers Directive, Opening Address by Commissioner Reding. Brussels: European Commission.

Rhodes, Rod A. W..1994. The Hollowing Out of the State. *Political Quarterly,* Volume 65, Number 2.

Smith, Paul. Summer, 1999. The Politics of UK Television Policy: The Introduction of Digital Television. *International Journal of Communications Law and Policy.* Universities of Yale, Milan, Singapore, Münster and the European University Institute, Florence, Issue 3, 1- 22.

Smith, Paul. November 2004. *The Politics of UK Television Policy: The Introduction of Digital Television* (Unpublished doctoral thesis). London: Metropolitan University.

Ungerer, Herbert. 13 February, 2002. *Media in Europe: Media and EU Competition Law*, Paper Presented at Conference on Media in Poland by the Poland Confederation of Private Employer. Warsaw, Brussels: European Commission.

Ward, David. 2002. *The European Union, Democratic Deficit and the Public Sphere: An Evaluation of EU Media Policy.* Amsterdam: IOS Press

Wheeler, Mark.1997. *Politics and the Mass Media.* Oxford: Blackwell Publishers.

Williams, Granville. September-October 2005. What is the Televison Without Frontiers Directive? Between Culture and Commerce. *Free Press: Journal of the Campaign for Press and Broadcasting Freedom.* London: Wernham Printers, 4-5.

Metaphoricity and the Politics of Mobility

Edited by Maria Margaroni and
Effie Yiannopoulou

r o d o p i

Orders @ rodopi.nl—www.rodopi.nl

This collection of essays investigates the convergence between the postmodern *politics of mobility* and a politics of metaphor, a politics, in other words, in the context of which the production and displacement of meaning(s) constitute the major stakes. Ranging from discussions of re-territorialization, multiculturalism, "digisporas" and transnational politics and ethics, to September 11th, the Pentagon's New Map, American legislation on Chinese immigration, Gianni Amelio's film *Lamerica*, Keith Piper's online installations and Doris Salcedo's *Atrabiliarios*, the collection aims to follow three different theoretical trajectories. First, it seeks to rethink our concepts of mobility in order to open them up to the complexity that structures the thoughts and practices of a global order. Second, it critically examines the privileged position of concepts and metaphors of mobility within postmodern theory. In juxtaposing conflictual theoretical formulations, the book sets out to present the competing responses that fuel academic debates around this issue. Finally, it evaluates the influence of our increasingly mobile conceptual frameworks and everyday experience on the redefinition of politics that is currently under way, especially in the context of Post-Marxist theory. Its hope is to contribute to the production of alternative political positions and practices that will address the conflicting desires for attachment and movement marking postmodernity.

Amsterdam/New York, NY,
2006 188 pp.
(Thamyris 12)
Paper € 40 / US$ 52
ISBN-10: 9042020342
ISBN-13: 9789042020344

USA/Canada:
295 North Michigan Avenue - Suite 1B, Kenilworth, NJ 07033,
USA. Call Toll-free (US only): 1-800-225-3998
All other countries:
Tijnmuiden 7, 1046 AK Amsterdam, The Netherlands
Tel. +31-20-611 48 21 Fax +31-20-447 29 79
Please note that the exchange rate is subject to fluctuations